Artist o

The Men

ARNOLD MACHIN

FRONTIER

FRONTIER PUBLISHING

This edition 2010
First Published 2002
Frontier Publishing
Kirstead
Norfolk NR15 1EG

British Library Cataloguing in Publication Data

Machin, Arnold
Artist of an icon
1.Machin, Arnold 2.Sculptors – England – Biography
3.Potters – England – Biography
I .Title
730.9'2

ISBN (10) 187291425X
ISBN (13) 9781872914 25 1

Acknowledgement for all copyright photographs are printed on relevant pages and constitute an extension of this copyright page.

Typeset by T&O Graphics, Bungay, Suffolk.

PRINTED IN GREAT BRITAIN
by Crowes of Norwich.

CONTENTS

1911	Born on 30th September at Oakhill, Stoke-on-Trent
1925	Began 7 year apprenticeship with Minton
1927-1933	Stoke School of Art, part-time student
1933	Moved to Derby to work for Old Derby China Works
1933-1935	Derby School of Art, part-time student
1935-1937	Derby School of Art, full-time student
1937-1940	Student at Royal College of Art, London
1940	Awarded the Silver Medal as top sculpture student RCA and a Travelling Scholarship
1940	Retained by J Wedgwood & Sons as a designer
1941-1942	Briefly Head of Stoke-on-Trent School of Art
1942	Moved to London to work for Voluntary Service for Peace
1943	Sent to Wormwood Scrubs Prison for 12 months as conscientious objector
1943	Employed full-time by Wedgwood
1944	Tate Gallery purchased his sculptures 'St. John the Baptist' and 'The Annunciation'
1947	'Spring' purchased by the Tate. Elected Associate of the Royal Academy of Arts
1949	Marriage to Patricia Newton. Moved to 'The Villas', Stoke-on-Trent. Son Francis born Nov.
1951-1958	Part-time Tutor at Royal College of.Art, Ceramic School
1956	Elected as a full member of the Royal Academy of Arts
1957	Moved to Offley Rock, Eccleshall, Staffs. Development of large scale garden design
1959-1966	Master of Sculpture at Royal Academy Schools
1959	Appointed Sculpture Assessor at the Scottish Schools of Art
1963	Won competition to model Her Majesty The Queen for decimal coinage
1964	Travelled to the Bahamas to design their coinage
1965	Awarded OBE
1966	Won competition to design the new definitive postage stamp
1968	Porcelain figures produced for Royal Worcester
1968-1971	Appointed to National Council for Diplomas in Art
1972	Designed the Royal Silver Wedding Commemorative Crown
1977	The gardens at Offley Rock filmed by the BBC for 'A Summer of Gardens'
1977	Designed The Queen's Silver Jubilee commemorative crown
1979	Advisor to Wells Cathedral on restoration of statues on west front
1986	Designed fountain figures and built grotto for Sebastian de Ferranti, Cheshire
1986-1999	Regularly exhibited at the Royal Academy Summer exhibitions
1998	Invited by the Royal Mint to enter designs for Millennium medal competition
1999	Died March

1

To stand today at the highest point of any of the roads in the centre of the conurbation known as Stoke-on-Trent is to look over a landscape which, denuded of its buildings, has undulations easily recognisable by the Romans who established themselves here in the first century AD. Archaeological evidence has been found of Roman roads, coins and other artefacts, including an abandoned kiln containing pottery discovered at Trent Vale in the 1970s.

Supplies of wood and then coal for firing and deposits of clay suitable for making red earthenware were abundant here from earliest times, when most communities would have had their own potter, and the Romans continued this old tradition by making their own pottery to a very high standard. It is intriguing to think that the influence emanating from the Seven Hills of Rome should touch the hills of this area of North Staffordshire, where eventually six pottery manufacturing towns became collectively famous as 'The Potteries'.

It is well known, of course, that Josiah Wedgwood, building a new pottery factory and village in the late 1760s on the banks of what was to become the new Trent and Mersey canal, named the area Etruria after the ancient name of a region in central Italy. It was there that 'Etruscan' black vases decorated with red classical figures were being unearthed in archaeological tomb excavations. Wedgwood admired them to such an extent that he copied them in black basalt with the same red decorative figures, proudly engraving in Latin on the base of each: *'Artes Etruriae Renascuntur'* – 'The Art of Etruria is Reborn'. It was mistakenly thought that the originals were Etruscan in origin whereas they were almost certainly Greek.

In a more frivolous vein, when car registration numbers were being chosen in the 1920s, an amusing solution was found by Stoke-on-Trent which adopted the Roman 'V' for five and ended local registration numbers with the letters 'VT' for 'Five Towns'. The latter name was taken from books, (in particular, 'Anna of the Five Towns') written about the Potteries by its most famous author, Arnold Bennett, after whom I was named.

Stoke-upon-Trent had always been the parochial centre of the original group of villages since the parish church of St Peter ad Vincula was built there, and centuries later it became the administrative centre of the region as well as the hub of its railway network. The discovery of abundant seams of high-grade coal brought great prosperity to the area through the mining, pottery and steel industries; but with industrial development came roaring furnaces and billowing bottle-kilns, creating a perpetual smog over the Potteries which was to last until the middle of the twentieth century and the introduction of the Clean Air Act.

The birth of the city of Stoke-upon-Trent was a laborious one, but in 1910, the year before I was born, the six towns of the Potteries – Stoke, Burslem, Longton, Fenton, Tunstall and Hanley – finally amalgamated to form the county borough of Stoke-on-Trent. Stoke continued to be the administrative centre, taking the status of 'city' in 1925 and its mayor becoming 'Lord Mayor' in 1928.

If, in 1911, you were standing in Stoke-on-Trent in the square known as Campbell Place you would see a bronze statue of Colin Minton Campbell, a previous Mayor and benefactor of Stoke. In 1869 he became High Sheriff of the county and an MP for North Staffordshire in 1874. His statue was later moved to a site near the modern Minton factory.

Your attention might be taken by 'The Wheatsheaf' public house, with the Spode china factory behind, or the splendid wrought-iron sign depicting a huge bunch of grapes hanging outside 'The Vine'. A short walk would bring you to the Quaker Meeting House and burial ground. Past St.Peter's church a road to the right would lead to Fenton and Longton, while the road to the left would take you out of the square towards Burslem and Hanley. Turn south along the London Road and you would find, running alongside, a canal serving Minton's flint mill, Minton's china factory, Minton's earthenware factory and a splendid complex, sponsored by Minton, comprising a library, a school of art and a public swimming bath. Much further along on the right would be the Minton estate of Italianate Victorian houses, known as 'The Villas' and eventually, as the canal veered off to the left behind the Oak Hill estate, London Road would continue towards the village of Trent Vale with the side roads of Sutherland Terrace, Rookery Lane and Flash Lane leading off it.

What memories are evoked by the place names, road names and surnames of our past: all weaving in and out in a creative tapestry and producing, finally, a most surprising pattern to one's life.

I was born on September 30th 1911 at Oak Hill, Stoke-upon-Trent, the ninth child of William James Machin and his wife, Sarah Ann. Father was known to his friends as 'Bill' and Mother as 'Sran', and they were both devoted to their large family which eventually numbered twelve: William was the eldest, followed by Albert and Percy; then came three girls, Elsie, Ethel and Hilda; next Wilfred and Henry, myself and Edwin. Sadly another sister, Vera, died aged seven from mastoiditis; also a tiny baby, Peter, who was unchristened. This left me and my younger brother, Edwin, as the youngest in this very loving family.

Soon after I was born the family moved from Oak Hill to the village of Trent Vale, about half-a-mile away and further from the centre of Stoke-upon-Trent. Number 813, where we lived, was in a terrace of about twenty houses on London Road, the first one being at the junction with Flash Lane. This was a 'corner shop' owned by Mrs. Dumelow and was a general store selling everything from bread and chocolate to paraffin and other household goods. In the middle of the terrace was another small shop selling toys, sweets, chocolate and sterilized milk, which we called 'paralysed' milk for fun. I remember 'Five Boys' chocolate bars in particular. Our house was two doors above the Post Office and these three shops are still in existence.

The story of moving day must often have been told in the family for although I was then a babe-in-arms I know every detail. It was general practice for families to move as much as possible themselves in a handcart, while larger and heavier items like furniture were taken by a carter in a horse-drawn cart. My father had several figures under glass domes and when the carter arrived he insisted on carrying the most precious of these himself. As he lifted it off the cart he turned and walked into a lamp-post, shattering it beyond repair.

The new house faced the main road. The front room had a bay window overlooking a brick-paved area about one yard wide, and this was surrounded by a low wall topped with triangular coping stones. The good, strong front door gave immediate access to the front room, or 'parlour' as it was always known, of which my parents must have been particularly proud. There was a rather elegant marble fireplace with a cast-iron basket surrounded by greenish-blue tiles decorated with painted flowers. On the mantelpiece above, my father placed his precious glass dome containing a colourful kingfisher, and a Copeland Parian figure called 'The Slave'. I remember being impressed by the chain which secured the slave to a post: it was made up of fine porcelain links which looked exactly like the real thing. Over the mantelpiece was a large gilt mirror with gas brackets each side and in front of this, in the centre, stood an elaborate gilded clock. The ceiling had a cornice surround and in the centre a rather nicely designed ceiling rose with a three-branched gas chandelier.

There were recessed cupboards on either side of the fireplace, one containing the gas meter and the other used for storage. I remember an old violin and a flute in a case, but no books. A table stood in the bay window with an aspidistra in an embossed green pot and a pottery swan which could also contain flowers, and I remember a Victorian settee and two armchairs facing the fireplace.

The décor was completed by two romantic prints taken from paintings by Glendening which hung against flowery wallpaper. Subsequently an upright piano was added but that came much later. It is interesting that

Glendenning's original paintings are today valued at several thousand pounds. This modern age which has despised traditional skills is now beginning to look back with admiration at Victorian and Edwardian painting.

From the parlour a plaster-moulded archway led into the kitchen where cooking was done on a cast-iron kitchen range. This had a central firebox with an oven on one side and a water container on the other. The window looked down a paved blue-brick yard to the back gate opening on to a cinder path known as 'the backs' which ran behind all the houses. Some of the more thoughtless tenants threw their rubbish here, which wasn't very pleasant for children playing. The other side of the backs contained stabling at the lower end, and there were allotments at the top end bordering on Flash Lane.

The local infants' school was also near here, attached to a chapel at the top of Flash Lane. When I started school I was interested to see a glass-fronted cupboard displaying selected models made by previous pupils and some of these had been made by my eldest brother, Will, although it was some years since he had left. This made me particularly proud. Another incident which I clearly recall was when one of the boys died of diphtheria and all the children attended his funeral. The service took place in the chapel next door and I remember vividly how we all filed past the coffin to take a last look at this boy. The lid of the coffin had a glass window inserted which enabled us to look at his face. Diphtheria was a terrifying illness.

The backyard of our house had high dividing walls for privacy, a small coal house and an outside lavatory; by the gate my father had built a small wooden workshop with a stove in it. In the summer Father shaved in the yard in the fresh air. I can see in my mind the hook on the wall where he hung a small mirror and the leather strap, known as a 'strop', on which he sharpened his cut-throat razor. In the cold weather he did this daily chore in the scullery or 'back kitchen'. Here there was an earthenware sink with a cold water tap, and a copper boiler with a small firebox underneath to heat the water for clothes washing, which was always done on Mondays. I can remember the dismay on wet Mondays when the washing could not be dried on the clothes line in the yard and the kitchen was full of wet sheets hanging from the ceiling rack: it made us all feel miserable. I can also recall the pleasure it gave me when Mother was doing the ironing with flat irons heated on the range; the raising and lowering of the rack with rope and pulley and the wonderful warm smell of folded linen hanging there to air. The scents of childhood are still very strong.

Normally we went down to the back kitchen to wash, but Saturday night was bath night when the copper boiler was heated up and buckets full of hot water carefully carried to the zinc bath standing on the floor by the range. Towels and night-shirts would be warmed on the overhead rack while we younger ones started the proceedings – and oh, how hot it was on the side nearest to the fire and how cold on the side furthest away, especially in wintertime.

The staircase to the bedrooms above led out of the kitchen, and underneath a larder was formed, but without any ventilation. At the top of the stairs was a small landing with the main bedroom on the left, over the parlour. This contained a large double bed, a wardrobe and two wicker chairs. There was a fireplace with a small hairy mat before it and a gas bracket over the bed. The window looked down on to London Road.

The bedroom to the right of the landing was over the kitchen and had a fireplace, and a window overlooking the yard. There were two beds squeezed into this room with five of us sleeping in the largest, three at the top and two at the bottom. This presented problems in cold winters when we had to keep warm with the oven shelf or hot bricks wrapped in a piece of blanket – did you put these at the top or bottom of the bed? The walls were usually papered with stripes or roses and a cupboard built in at the side of the fireplace formed a wardrobe. There was a small gas light to the side of the window. I am now convinced that these gas jets upstairs contributed to many of our ailments. The ceilings were very low compared with those of the downstairs rooms and the gas fumes were therefore held at a lower level. Another small bedroom led out of this one, situated over the back-kitchen, with a small window overlooking our neighbour's yard. This room did not have a gas light, so either an oil lamp or a candle was used.

Life was hard in the early 1900s, with large families, sickly children and very low pay for long hours of work. The child two or three doors away suffered from congestion of the lungs and it was common practice, when the roads were being tarmacked, for mothers to hold their afflicted child over the steaming pitch, heated in a tank on wheels, which was nicknamed 'puffing Billy', hoping that this awful treatment would bring some relief. I was astonished when I saw our neighbour take her small child out to the workmen, who lifted the lid of the tank so that the child could be held over the fumes. It appeared rather drastic treatment to me.

Next door lived a couple on their own and they had a lodger with cancer. I remember listening, terrified, as my mother and her neighbour exchanged graphic descriptions of 'cancer being a growth which branched out like a tree'. In bed that night I found radiating lines on the fleshy part of my legs and was convinced that I had cancer. Of course it was only the temporary lines caused by the creases in my trousers but for a time I was unbelievably distressed. The regular chatter of the two women used to enter into my mind and cause me great consternation, for they always talked about disaster and illness, never pleasant things.

In these early years there was no such thing as social security or free medical treatment; consequently poor families never called in a doctor, and when on the rare occasions they did it was usually a sign that the patient was dying. I remember Dr Johnson, a tall, very dignified white-haired gentleman who tended to shuffle along, but I think he came only two or three times: once when the youngest baby was ill. I remember this tiny boy lying on a couch in the kitchen and my mother periodically rubbing olive oil on his lips to moisten them. He died before he could be christened.

Another occasion was when my youngest sister, Vera, was very ill with earache. The pain was unbearable and eventually she was taken to Hartshill hospital where she died from mastoiditis. She was a sweet child aged seven and we all missed her very much. She was brought home in a coffin which was placed in the parlour on the night before the funeral. I can see now this small figure lying there with hands folded on her chest looking like a beautiful marble carving, and I was lifted up to kiss her forehead before the lid was screwed down. I remember how cold she was. All the family kissed her before she departed from us for the last time. It was one of the saddest days of my life and I will never forget the scene in our front room and the peculiar smell of death that seemed to permeate it.

Death was a dramatic event in which we all took part. Generally people were nursed and died at home but if not, the body was brought home to lie in state in an open coffin so that family and neighbours could gather round to pay their last respects to the deceased and give support to the family. At Trent Vale there was no graveyard and all were taken to Hartshill cemetery for burial. The hearse was a coach drawn by two black horses, and smaller coffins were put into a small compartment under the seating. The cost of burial must have been very expensive for poor families as there was no help from outside. There was also very little opportunity to visit the grave once the funeral was over: it was a very long walk there and back and our lives were one long struggle for survival.

About this time in my life I recall another incident involving Dr Johnson. My mother had a sister, Mrs Littler, who lived in Flash Lane. Her husband was a potter working in Stoke-on-Trent but he was dying of silicosis caused by clay dust in the lungs. It was a terrible affliction, and many who worked in the pottery industry and in the mines suffered from it. Before there were regulations to control this lethal dust many young people died before they were thirty. One day I was taken to visit this aunt and my cousins because they needed family help. The eldest boy, Gordon, who was about my age, had pulled a pan of boiling liquid off the hob and had scalded himself badly. When Dr Johnson arrived I watched as the boy's stomach was exposed and the doctor, taking out a pair of scissors, carefully cut each huge blister. Gordon eventually recovered, but his father died not long after this event.

I was a sickly child myself, often away from school and consequently rather solitary, and never happy in a crowd. My sister, Hilda, became a nursemaid to us and she was very dedicated to me – as indeed they all were. I must have been born with a pencil in my hand for I was drawing from the very earliest days and I used to sit on a little stool, made by Father, using his armchair as a work table. The entire family would stint themselves to provide me with books, pencils, watercolours, scraps of paper and wrapping paper with which to work.

When I was ill my mother would light a fire in the bedroom where she and my father slept so that I could be warm while I was recuperating. She had to be very economical and could not afford many fires. During one period my hair fell out, and I spent most of my time indoors. I preferred to construct things, draw or simply daydream rather than play outside. I remember that once when I was away from school, Hilda made me a pair of cowboy trousers from a rather hairy old rug, and a stetson from an old trilby hat. I also had a wooden toy gun with a holster, of which I was very proud. Our eldest brother, William, obtained from somewhere a magic lantern to entertain us all. Sometimes we watched it in the shed in the yard, with a blacked-out window and an oil lamp, but if I was recovering from one of my bouts of illness I was allowed to have it in the bedroom. I placed it under the bed where it was darkest and lifted one part of the sheets to allow the sun to filter through and this beam I directed into the lens. We only had one film, black and white of course, entitled 'Man and Beast'. It was wonderful to be the projectionist and entertain myself with pictures of animals and men. The spool of film was very large, about eight inches in diameter, and I cannot recall that I ever reached the end of it.

On Saturday mornings, weather permitting, we younger children were cleared out of the house to go for a walk, usually with Hilda in charge, while the older ones helped Mother to give the house a thorough clean-up. Everything was tackled: the carpets were taken outside and beaten, the floor scrubbed, the windows cleaned, but the major operation was the cleaning of the grate in the kitchen. The ashes were taken outside and riddled, the fire-irons polished and all the ironwork black-leaded. The steel knobs on the oven door and the water container together with the moulded front edge of the range were highly polished until they shone like silver. The effect when the fire was newly lit was heartening, and I am sure that it was a welcome sight for my father when he returned from work at lunch time, for everyone worked on Saturday mornings in those days.

Mother's family were possibly of gypsy stock and she herself was rather tall and erect with dark hair. She was immensely strong: it was no trouble to her to chop wood, except that one day she chopped across her thumb, which was permanently dislocated as a result. She was devoted to her family, every single one being loved and well cared for, but she was a very determined woman and was the real boss of the family.

My father was smaller than her physically and of a very quiet disposition. I never heard him say a rough word in the house and he was silent when she tried to argue with him, but he must at times have been very irritating to my mother with his go-as-you-please temperament. He liked a drink of beer, of course, and would frequently go down to the pub after his evening meal. I can't really blame him, for with a house full of children he must have felt the need to get away from the noise, but he was a good father to us. Ranged round the table were the stools he had made for each child and every Sunday, after cooking an early breakfast for himself when all was quiet, he would take breakfast in bed to my mother so that she could have a rest. He would then seat us children round the fire on our little stools while he cooked something for us. Eggs were too expensive to have often and we never had one each. I think that many poorer children in those days had only half an egg. Mother had great difficulty in dividing them equally. Father obtained a blacksmith-made tray of open bars which could be hooked on to the front bars of the fire grate. This grill had a slide plate controlling the distance from the fire, and also a domed tin plate which was placed behind to reflect the heat on to the rear portion of the food being cooked; it was known as a 'tin bonnet'.

I never remember my father being ill; he never seemed to catch cold or have to stay away from work. The only time that my mother took to her bed was when she was giving birth, always with a neighbour to act as midwife. Normally she was busy about the house, salting kidney beans in stone jars in the summertime, pickling surplus vegetables and, when eggs were plentiful and cheap, preserving them in isinglass. She made interesting drinks like nettle beer and ginger beer and something called 'Bees wine' which was started with ginger and left to ferment. Cousin Gordon's mother was very good at making a drink from dandelions and burdock, and I remember that she used to sell it at twopence a bottle, which helped a little with their income. At home, in hot weather, there was often a huge bowl of lemonade with a cup to dip into it. In wintertime father made ice-cream for us. He used to put a tin container inside a larger one and fill the space between with ice and 'freezing salt'; then cream was put into the smaller tin and the whole thing made to revolve with a handle which he had fixed to it. This was a great treat.

Father was very skilful. I recall that he kept a bottle of 'quicksilver' in a locked drawer in order to restore mirrors. I was fascinated to see this amazing liquid rolling around. He had his own last and bought leather and nails so that he could repair the family's shoes. He was the family barber and would sit us down with a cloth round our shoulders to cut our hair – outside in the warmer weather. Then there were the little stools he had made, one for each child, and a wooden scooter for us to play with.

Our parents never stopped working, so that we ourselves felt guilty if we were not busy too. Young people today do not seem to have the same sense of urgency but I think it is rather nice to feel the necessity to be doing something. If we went for walks it was not a simple outing but an opportunity to collect sticks for the fire, mushrooms, blackberries, bilberries, hazelnuts – it was in our nature, I think. We would come back with wildflowers for Mother: I especially remember our picking huge bunches of bluebells and primroses. In those days anything free and edible was valuable food, and there was fierce competition in the neighbourhood to find the mushrooms first. When brother Percy went to work in the local coalmines he would often arrive home at about three-o'clock in the morning after a night-shift. One of us would tie a long piece of string to our big toe and then let the string dangle through the window. Percy's job was to tug hard on the string to waken us so that we could be off mushrooming really early.

At Trent Vale we lived on the edge of the Potteries, within walking distance of the lovely Hanchurch Hills and the caves at Beech. At weekends or during holidays we would sometimes take food and a rope to this exciting place and lower ourselves down into the caves. I remember burning my hands as I slid down the rope: it was terribly painful but I dared not tell my parents, so one of my brothers secretly brought me a bowl of water when we reached home so that I could immerse my hands. Beech caves had been a quarry and the stone used to build local cottages. Stone pillars had been left to support the roof and this made it interesting and a great place to explore. Munitions were stored there during the last war.

Trentham Park, owned by the Duke of Sutherland, was also not far away. At certain times it was open to the public and once a year, during the bank holiday, came a day known locally as 'Trentham Thursday', when many people either walked or rode in wagonettes to the park. Sometimes we used to sit with Mother in the bay window, concealed behind the aspidistra, and watch this motley crowd passing by in their finery; but if possible she would make the effort to take us there, looking upon this as her annual holiday. It was quite a long walk for small children and I can remember Mother putting the smallest in the pram and two or three of us hanging on to the side, feeling that by so doing the journey would be made easier for us. At Trentham, stalls were set up by the enterprising, selling orange juice, lemon juice and cold milk. I remember one occasion when someone told the stallholders that the inspectors were coming and the man selling milk emptied it all away and disappeared. Mother told us that he must have watered it down and was liable for prosecution. She took her own bottles of water, milk or homemade lemonade and some sandwiches.

There had originally been a mansion in the park approached, so I was told, through huge gilded iron gates of great magnificence. The river Trent flowed through the grounds beside a lovely lake, but unfortunately for the Duke and his family, a great deal of effluent from the Potteries entered the Trent upstream and the resulting stench eventually drove them away. They moved back to Scotland, taking the 'golden gates' with them. In the year that I was born their stately home was demolished, leaving only part of the west front and the stable block intact. As I grew older I became fascinated by this old stabling built of beautiful stone and with its own splendid smithy, the doorway of which was formed like a great horseshoe; on either side rose huge masonry columns, each capped with an impressive vase emitting stone flames. This spectacular design always entranced me.

Beyond the entrance was a long walk leading to the lake in 'Spring Valley' where fewer people went, and it was here that Mother took us to enjoy our refreshments and then to play or explore under the magnificent trees. Nearby a little stream meandered under a bridge carved from one enormous stone with two steps cut into it and I always made for this as it impressed me no end. Our day ended with a long and tiring walk home, Mother knowing that we should all sleep well that night.

Those who could afford to do so would spend a few days away during the holiday week in summer, which later became known as 'Potters' Week' and in more recent times as 'Potters' Fortnight'. We would peep through the window as the holidaymakers went past with poorly-made yellow cardboard trunks – handles tied with string or with rope to bind them, struggling to get it all to the station; going away with white faces and coming back looking like turkey cocks, some wearing funny hats. There was always a strangely quiet atmosphere in Trent Vale during this period, when we felt that everyone had gone away and we had been left alone. When we had a family day out I cannot remember that Father ever came with us – his holiday was probably spent peacefully tending his allotment.

My father was reared by two aunts and little was known about his ancestry, but it must have been quite remarkable, and I am proud to have his genes. He was always a Conservative, which made my mother very cross. "What are you but Labour?" she would say. Mother told me that he once set off for America to make his fortune and he baked a great box of dry toast to eat on board ship. However, having worked his passage, he must have decided that America was not for him, as he returned almost immediately.

Father was originally a freelance modeller and when William left school, (which all children did at the age of fourteen) he worked with our father in the shed at the bottom of the back yard. They designed small models similar to Goss China, making windmills, motor cars, little presents from Blackpool, egg cups, and oval salt and pepper pots which were turned on a lathe and then sealed at the bottom with a screw cap. I used to watch them working and was fascinated to see Father colouring the salt and pepper pots to look like eggs. He also designed a china canary with a hollow tail which he filled with water and blew down so that the bubbling water warbled like a bird. Will was skilful and inventive and also a very good watercolour artist. When he was working in the shed he used to show me how to model little figures and, with small metal tools which he had designed himself from stainless steel knitting needles, how to make the eyes and finger nails. Later on, when I started modelling seriously, he gave me my own set of modelling tools which he had made most beautifully and I still value them.

Father and Will were ambitious and tried to survive by producing these small models for the pottery industry but they did not realise the difficulties involved: having produced a model they then had to travel on foot round the factories trying to sell it but, even if they did so the remuneration was so little that it was impossible to make it worthwhile. Eventually they were forced to give it up and each get a job with a reliable source of income. Will found work as a modeller at a local factory and my father became a turner at Buller's Porcelain Factory, making huge insulators. (Oddly enough a girl who in later years became a great friend of mine as a student, latterly came to work at Buller's. Her name was Nita Hoy: she was Danish, and her work is in the V&A Museum).

After the family moved to London Road my father had to walk seven miles to work and seven miles back each day. In spite of this he continued to work industriously every weekend on the allotment which he kept about a quarter of a mile from the house. Here he grew a great deal of food for us, which must have helped considerably with the housekeeping bills. Water for the allotment had to be taken from the tap in the house and he had a 'carrying hoop' which enabled him to carry two buckets at a time without strain. We always thought he had invented the idea, but I am not certain of this. We children had to help by following the delivery horses with a bucket and shovel to collect the manure and also collect autumn leaves for rotting down in his garden. I remember that once my brothers had a bit of fun with him by trying to grow a prize marrow: they inserted a tube into it and injected artificial manure, but without success. Father was furious with them for, as he put it, "mucking about with my marrow."

We all had to help with weeding, digging, or carrying the vegetables home for mother to make a tasty stew with cheap cuts of meat. She was a remarkable manager and I never felt hungry or deprived. She had an old sewing machine, cutting down and remaking outgrown clothes for the younger children. When we were old enough we helped by selling newspapers, helping to fill coal-sacks for the coal merchant who lived opposite, or bundling up sticks for a man who supplied these to local shops as firelighters. He had a clamp, operated by a foot pedal, which held the sticks tightly together while we bound them round with wire.

I always remember how exciting it was, at the end of the Great War, when a local coalman bought a pair of wonderful black 'War horses' to pull his wagons. We helped to feed them by collecting hay in return, perhaps, for a few bits of coal. So in this way we were all expected to help with the economics of living; but in spite of this and of school work my passion for drawing and modelling continued to grow, encouraged and nurtured by the family.

Although the house was very congested we rarely used the front room, but we had marvellous times there at Christmas when the girls decorated it with festoons of coloured paper which they made themselves and glass balls which were carefully packed away when the festivities were over. I can remember them making dolls from wooden pegs and sewing tiny garments for them, and other 'peg' toys which we used like boxers or acrobats which swung over on a wooden frame. At Halloween father used to make a turnip lantern, hollowed out with a candle inside, and on Guy Fawkes' night we always had a few simple fireworks, like 'bunters', which were as thick as a cigarette with a wick to light which banged harmlessly and, of course, a few sparklers.

I don't think that birthdays were celebrated particularly, doubtless because there were so many of us, but the girls made a fuss of us younger children, and there was perhaps something special to eat at teatime. We may have had 'new' clothes, which would not be newly bought but handed down from older brothers or sisters, or those cut-down and altered by Mother. I expect that the older ones had to wait until they started work to buy brand new clothes. Certainly I remember being taken by Mother, shortly before I started work at fourteen, to buy my first suit from 'The Co-operative Emporium' in Stoke – it was a great day for me.

A very pleasurable occasion was the annual carnival when children were dressed in fancy costume and driven round the village on tradesmen's wagons drawn by horses. The wagons were beautifully decorated and the horses groomed until their coats shone, then hung with ribbons and rosettes. It was a most exciting event for everyone in the village and my sisters in particular had great fun making costumes from bits and pieces. When I was about three or four they made a very attractive Pierrot costume for me to wear.

Once a year Pat Collins's Fair came to the area, an event which was very exciting; not that we had any money to spend, but there were sideshows and stalls which we could gaze at and there was a special atmosphere which only came with the Fair, or the circus; our entertainment with the latter was to wander round the tents, caravans and wagons looking at the animals and the people who trained them. We found the animals particularly interesting as few people kept pets at home in those days, although my younger brother Edwin eventually had a cat; possibly by then Mother could afford a little extra food to feed it.

Not far from where we lived was a disused marl pit which had been used for quarrying clay for brick-making. It was gradually being filled in with rubbish from the Potteries and on this site were pieces of broken moulds from pottery working which we regularly collected: bits of figurines, cup handles, teapot spouts. It was a treasure trove for children and we pressed soft clay into these pieces to make our own models.

The pit however, which was always full of water, was said to be ninety feet deep, so that it was a treacherous playground. Iron railings surrounded part of it but these had been bent and twisted and were no deterrent. The marl pit was a death-trap and several children had died in it. I myself almost drowned in it. I was only very young and had been sitting with other children on a bank close to the water when suddenly I was accidentally pushed and slid into the deep water. No one could help me as I gasped and struggled and it was only by some miracle that a man who happened to be bringing rubble with a horse and cart was told by the children who ran to him, and he rushed to the spot and pulled me out unconscious. He held me upside-down and shook me to try to empty my lungs of water, then quickly carried me home. I clearly remember being propped up under the kitchen window and being given grapes to aid my recovery: goodness knows how Mother could afford to buy them.

On another occasion I was at the marl pit with other children coming home from school in wintertime. There was ice on the pit and some children had been sliding on it, but at the end where the warm rubbish was tipped the ice was thinner. A small girl, not knowing this, ran straight on to the thin ice and was drowned. I still feel the horror of it as I see again in my mind the little body, splayed out in a wheelbarrow, being wheeled past us to 'The Swan'; maybe I felt that it might have been me. Years later as a young student I had travelled back from London by train to Stoke where I caught a bus home. Sitting opposite me was a girl and an elderly lady who looked at me very intently before the girl asked, "Is your name Arnold Machin?" When I replied in the affirmative she said, "My father saved your life when you were drowning in the marl pit." What a surprise, and what a shock to be suddenly confronted by an incident so long forgotten. It reminded me of how fortunate I was to survive when a number of children had perished in that same pit.

By now the 1914-18 War had begun, and William and Albert – my two eldest brothers – joined up together, both barely old enough to enlist. Will was in the Royal Artillery, and I remember that his letters home were most graphically illustrated with horses pulling gun carriages and with sometimes very amusing, even rude, drawings. One Christmas, when he came home on leave, I was so excited that as he arrived I promptly fell downstairs from top to bottom. He brought his spare puttees for us to wrap round our boots to protect us from snow. To our great relief he survived the war without mishap. Albert was not so fortunate: he was gassed when mustard gas was first introduced, and was sent back to work in the mines in Pontefract. My brother Percy was stationed at historic Nostell Priory in the West Riding of Yorkshire, about which he used to talk a great deal when he came home on leave. It is now owned by the National Trust.

Various memories remain in my mind from that period. I well remember when the first Zeppelin airship came over the Potteries looking for the blast furnaces of Shelton Bar Iron Works which produced steel for the manufacture of ammunition. Mother picked me up and took me to the front door to watch this great 'cigar' going across the sky. We heard one or two explosions and then it disappeared, but it did no damage and no one was hurt that I recall.

After Hilda left school she worked for a time at a chemist's shop in Stoke, called 'Tippers' and she sometimes took me with her. Her job was to count pills into bottles and to break up 'Spanish juice' – a hard, black, brittle substance tasting like aniseed. We used to buy liquorice root from the shop, chewing it to break down the fibres and extract the liquorice. Afterwards the fibres looked like paintbrush bristles and we pretended to use them as such.

Mother continued to manage the household in her usual efficient way. Once, when I was old enough, she insisted that I go to the Co-op instead of her as she was too busy. It was a quarter of a mile away, and my visit caused a sensation because I had to ask for a special cut of gammon costing as little as possible. The staff joked about it, causing me great embarrassment.

I was always impressed by the system of payment used there. One of the staff used to sit in an elevated compartment in a corner of the shop from where a series of double wires led down to different sections of the serving counter; the assistant serving would then put one's payment into a metal cup attached to the wires, screw on the lid , pull down a handle, and the cup would be ferried along the wires to the cashier in the elevated office. There, the bill was made out, any change put with it into the cup and the process reversed , the contents being returned to the appropriate customer. I believe that this system was unique at that time and heard that it was produced and installed by 'The Dart Cash Carrier Co. Ltd' of Campbell Road, Stoke in most of the shops belonging to the North Staffs Co-operative Wholesale Society. On these errands to the Co-op it was imperative that we call at the newsagents afterwards, not to buy a paper, which we couldn't afford, but to memorise the notice boards in order to tell Mother the state of the war.

The poor in those times were greatly impoverished, however hard they worked; the rich, conversely, lived in a world far removed from the rest. One such was a man named Patzer who lived at Clayton Hall (now a school). He rode along Flash Lane to the Potteries every morning in a coach pulled by two splendid horses, on his way to business. He was German and during the war there were rumours that he was a spy and was signalling with lights from the top of the hall.

A man who had aspirations of greatness was Mr Sharpley, the Town Clerk for Stoke. He had a farm below the Hanchurch Hills at the back of the Trentham estate laundry. Every day he rode on horseback to the Town Hall. Tall, slim, dignified but very autocratic, he always rode on the pavements so that people on foot had to make way for him. He presented a striking figure but, according to accounts, he was also a bit of a rogue. It was said that because he had prior information about land that was going to be requisitioned by the Government in wartime, he would acquire it at a very low price and later sell it to the Government at an enormous profit.

The local butcher could never get Sharpley to pay his bills, which eventually added up to a considerable amount so he hit upon an unusual way to reimburse himself. There was a slaughter-house on the London Road, not far from the centre of Stoke and periodically Sharpley sent his sheep and cattle there. On the way the drover had to pass the butcher's shop where, by prior arrangement, he managed to leave a sheep or cow to compensate the butcher for unpaid bills.

We knew a land girl who worked for a time on Sharpley's farm and she told us that one day he had the sweep to clean his chimneys. When he had finished, Mrs Sharpley told him that she hadn't the money to pay him. Immediately he threw his bag of soot forcibly on to the kitchen floor, creating black dust everywhere, and saying: "I don't move from this bloody house until I get paid"; which presumably he was! When Mr.Sharpley eventually retired as Town Clerk they tried to arrange a special benefit for him, but so many people had suffered during his administration that there were objections and he had to leave unrewarded. It was said that he was lucky not to find himself in prison.

In those days there were trams passing through Trent Vale to transport workers along the route from Hanford to Stoke. The trams had to negotiate a bad bend in the road outside 'The Swan' where periodically they became derailed. This event did not seem to unduly perturb the driver who would ask the passengers to alight, then fetch a bucket of water from the pub and throw it under the wheels of the tram; the force of the resulting electrical charge caused the tram to 'jump' back on to the rails. Later the tramlines were taken up, and omnibuses used instead.

Ambulances frequently brought injured troops to and from Hartshill hospital, travelling down London Road and Flash Lane. One night an ambulance took the wrong turning and began to drive down Sutherland Terrace towards the marl pit. Horrified onlookers who took a short cut, shouting and flashing lights, managed to bring it to a halt before it plunged into the pit. One day I saw people running alongside a number of ambulances, throwing in socks and cushions to the soldiers as they passed.

Knitting socks for the boys in France was a regular pastime, for in this way those at home felt that they were 'doing their bit' towards the war effort. One of those who knitted socks was a wealthy member of the Minton Pottery family known as 'Minton-Senhouse' because he came from a different branch of the family. My eldest sister, Elsie, started work as a nursemaid at his large house along London Road and occasionally I would go with her. The long, deep drive was edged by ferns and rhododendrons and it is impossible to imagine the pleasure that I derived from the scent of these plants: it still lingers in my memory. The house itself was so out-of-this-world that I could not help but be impressed by the imposing magnificence both inside and out. I recall a huge rocking horse in the nursery which to my child's eyes was almost life-size, and the scale of the room seemed enormous. Little did I know that in later years the owner was to become my 'boss'.

2

When I was seven I moved to the main school at Trent Vale which was situated on the Newcastle-under-Lyme road opposite 'The Swan'. It was a Church of England school and every morning the vicar of St.Michael's came at nine-o'clock to take a short service. On special saints' days the whole school went to church. I found this interesting as the church had a spire and the walls inside were stencilled all over with Victorian fleurs-de-lys which seemed to create a special atmosphere. In later years, I visited Pugin's church at Cheadle, also decorated, but much more elaborately.

Unusually for that era we were given swimming lessons, regularly walking, as a school, to the Minton baths in Stoke. To reach the baths we had to go along a passageway behind the library where two life-size terracotta figures were on display. I was very taken with these: one was of Shakespeare I remember.

On my walks I absorbed everything that was new to my eyes. Swan Lane led down to the canal where there was a picturesque drawbridge and some very clever engineering had counterbalanced the bridge with huge oak beams so that a man could, with the slightest effort, operate the lifting and lowering of the bridge. It was aesthetically beautiful, one hundred per cent effective in operation and yet simple, like all the devices invented when the canals were built. I also remember a brick-built bridge, not far from here, which had to be built at an angle. I was first attracted to it by the decorative effect of the castellated brickwork, thinking that it was merely decoration, but when I looked more closely and examined it from underneath on the towpath I saw that in order to build the bridge on the skew they had to start the arches at an unusual angle which, when completed, automatically formed the castellated effect.

It must have been about this time that a travelling salesman called and persuaded my mother to buy, by instalments, twelve massive volumes of Arthur Mee's Encyclopaedia. What a godsend this was. My horizon was suddenly widened beyond anything I could possibly have imagined. The books were profusely illustrated and provided an endless source of pleasure and enlightenment. I was excited to find a section on fossils and was introduced to great paintings, sculpture, architecture, poetry, literature, invention, as well as Greek and Roman art and all their enchanting myths and legends. I copied some of the pictures and remember especially drawing 'Hercules and the Python'. It was like entering a new and magical world. Previously the two Glendening prints had been my only means of escape from a barren cultural atmosphere, although they had served their purpose – the elegantly dressed figures, arm in arm, descending moss-covered steps to a boat which would enable them, and me, to glide away into the unknown, into the world of imagination.

It did not take much to start my imagination working as I was something of a dreamer. One thing that stirred me was the fossils to be found in lumps of coal. In those days coal was delivered in much larger pieces and it really did glisten like 'black diamonds' and had varied fern fossils embedded in it. Studying these and reading about them in the encyclopaedia kept me enthralled for many hours.

My older brothers and sisters were all working by this time, which must have eased the strain on the housekeeping budget. Young people in those days were expected to hand over their pay packet if they still lived at home and were given 'pocket money' for their personal expenditure. Mother probably took the opportunity to put by a few savings.

There was a little shop in Stoke called 'Heads' which supplied artists' materials. My brothers and sisters would spend hard-earned pence there to buy for me, amongst other things, postcards to copy. These included romantic Italian gardens by moonlight painted by Tom Mostyn (just recently, in Kensington High Street, a picture dealer produced a large and magnificent painting by Tom Mostyn with an asking price of £6,000). He was a very fine painter: although he was almost ignored by the artistic world of the time he had a tremendous influence on my own artistic development.

Elsie, who was a very dear person, later ran a children's home at Penkhull where she had about twelve children to look after. I used to visit her there and help with the cleaning. Eventually she married but because only single people were employed she had to give up this work. Poor Elsie, who so loved children and would have made a marvellous mother, died in childbirth. My mother was called out and had to walk about two miles to see her, but before she died she was hallucinating. Mother said that Elsie was terrified because she could see black beetles running all round the room. Then she fell into a coma and died during the night. Mother walked home very early the next morning while we were still in bed. She came upstairs with tears in her eyes and said: "Elsie's died, with the little baby." I groaned and turned over; I couldn't speak and I am still filled with emotion when I recall that day.

Life brought many tragedies to most families and ours was no exception. One Saturday my next eldest sister Ethel, who was now married, came home in a terrible state. Her husband Bill, a miner, had consumption and was in a very bad way. Ethel said that he was hysterical and his mind was wandering, and then she fainted away in front of us all. Bill had been in a mining disaster and could not forget the flooded mine, the escaping gas and the young miners who had been trapped and could not be rescued from the pit. Ethel could not quieten him as he shouted, "Let them come up! Let them come up!" Towards the end he said, "My nose feels big", and when he was examined it was found that the disease had eaten away the division between his nostrils, forming a large cavity. He died leaving Ethel with one son, William.

Ethel started back to work in the pottery industry where she had trained as a paintress, at Wilshaw's factory. Of all my sisters she was probably the most attractive and certainly had a flirtatious nature which gave her many admirers. One of the directors of the factory who was engaged to be married, persuaded Ethel to go out with him the night before his wedding. She was very honest and told our mother about this. Mother was not at all happy about the situation, but Ethel was flattered to be asked out by the boss and besides this there was always the chance that she would be 'given the sack' if she refused. So Mother grudgingly agreed to look after William while Ethel had her night out. In the course of time Ethel remarried and moved to Derby.

Hilda was closest to me in age, with only Wilfred and Henry between us. She it was who was given charge of us when Mother was particularly busy. In our younger days we all shared the same bed, plus young Edwin, but later Hilda moved into the little back room and one night she was extremely ill. I didn't really know what was wrong with her, but now I think it was probably due to her monthly periods because the doctor could do very little for her. Some of us were up all night warming a lot of salt in a frying pan, the salt then being put into a linen flour bag to make a poultice to ease her pain.

Eventually Hilda became attached to a young man named Charlie Hudson who was a tile-maker. His father was the manager at the Trent Vale Brick and Tile Works, so he was considered to be a superior fellow. Unlike his father he was a simple man, but very kind and devoted to Hilda. Before they were married they used to go on holiday to Blackpool every year and always brought a present each for the younger ones. Once they gave me a wristwatch. I was rather small, as my family called me 'Titch', but to own a wristwatch made me feel very important – it was a great treasure. Brother Henry became a brickmaker when he left school, a job possibly found through Hilda's influence. Wilfred worked in engineering.

When I was ten there were miners' strikes because of low pay and poor conditions in the pits. Naturally this affected the pottery industry which relied so much on coal, so that many of the men were 'laid off'. With families deprived of their income the local authorities were obliged to organise communal soup kitchens to keep people alive. Our soup was provided by a local butcher and made in his wife's copper wash-boiler, except on washday when sandwiches were provided instead. The food was distributed in the school where we took a bowl and spoon from home. For the first few days I was too ashamed to go, feeling it a great indignity. I played near the marl pit instead but Wilfred and Henry, who were still at school, found out that I was missing my meal and told our mother. She was very cross and upset about this so that my brothers escorted me each day afterwards.

At that period in history work-people in the Potteries had little or no entertainment and consequently many of them took to drink; they used to send out a young apprentice with a large jug to buy beer so that their drinking began even before they left work.

These conditions encouraged well-meaning citizens to set up Temperance Societies which held lectures in the evenings in local village schools or institutes. There was a series of such lectures run by The Band of Hope in the school opposite the shop owned by Mrs. Dumelow; but there happened to be a gas street-lamp outside which attracted children with nothing better to do and they gathered round it in gangs, making an unbelievable noise as they fooled about. It must have been hell for poor Mrs. Dumelow who condemned them as a 'Band of Devils' rather than a Band of Hope. When eventually the lecturer arrived everyone filed into the school to hear his talk and be shown slides of bottles of spirits containing mummified food, apparently to show that food would not dissolve within the body of a heavy drinker. Such events brought a little interest into the lives of a deprived community.

We boys had other means of making life interesting. My father once gave us a powerful magnet, used in the pottery industry to extract iron particles from the liquid clay known as slip; discovering that it would move small metal objects, we took it to the little grocery shop in the middle of our terrace where small tin toys were displayed on strings stretched across the window and found that we could move them from outside. This caused great hilarity on our part and great consternation on the part of the shopkeeper, until she discovered the cause of this alarming disturbance. We saved up our pennies for Christmas at this shop, recording our savings in a small book. When the time came to spend it, one of the things we looked forward to most was Brazil-nut chocolate which was considered a great treat.

Later on, when the first cinema came to Trent Vale, films were shown in a tin hut grandiosely called 'The Kozy Cinema'. We could never afford to go in, but stood outside and, each time the doors opened, jumped as high as we could to catch a glimpse of these new 'moving pictures'.

Lower down Flash Lane stood the remains of a demolished cottage, known as 'Bogey Moreton's corner' where there was another street-lamp, and sometimes on Saturday evenings I would join a gang of friends here to play very simple games, which were often invented as we went along. We had small bags of buttons of various kinds which we spread out on the pavement and then picked up as quickly as we could on a wet thumb. We found glass marbles from discarded 'pop' bottles, and 'taws' which were soft-fired clay balls of different colours. One game was to draw a ring on the ground and place our marbles inside then, with a special marble, flick at those in the circle; those which you flicked out were your winnings. Sometimes we used a heavy ball-bearing which would scatter a lot of marbles at one time. We collected cigarette cards, trying to collect a set by swapping as children still do today. I was enthralled by those of the kings and queens of England. We also skimmed cards to see who could go the furthest.

Often a child would bring a newspaper showing lists of football teams; he would call the initial of a team and the rest had to guess which team was intended. If someone guessed correctly he would then drop his paper and run like mad to avoid capture. Whoever caught him gave out the next initial. The imagination can transform even a puerile game such as this into a magical world of make-believe. I can remember being fascinated by the names of Scottish football teams: wonderful names like Melrose, Heart of Midlothian, Elgin and Ecclefechan. In later years I would read the novels of Sir Walter Scott who wrote about Melrose and built his house nearby at Abbotsford; learn of the Earl of Elgin who brought the 'Elgin marbles' from Greece to the British Museum, and of Thomas Carlyle who was born at Ecclefechan. These place-names stirred my imagination as a child and I wonder, now that I know about the famous people connected with them, whether it was not some instinctive premonition of the excitements in wait for me.

3

At about eight years old I had begun to visit a family named Capewell. Mr Capewell had been a china painter at Cauldon Place but became involved with religion; in fact he was generally considered to have 'religious mania'. He gave up his work and started a fruit and vegetable business, travelling round the district with a horse-drawn wagon. He also had a small shop looked after by his wife. They sold newspapers as well and I used to help by delivering these for fourpence a week, my first earnings, which was very exciting. I was fascinated by Mr Capewell because he used to make his own wagons. He used a spokeshave most skilfully, creating lozenge-shaped cavities where two pieces of wood were joined and eventually inscribing a series of different colours into them which was very effective. Everything was beautifully made, but the highlight as far a I was concerned was the making and decorating of the tail-board which had baroque curves later embellished with fruit and flowers. Then, with a long brush he would write his name and address in elegant copper-plate writing. I spent hours, enthralled, watching him. He obviously used all the techniques he had learned at the china works and to me the result was a real work of art.

Grandfather Capewell, who also lived nearby, was a retired 'crest' painter. When I was taken to visit him he showed me a number of watercolour designs of heraldic devices which he had painted as patterns for china plates supplied to titled gentlemen. His designs were minute and exquisitely painted in colours and gold. It gave me a lot of pleasure to see them.

The Capewells were an interesting family, what was known as 'a cut above the rest'. Mrs. Capewell had blue eyes set in the whitest face I had ever seen. She was not one of the ordinary chattering women I knew but rather aloof and dignified. The family lived at the end of the terrace in Flash Lane, but being the end house they owned a longer piece of land, stretching as far as 'Bogey Moreton's Corner'. This was where a cottage had been demolished with only the chimney left standing. The rest of the garden enclosure was a wall formed by ridge tiles called, for some reason, 'chrissies'. These had been left behind from the disused tile-works beyond, which was now a derelict site with remains of ovens still standing and the treacherous marl pit.

Mrs Capewell ran the shop in the converted front room, with the family living in the kitchen and scullery behind – as was often the way with these small village shops. She and her husband had three sons: Arthur was married and ran a small wireless shop in Stoke, Reginald was a schoolteacher and also lived away from home, and the youngest, Bob, helped his father on the delivery rounds. Bob was a poor fellow who had some spinal difficulty: he walked with a bent back and had to swing partially paralysed legs. But he was a jolly boy in spite of his disabilities and there was always a great deal of laughter when he was around. There were a number of outbuildings and wooden sheds adjacent to the house which were used to store fruit and vegetables, provide shelter for the wagons and stabling for two horses. Bob cleared out one of these and installed a billiard table where he and his friends entertained themselves.

Mr Capewell made and decorated his wagons in one of these useful buildings. He also had a vegetable plot and a pigsty. To feed the pigs he kept a huge barrel into which was put not only the waste from the house and shop but that of everyone else in the area. For some reason they used to groom their horses in this corner and on one occasion, when their frisky horse was being groomed by Arthur, it lashed out at this 'pigwash' barrel, splitting it from top to bottom and releasing obnoxious odours all over the neighbourhood. In his attempt to control the horse Arthur leapt on its back and very stupidly struck it frequently with a leather belt. Unfortunately for the poor horse he hit it in the eye with the buckle, doing untold damage so that they had to get rid of it.

The pigs were sometimes let out of the sty to roam at will on the waste ground near the house. I watched the Capewells feeding them and talking to them and to me they seemed like family pets, almost like friends. Imagine my horror when one day I heard a pig squealing frantically and watched it being dragged into the yard, stretched across a pig-bench and slaughtered by someone I had considered to be its friend. To my astonishment it next had boiling water poured all over it to facilitate the scraping of hairs from its skin. I was horrified, but silent. I am not sure if it was this incident which eventually led to my dislike for meat.

From time to time the Capewells drove off in a horse-drawn trap for family outings and to my delight I was often invited to go with them. A favourite spot was Rudyard Lake, near Leek. In 1863 John Kipling, an architectural sculptor who worked on the design of the Wedgwood Memorial Institute in Burslem, met Alice MacDonald for the first time at Rudyard Lake. They married, and loved the lake so much that when their son was born they named him Joseph Rudyard Kipling. At the lakeside the pony would be tethered to graze while the family unpacked a picnic and I revelled in this unusual treat. The food, fresh air and holiday atmosphere made a lasting impression on me. I was also invited to stay at their house for tea sometimes and tasted the new delight of fresh strawberries with sterilised milk. They had a piano and sang songs around it. I can remember still the tune of 'Touch the harp gently, my pretty Louise'. Usually Bob played, or one of his visiting cousins who also sang well. I got on very well with the Capewells, so much so that at one time Mrs Capewell wanted to adopt me but my mother was not at all agreeable to this suggestion.

One of Mr.Capewell's jobs was to go round country districts collecting fresh eggs, vegetables, rabbits and so on. At the same time he would sell bananas and tomatoes – anything which could not be obtained in rural areas. Every Thursday Bob did these runs in order to help his father and later on my mother sometimes allowed me to miss school to go with him, which I loved.

The wagons we used were two-wheeled and we generally sat on the front box together. When motor cars began to appear on the roads, Bob fixed an empty barrel in front of him on the wagon and pretended that it was a steering wheel, driving the horse very badly from side to side of the road. On one occasion I was sitting on the back with my legs dangling down when suddenly the wagon began to tip and I fell off, plus the heavy weighing scales and various sacks of potatoes; but there was no harm done and we had a good laugh. Bob was a great tease.

We used to set off very early in the morning, travelling along the main road to Trentham, then Tittensor where we turned right for Swynnerton. Along this road was Groundslow sanatorium which was one of our stops. It had very lovely grounds where the patients, who all seemed to be young women, were accommodated in small chalets. Those who were well enough crowded round the wagon to exchange chat and cheeky banter as they bought fruit from Bob. Although he was bent with his deformed back, he was very good-looking and obviously attractive to the girls who chattered to him excitedly.

Having reached Swynnerton we went first to the smithy which, as in the song, stood under a spreading chestnut tree. It was very picturesque standing in the centre of the village with the skilful smith hard at work shoeing horses or making a decorative wrought-iron gate. We never had time to visit the Anglican church, but in later years when I was studying sculpture I went there to see a magnificent carved Christ situated in a side chapel at ground level. It had obviously been designed for an elevated position, with its large head and elongated lower part of the legs to counteract the perspective when seen from below. It has been suggested that it was taken to Swynnerton from Lichfield cathedral to preserve it during the Reformation but, as far as I know, no one has been able to confirm this.

The next call was Lord Stafford's kitchen garden at Swynnerton Hall. Bob may have sold bananas, oranges or lemons to the head gardener, but the chief reason for our calling was to buy vegetables, apples or pears in season, all of excellent quality. I remember how well-organised the garden was, being divided by pleached fruit trees trained on wires – all very tidy, as well as being decorative. Sadly it has now disappeared, having become a housing estate.

We headed towards Eccleshall, but did not visit this little market town, following instead the country lanes which took us to more isolated areas. I remember one farm – it could have been Greatwood House near Offley Brook – where two brothers lived. I think they were twins, but in any event they were enormous fellows well over six feet tall, and they used to take whatever they wanted from the wagon without paying. Bob's answer to these intimidation tactics was to take me into the dairy where we drank as much milk as we could hold, but I think it was all done with good humour. Bob usually bought a lot of eggs from here and sometimes we would go round the hay barns where the hens frequently made their nests, collecting the eggs ourselves. What a joy it was for me to travel through this remote countryside and to see various farming activities.

A fascinating lane led from Greatwood to Bishop's Offley. It was in a deep cutting through sandstone rock, the banks each side lined with trees which formed a dark tunnel below. Bob called it, 'The Dark Rock'. A steep rise led out of the tunnel and shallow steps had been formed to facilitate the passage of horse-drawn traffic. I heard recently that the road through this cutting had been made by the farmers at Greatwood, in order to reach more easily another farm which they owned at the top of the hill. Nowadays, of course, the surface of the lane has been levelled and tarmacked. Leaving Bishop's Offley we came to the hamlet of Walk Mill where we saw a fine water mill and an interesting house overlooking the mill pond. From here we started back on our return journey, crossing the railway line to Mill Meece where Bob had an uncle who worked on the railway. He and his wife lived in a railway cottage by the side of the line with a long, narrow drive to get to it. We always arrived here in the late afternoon for a cup of tea and a sandwich. I was impressed with the silence in the small room, which seemed to be intensified by the rhythmic beating of the grandfather clock.

There were only two more calls to make before setting off for home. A few hundred yards away was Hatton Water Works with its magnificent engine pumping water up to the tower at the top of Hanchurch hills where sufficient fall was created to supply the Potteries with water. Nearby was Paddock's farm where the farmer's four young daughters used to crowd round the window when Bob arrived, doubtless expected at this time on Thursdays. Their mother was a fussy, friendly woman who always called Bob 'Roberty', which tickled Bob no end and caused him to laugh hilariously. The girls peeped through the window whilst their mother was doing her shopping and they thought that Bob was laughing at them, so they reciprocated with shrieks of laughter from inside the house. He was obviously one of their favourite callers.

We then started off up the steep bank to Beech and Trentham on our way home to Trent Vale. This latter part of the journey often took place in darkness so we had candlelit lamps on the wagon. It was a long day; we were very tired and if it was wintertime also very cold. By modern-day standards we were most inadequately clothed for this work and I remember the effects of the freezing temperatures even now. I would pull an empty potato sack over my head and shoulders in an attempt to keep warm and dry. On one occasion when Bob tried to skin a rabbit for a customer it was frozen stiff , breaking in half as he pulled. The winters must have been a great deal colder then, for most people skated. I can remember people gliding elegantly over Trentham Lake and even fires being built on it.

One Thursday when Bob was not well his father went on one of these journeys instead and wanted me to accompany him. Mother, however, wouldn't let me stay away from school. As it happened it was very fortunate for me because Mr Capewell was driving a horse that was inclined to be unpredictable and would shy at the least thing. Later that day the horse and wagon were found upside down with Mr Capewell dead in a ditch. I could have been with him. After this they got rid of the horse and Bob replaced it with an old black funeral horse. We were intrigued because, on the outward journeys the horse could hardly be made to move but walked at a sedate pace, whereas the return journey was quite the opposite – the horse couldn't change his habits and trotted all the way home.

A lot of houses had been built on the new Harpfield estate, stretching from the bottom of Flash Lane, along the London-Newcastle road, behind Trent Vale church and across to the beginning of the Penkhull hills. I remember that when they were in process of construction the first operation on the building site was to dig a hole, about ten feet by eight feet and five or six feet deep, into which they would tip rock lime. This was then covered with water which, when slaked, was mixed with sand to make lime mortar. The lime was intensely hot during the slaking process, but there was never any protection provided to prevent anyone from falling in. We used to play on the scaffolding and round this hole and, as far as I can recall, no one ever did fall in but it would have meant certain death if they had done so.

When the houses were eventually occupied the people who bought them were, generally speaking, much better off than the original village people so that it was a prosperous district in which to sell fruit and vegetables and most of Capewell's trade was now in this area. Living in one of the houses was the engineer, Mr Wallett, who developed the cash-carrying device used by the Co-op, and when I called one day with Bob Capewell I was confronted by a girl of staggering beauty. This was his daughter, who had the unusual name of Hulsie; I don't think I have ever met anyone who impressed me so much, but although I lost contact with her when I left school, strangely we were destined to meet again many years later.

Bob grew worse as time moved on, sometimes having great difficulty in walking, so that when I was about twelve or thirteen they asked me to do the local rounds myself at weekends or holidays. They trusted me to drive the horse and wagon and deal with the customers. I was given an apron to wear with two large pockets in front – one for copper coins and one for silver. I was paid sixpence a week but I also had a lot of meals with them and took fruit and vegetables home for Mother. I remember Bob with great affection as a most humorous and courageous man. He finally had an operation on his back but his chances at the outset had only been fifty-fifty and sadly he became bedridden. However, nothing daunted, he had his bedroom fitted up as comfortably as possible and kept himself going by repairing wireless sets for people. His friends visited and played card games and there was still much laughter around him.

Before I left school, my father took me as a treat on a day trip to Liverpool where we visited an art gallery. What a wonderful experience this was. I had never seen paintings in the original before, and the only original sculptures were those near to Minton's library. Here I could study a number of sculptures one of which, a reclining woman with a veiled face, filled me with wonder; it was amazing how the sculptor had created the suggestion of a face behind a concealing veil. There was a painting which made a lasting impression on me: 'The Stone Breaker' by John Brett depicting a young boy breaking stones by the roadside in readiness for repairs. I have never forgotten the brilliant colours and dazzling light across the landscape, and I still liked it when I saw it more recently. We also visited the docks and Giles Gilbert Scott's Anglican Cathedral, as yet unfinished. The latter was a most moving experience. Little did I know then that one day I would have close contact with the architect of the even newer Roman Catholic Cathedral, Frederick Gibberd.

I was not very distinguished at school but I was particularly observant. This came out one arithmetic lesson when we were asked how many oranges would fit into a box of a certain size. The others worked out the volume of the oranges and the volume of the box and how many times one would go into the other. They were all wrong! Because I had worked so long for Capewells and had packed many boxes of oranges I could visualise them in my mind as spheres with spaces between, so that I was able to calculate the correct number. To my eternal disappointment I did not receive the praise I had expected for this achievement. However, during my last few weeks at school I was allowed to draw and paint the whole time, much to my delight. The teacher who had a special interest in art gave me help and encouragement, one day bringing in a bunch of flowers from his garden for me to paint. He took a great deal of trouble to make a suitable arrangement, placing the flowers in a green vase on a ledge in front of the blackboard, then draping a blue duster behind and securing it with a drawing pin.

At the age of fourteen I was interviewed by an employment officer from the Education Office who recommended Minton's China factory and told me to take my drawings with me. Naturally I took my most recent one of the vase of flowers, and afterwards my sister Hilda carefully preserved it.

I saw the manager at Minton's and he set me on immediately. I found that we were expected to buy our own brushes, so my first week's wages were spent on these. Between leaving school and starting work there was no holiday break; in fact one was considered fortunate to find a job with such alacrity. So the following Monday I changed from a schoolboy to an apprentice earning four shillings and sixpence a week.

4

The Minton factory was built alongside London Road for about two hundred yards. It was a stylish building on three floors with the top-floor windows on a smaller scale and a central archway in the middle giving access to a narrow strip of yard where the kilns were situated. The boundary on this side was the canal, which was used for bringing in the raw materials necessary for the pottery industry and also for transporting finished products. The main works' entrance was through gates in the large archway and through this the men who worked in the 'clay end' filed off to the right to 'clock on'. Here the raw clay was unloaded from canal boats, treated, graded and stored. The storage units were on the far side of the canal, which at one point was narrow with graceful curves so that boards could be laid across and the refined clay taken across in wheelbarrows. I remember that the workmen made their lunch hour exciting by competing with one another in jumping this narrow section of canal. At this end too the basic 'ware' was made: plates, cups, bowls, vases and so on and the first clay firings were made in the nearby kilns. It was customary for wives to wash the white overalls and white aprons worn by the men and these they often put on before coming to work, rolled up under their jackets to save time on arrival. Many of the labourers carried a red-spotted handkerchief inside which was a basin containing their hot dinner and this they would put on the stove at lunch time. Because firing is a very long process the stokers needed to be there all night. I remember how highly polished their shovels became so that at breakfast time they could be used as frying pans on the stove to cook their bacon!

Firing the clay ware is the most vital part of the china-making process and the supervision of the temperature the most important job in the factory, otherwise weeks of time-consuming and valuable work can be lost in its final stages. The chief fireman was in charge of the ovens and was very highly paid, which is not surprising considering the thousands of pounds worth of ware for which he had main responsibility. Originally he wore a top hat in deference to his exceptional skills. No thermometers were used: the traditional method of gauging the temperature inside the oven was all done by eye through a small spy hole and an expert fireman knew by the colour of the glow whether or not the heat was correct. A later development was to put small cones of clay, which collapsed at certain temperatures, inside with the ware, but again it was necessary for keen observation by a well-trained man.

The 'decorating end' of the works was through the gates and to the left, as far away as possible from the dusty, dirty clay end. Here there was no need to clock on as everyone was paid piecework, but even so it was in our own interests to arrive by 8am and to work until 5-30 pm, as well as Saturday mornings, for pay was very poor. The modelling shop was at ground level, the gilding shop on the first floor and the second floor used by the engravers and as storerooms. At 8-o'clock sharp the main gates were locked and anyone arriving after this time had to wait outside for almost an hour until they were opened again. The latecomers were then admitted but lost an hour's pay.

I was put into the gilding shop on the first floor, overlooking London Road; this had long windows to give as much light as possible for the painters. I had been taken on as an apprentice for seven years, learning to decorate china, but for the first two years I was to work with five or six trained gilders under the supervision of Mr.Goodall. He distributed the work, inspected it for acceptance when completed and, if it was a new design, discussed the price with the management. He sat at one end of the shop, near the stove, with a large board in front of him so that he could never be seen unless standing at the side of his table.

The work benches were extremely solid, avoiding any movement which would have been detrimental to the fine work expected of the gilders. They were fixed right up to the windows, with provision made for two operatives each side; senior gilders sat by the window to catch the best light, apprentices further away. In poor light the room was lit by gas lamps. Each operative sat on a three-legged stool made by the works' carpenters and each had a wooden rest – a board about 2'6" long and 5" wide – screwed to the table with a nut and a long bolt in such a way that the angle could be adjusted according to the work being done. There was also a very finely pivoted wooden wheel on the bench in front of each operative, mounted on heavy cast-iron legs to stabilise it. We called this a 'banding wheel' and it worked very silently and accurately; I believe it was made of rosewood. The operative would lean his right arm on the rest, spin the wheel with his left hand and then, periodically touching the plate or cup to get it perfectly centred, he would apply the banding, or edging, in the correct place.

The processes through which a piece of china passes before completion are surprisingly long and complicated. After the initial firing the ware is sent to be decorated: a design is applied and another firing, known as 'washing it in' is made. This is followed by yet another firing before arriving at the gilding shop. The gilding was done in pure gold, supplied to each of us in a small round tin similar to those which hold shoe polish. It came as a dark grey paste which had to be mixed and adjusted by oils before it could be used to decorate china. When the ware had its final firing this grey vegetable stain disappeared, leaving the gold with a matt finish. It was then sent to the girls whose job it was to polish it with pencil-shaped pieces of agate, or bloodstone – a process known as 'burnishing'. The gold then came into its own. A highly decorated or exceptionally expensive piece of china might require further firings.

At first I had to sit for hours and hours making Chinese pot-hook shapes round the rims of plates, freeing the wrist and training it to move fluently: a method used by the Chinese for thousands of years. It was not until later in life that I realised how beneficial this practice had been. Next I was given plates with flower designs already on them and I had to practise colouring them with the cheapest paint, which was a rusty-red colour. Later, when I became more proficient, I was allowed to decorate plates as I wished, write my name or initials on them and then pass them to Mr. Goodall for his approval or otherwise; this method gave apprentices the freedom to express themselves and experiment to a certain extent. I still have my very first two trial plates signed by him most beautifully in copperplate writing on the back

To apply gold or colour to highly glazed ware required very precise skill and knowledge of how to adjust the colour. I was most intrigued by the arrangement which enabled the gilders to make these fine adjustments. Each operative was supplied with a cup and saucer; the required colour was put into the saucer and turpentine poured into the cup and allowed to overflow; because the turpentine was more thinly spread in the saucer evaporation increased and gradually the colour began to thicken. This was known as 'fat oil'. At the end of each day the cup was topped up and again allowed to overflow, replacing the turpentine which had evaporated during the day. Eventually another saucer was placed under the first, separated from it by three bits of wood about half-an-inch- thick, then another, and another, until each saucer contained fat oil of different grades of viscosity. Some of the older workers had as many as six saucers, enabling them to produce colours and textures of amazing variety.

A touch of glycerine was sometimes added when working on long strokes and aniseed oil was also used in order to keep the colour 'open' and facilitate application; in fact, aniseed was the dominant smell in the painting and gilding shops. Another type of oil was used to dry up the colour. The colours came in powdered form but, although they were already finely ground, each operative ground them again on a tile with the turpentine. He would start the day by mixing the colours he required with a palette knife and placing them at the top of the tile ready for use, covering them with a saucer to keep them soft and to prevent dust from settling. Because pure gold was used for gilding it was necessary for all the waste to be conserved and periodically the rags we used were burned to extract the gold.

The rose was used extensively in china decoration and each painter developed his own style of forming a rose, but at that time the method used at Minton was one invented by William Billingsley in Derby. His technique was to apply the full-strength rose colour to the glazed china forming a sphere with a dark blob in the centre: this would become the heart of the rose. He then loaded a square brush with the correct fat oil, worked it on his tile and with deft strokes shaded the rose colour on his plate from dark to light, using the china itself for the lightest part of the flower. With smaller brushes loaded with the correct grade of oil he then lifted out smaller areas of colour to form the petals. This method was known as 'cutting up', and breathing on the colour would dry the oil in some way so that it could be lifted off the plate more cleanly. It was very skilled work, but a good painter with the knowledge of the structure of a rose could quite quickly paint a realistic one. Similar techniques were used for other flowers, but the rose was so often used as a central feature that it was essential to produce a good effect.

In the early days all the main china factories produced their own distinctive colours and jealously guarded their recipes. Rose and purple, for instance, obtained their brilliance from a certain amount of gold in the manufacturing process, and brilliant yellows from the addition of uranium. Today the colours are produced by large manufacturers like Wengers at Etruria.

Very much later I was privileged to meet old Mr.Wenger who, through the years, had built up an enormous collection of ceramics and glassware illustrating the use of his colours. He had a wonderful museum full of absolutely everything that had colour on glass or ceramic, including such mundane objects as milk bottles; but amongst this motley collection of objects were some very fine examples of the work produced by the great factories including Spode, Wedgwood, Minton, Worcester, Coalport and Derby. He even showed me a fragment of the Koran which he had collected during the war. He was an officer in the Middle East and he ordered one of his more audacious men to hook this bit of the Koran off the wall with his bayonet. Sadly, after he died, the museum contents were all sold and scattered far and wide.

I was not sorry to have left school, but the next few years were to be the most distressing in my life. From the age of eleven or twelve I had been losing my hair, but now it began to fall out at an alarming rate. Treatment prescribed by the hospital was ineffective and I recall my distress when I woke up in the morning to find yet another pile of hair on the pillow. Perhaps I was unreasonably sensitive about it, but just at the time when my contemporaries became interested in girls I would do anything to get away from them. If I had to ride on a bus I always endeavoured to sit on the back seat so that no one could sit behind me; if I was walking and someone was following, particularly girls, I would cross over to the other side of the road. I bought a cap which I never took off except at home. The misery it caused me was unimaginable. As I walked back and forth to Minton there were always a lot of girls on the same mission and these journeys became a nightmare.

For the first two years I had to walk through a shop of about twenty young women paintresses who terrified me, having to run the gauntlet several times a day. Some of the more forward girls would try to snatch off my cap as I went by. However, it so happened that one of my friends had a sister who was married to the local barber and he had recently invested in a vibratory electric device to massage the scalp. He agreed to try and stimulate the growth of my hair, generously giving me treatment every day when I was returning from work. His shop was on London Road midway between Stoke and Trent Vale so that it was very convenient. To compensate him for all his kindly effort I painted a sign to go outside his shop showing his name: Broomhall. It was on a box with a glass front which could be lit from inside. In the course of time his treatment began to have some effect and very fine hairs began to appear in the bald patches. I was also moved into the painting studio which was isolated from the rest of the factory, and my tormentors. It all seemed like a miracle. My constant anxiety began to abate and, now aged sixteen, the quality of my life improved.

In the studio were two men painters and three apprentices. The men were extremely skilled: Joe Colclough specialised in flower painting ; Teddy Dean, whom I considered to be a real artist, was a very talented water-colourist and could paint anything. Both were employed on a piecework basis, so every minute was precious and consequently they refused to help the apprentices. They sat at separate benches at opposite ends of the studio with a large hood erected in front of them so that their work in progress could not be seen. We apprentices had to glean knowledge as best we could, which was a ridiculous system. Of course the men painters were justified in their attitude of non-co-operation as they did not trust the management and realised that as soon as the apprentices could produce an equivalent standard of work at a cheaper rate they themselves would be deprived. The system of producing designs differs from that used today. Because these qualified painters were so experienced the Art Director would not attempt to interfere with their natural talent but present them with a plate or vase and ask them to paint a landscape, flowers or fruit, indicating the size and position required. Afterwards the work would be completed with gilded borders and so on. The painter who had created the original design executed any orders which developed from it.

Minton produced a very fine embossed gilding known as 'raised gold'. 'Adeney's Raised Paste', which was ochre-coloured, was quite stiff and when applied with a brush could be lifted to form certain shapes like the edge of a leaf, small dots, or a central spine and veins, before being fired and gilded. It was influenced by the illuminated manuscripts produced by mediaeval monks and looked similar. On some broad areas, such as leaves, water was added to the paste to enable it to flow at a a lower level before the raising was done. The final effect was most realistic.

Acid gilding was also used, although this ware was much more expensive. For example, a white china plate might have a very fine pattern engraved round the edge; the entire plate, except for the pattern, would then be painted with a 'resist' of black, acid-resistant wax and the plate dipped in acid. The acid would eat away the exposed glaze and after the wax was was removed the 'acid band' round the edge would be gilded.

Teddy Dean, who travelled in from Cheadle, was an interesting character: he was crippled with a club foot, and because of this was allowed to come into work through a side door instead of having to walk the long distance from the main gate. Even so, he hobbled down to the basement if there was a storm in progress as he was frightened of thunder. His work was excellent: I remember in particular his hunting scenes, aeroplanes, great tiled panels for a butcher's shop and a magnificent dinner service for an Indian potentate. While he was painting hunting scenes my imagination worked so that in my mind's eye I could see everything happening. He once copied Landseer's picture, 'Shoeing the Bay Mare' on to a plaque. The quality of his work did not receive the remuneration it deserved.

But Teddy had another string to his bow. He made contact with a Mr Fenton who acted as an agent for the sporting fraternity and from time to time he visited Teddy at the factory and commissioned him to paint racehorses, greyhounds or fighting cocks on small china plaques which were framed after firing. Teddy contrived to have an attack of gout when a commission was in progress, staying at home to do the painting and returning to work when the plaques were ready for firing. I usually took them down to the kiln for him. This was done surreptitiously, without the management's knowledge – or perhaps they turned a blind eye, but it was too risky to do much private work. Mr Fenton called one day for two plaques of fighting cocks and there was always good-humoured banter between them when he came. "Now then Teddy, what do you want for those?" he enquired. "Five pounds" was the reply. The agent spun round with a look of disbelief. 'Five bloody hells Teddy!' he blurted out, but in the end he was pleased to pay. Interestingly these two plaques were recently sold by Louis Taylor of Stoke, fetching an incredible £2,000.

There were two boys in the design shop who were paid piecework and because I worked quickly they generously allowed pieces of my work to go on to their pay sheets, later giving me some of their money. It was a fiddle of course but of enormous help to me as a poorly-paid beginner.

A retired director of Minton, John Campbell, who sported a large beard, used to walk round the factory every day for exercise and most likely to keep up-to-date with progress in hand. He was accompanied on these occasions by the manager of the decorating department, named Mason. Campbell and Teddy Dean got on very well together and used to amuse one another with cheeky stories. Mason was a churchgoer and conducted the choir at Penkhull church. We noticed that he rather pointedly walked away when these risqué stories began and Teddy, always one to make us laugh, remarked once that Mason looked 'rather like an owl throwing up!' when he was conducting the church choir.

A corridor led to the studio where we worked, at the end of which was a window looking down on to the flint mill belonging to the company. The canal alongside London Road ran through a deep cutting at this point before disappearing under the central square in Stoke and this rather romantic-looking building rose up to a height of four storeys from canal level. There was very little spare time during the day but I managed to do a water-colour drawing of the view when I was fifteen, which I still have; it always impressed me as I imagined that it must look similar to scenes in Venice. It was a relief sometimes to look through the window. Generally the people walking past were roughly dressed but one regular passer-by used to intrigue me. He was a black man – they were rarely seen in the Potteries – who was immaculately dressed, with yellow spats and gloves and who had a most dignified manner. I never discovered who he was, but what a contrast he made to some of the local people. I used to see children without shoes or stockings standing at the gates when the work people were leaving, waiting to see if there were any fragments left over from their lunch packets.

Many of the social problems of that time were caused by drink. For many men the responsibility of feeding and clothing an ever-growing family was too great; the only escape being to the local public house where they became drunk on their meagre wages and returned home to hungry children, an irate wife and constant quarrelling. It was these conditions which led well-meaning citizens to set up Temperance societies, and factory owners like Minton to provide alternative educational facilities. They also ran lectures on the work of Marie Stopes into Venereal disease, but although the young men at the factory attended they mostly did so for titillation, not caring about the outcome of the disease.

I was the youngest apprentice and it was my job to make up the fire, go and buy ground coffee from a nearby shop and heat it up in a saucepan on the stove. Looking back I always feel amazed that we were treated to such an expensive beverage; it certainly gave me a taste for ground coffee at an early age. Minton had a wonderful collection of volumes in which they entered every china pattern used at the factory. Each painter hand-painted his own sample with its number, making a unique and valuable record. I used to borrow these to study in the workshop and found them of absorbing interest.

At the end of each day I walked home along a route which became memorably familiar over the next five or six years. First I passed a long, narrow building, similar in many ways to Minton which was Campbell's Tile works and then, for about 300 yards, came a row of shops on either side of

London Road. On the right was a butcher's shop and slaughterhouse. Sometimes I saw cattle and sheep being driven along the road from Trent Vale and saw how reluctant the animals were to enter the gateway which led to their slaughter. The butcher's shop was splendidly designed and very hygienic with a fine Minton-tiled counter and, on the wall behind, a magnificent glazed tile panel depicting a country scene with cattle. This was most likely Teddy Dean's work. Soon after this I passed an interesting swing bridge enabling traffic from Boothen to cross the canal and join London Road. On a wall a little further on was some decorative brickwork and a drinking fountain with an iron cup on a chain for the refreshment of weary travellers. Here, where the canal runs parallel to the road, is a small plantation surrounding an obelisk recording the bravery of a tram-driver named Timothy Trow who, many years before, had leapt into the water to save a child who had fallen in, but sadly he cold not swim and was himself drowned.

Across the road, before it began to slope towards Oak Hill, was an enclosed estate of large houses named The Villas beyond whose high boundary walls was a right of way up a back lane. At the top of this was a flight of steps known as 'The Monkey Steps' (though why this name I never discovered) leading to a steep field and the village of Penkhull. The 'Flash' stream rises in this field, giving its name to 'Flash Lane' and as children we used to find orchids there, and watercress. From Oak Hill I could clearly see on the skyline the Sideway coal-mines where huge tips had built up, red-hot inside and smouldering the whole time. Once, when I was passing, one of these mounds collapsed causing an inch of dust to settle over the entire surrounding area and ruining a new copperplate sign recently painted and varnished. I recalled the days when there had been a miners' strike and we used to scrape about at Sideway collecting fragments of coal, very bright with many fossils, and wheel them home on an old bicycle. Soon came the road junction to Penkhull where the Co-op was situated, with the newsagents opposite; then Rookery Lane, the brick-and-tile works and the allotments. Opposite Sutherland Terrace was the lodge with a long tree-lined drive leading to 'Highgrove', Elphinstone's house, and then came Flash Lane and home.

On Saturday afternoons the other apprentices and I would sometimes take our lunch with us and go to watch Stoke City Football Club when they had the brilliant seventeen-year-old Stanley Matthews playing for them. He was a remarkably skilful footballer and I do not think he ever fouled another player. Had he been playing today he would have earned vast sums of money, but in those days football players were paid very little and special skills were not specially rewarded. With my friends from Trent Vale I often met him. He later married the daughter of the Stoke football manager – a shrewd Scotsman – Jimmy Vallance, and to supplement his income Vallance rented a field along the road leading to Trentham Park where he created a putting green. Trentham was still as popular as it had been in my childhood days, especially at weekends, and quite a few of us were attracted to this new form of entertainment. Twopence was charged to hire clubs and golf balls to go round an eighteen-hole course and ,to stimulate our interest, if we could afford it, we sometimes arranged a foursome and played for one penny. The entire Vallance family, including Stanley Matthews, used to help to run this enterprise, mowing the grass, playing with customers and storing the hand-propelled mower and golfing equipment in a small wooden shed. How times have changed!

Stanley Matthews was very keen to win the FA Cup medal but he realised that Stoke City, who lacked the enthusiasm for major football events, were never likely to win the cup, and much to the disappointment of all his friends at Stoke, he managed to get a transfer to Blackpool where he thought he would stand a better chance. He *did* get his medal, the event was recorded on camera, and it was entirely due to Matthews's determination that Blackpool won the cup. He was subsequently knighted, the first footballer ever to receive this honour. Eventually, in 1961, he came back to Stoke City and helped them to get promotion to the First Division in 1963. After living in Malta for several years with his second wife he finally returned to The Potteries and lived in Sir Oliver Lodge's old house at Penkhull.

Opposite the factory Minton had built an impressive complex of art school, library and swimming baths with money raised by public subscription, but designed by them and all available to the public. Eric Owen, a modeller for Minton, taught at the art school in the evenings and since he took an interest in my work he advised me to go there; so when I had the chance I slipped into the library or made models in the art school. Eric Owen was very good to me and took me on my first trip to London – a tremendously exciting event. However, his main interest was in ceramic modelling so, rather than the museums and art galleries which I had hoped to see, we went to shops such as Heals to search out modern ceramics. Heals encouraged work from abroad, especially from Denmark, and I came under this influence for a time and made modernistic little figures. They were building new offices for the Daily Express in Fleet Street in black glass which was most unusual. Eric Owen managed to get us inside to look round and I noticed that they had used silver leaf in the decoration rather than the usual gold leaf, which was much more effective against the black glass. I was very impressed by this extraordinary building. I remember that Owen's house in Penkhull reflected this modern trend, for he named it 'Neuways'.

The meeting with Eric Owen was the beginning of my interest in sculpture. In the main the students at the art school were concerned with making small ceramic designs of figures and animals, but I began to take a serious interest in anatomy and studied carefully some plaster casts of Greek and Roman work which were available. One day, at the factory, the men pulled the body of a young girl out of the canal and, seeing her lying there with her wet clothes emphasising the contours of her body and her face as white as alabaster, she looked like a Greek marble. It was obvious from her full breasts and rounded body that she was pregnant. Unlike today, young girls who got into trouble were made to feel ashamed and in some cases the strain was too much for them to bear.

During my time with Minton I took every opportunity to visit their library opposite, where I read avidly during my lunch break. It was usually pretty empty and I could look round the bookshelves in comfort, gradually progressing from boys' tales of adventure to the more adult world. When I was about seventeen or eighteen I came across a book which was unlike any I had seen before: both the reading matter and the accompanying illustrations were so striking that I was immediately intrigued. It was by William Blake. I felt an immediate empathy with him and I began to delve into books about the people he mentioned, in particular Descartes, Rochefoucauld and Dante. Blake continued to influence me all my life.

Blake was said by many to be mad because he saw visions of angels, but he also had an appealing sense of humour. On one occasion he was with some scientific friends who were discussing the distance of the moon from the earth and Blake's comment was: 'Nonsense, only yesterday I reached up and touched it with my walking stick!' He was certainly a visionary and had unusual insight, but it is interesting that he had some very good friends including Flaxman, the sculptor, who said of him: 'His drawings will be as famous as Michelangelo's and his poems are just as grand.' Wordsworth said that he preferred Blake's madness to Scott's sanity and Flaxman believed that Blake was as sane as he himself. Flaxman tried to get work for his friend and at one time Blake illustrated a catalogue for Wedgwood, but he didn't bother about work unless he needed food.

Before the Franco-Prussian War of 1870-71 a number of French intellectuals and craftsmen came to Britain and Minton employed some who were experienced pottery designers, building for them the rather grand complex of houses called 'The Villas', each with its own coach-house. The complex, on steeply sloping ground, was completely enclosed by a wall with splendid wrought-iron gates opening on to a wide central drive. Originally a gatekeeper was employed to open and close the gates. Halfway along, the drive widened to form a circle, in the centre of which were circular stone steps surmounted by a stone plinth and on top of this a fine Victorian gas lamp, the whole making a most interesting feature. The gardens were thickly planted with trees. All the houses were rented from Minton, the occupying family paying for its own gas-lighting.

The most talented of these French immigrants was Louis Solon, an intellectual and writer, as well as being a gifted potter. He had come from the Sèvres Pottery and had written a book on the history of ceramics. He devised a unique method of decorating china with glazed relief panels, resembling cameo work, in fine white paste on a coloured ground, a method called pâte-sur-pâte (paste on paste). He designed vases which were uniquely his own – shapes, decoration and gilding – and these now sell for thousands of pounds. He was a remarkable man who set the pace which others followed. Leroy imitated the pâte-sur-pâte method by using white enamel on a brilliant turquoise ground and this theme became a bestseller. This is not done any longer because it would be too expensive. There was also Leon Arnoux, a modeller, who developed new coloured glazes for Minton, called Majolica. He became the Director of Art, designing their display at the Great Exhibition in London in 1851. I have a picture by a designer named Mussel who painted roses most beautifully but in my opinion Solon outclassed them all. He lived in the bottom house at the Villas and designed items for use in his home, including a writing cabinet. The skill of these French designers still influenced our work sixty or more years later and there were examples of their work still lying about in our workshop. In 1932, when I was just out of my apprenticeship, I remember making a small panel of white enamel on a coloured ground.

There was a small museum above the library where I discovered an exhibition of the fine work done by these ceramic artists. It also contained some very delicate pastels of flowers by a German named Hürten who had worked for Copeland China from 1859 until 1897. But the exhibit which really caught my eye was a large Spode dish painted and signed by Daniel Lucas. The scene depicted was of Lake Como and I went to look at it frequently, for both sky and lake were painted a most amazing shade of blue – a colour which I never came across at Minton.

Now that I had a little money of my own any spare cash was used to buy books: Blake, Heine, Goethe, Trollope, Dickens, St.Thomas Aquinas; books on mathematics, metaphysics and philosophy. I found unusual lives fascinating: George Fox, the founder of the Quakers, who once said when threatened by a man with a stave, "Put it away – it is no more than a straw in thy hand"; Montaigne, the writer of aphorisms such as: 'Six doctors, six different opinions, so diagnose yourself'. He also described how he was once attacked by brigands and was so fearless that they didn't know what to do with him; Louis Pasteur, who was working for the wine industry when he discovered the micro-organisms which cause fermentation – a discovery which eventually led to the pasteurisation of milk. It has been said that our real education begins after leaving school, and this was certainly so in my case.

I had been getting on quite well with my work for Minton and customers began to ask for china painted by me, but in 1926 there was a General Strike all over Britain causing an enormous slump in factory production. This time the owners of potteries in the area had bought in mountains of coal to try to offset any detrimental effects on their own production of strikes in the pits, but work gradually petered out and during this time things were pretty desperate for everyone. Mr Elphinstone allowed two of the large trees lining his drive to be cut down and sawn up as logs for the villagers to use. He was reputed to be related to Royalty, which is possible, since the Queen Mother had cousins named Elphinstone. I remember, as a small boy, with a lighted candle in a jar, going with a gang of children carol singing to his house and standing at the door while he listened benevolently before giving us a generous donation. Eventually his house was to become a Roman Catholic school run by the Christian Brothers and re-named St Joseph's College.

The Wall Street Crash in the USA in October 1929 brought about a worldwide economic crisis, which became known as The Great Depression. There was little or no financial help for the unemployed in Britain – the Welfare State was not introduced until very much later – and the tremendous hardship and poverty were far worse than anything known today. This period from the First World War to the thirties caused widespread despondency and a glut of soporific songs circulated that seemed to express the feelings of the unfortunate unemployed. Those who had gramophones or radios would listen to the tremulous voice of Al Bowlly and phrases from these songs still spring to mind: 'there's nothing left for me except a memory', 'It's raining all the time', 'You've got to smile when you say goodbye', 'Brother can you spare a dime?'. In 1927 the American, Al Jolson's first 'talkie' appeared at the cinemas – 'The Jazz Singer' – in which he sang: 'Keep smilin' at trouble' and in the following year he appeared in 'The Singing Fool', singing a song that was to be hummed and whistled nationwide, so great was its popularity: 'When there are grey skies, I don't mind the grey skies, You make them blue Sonny Boy'.

We had a cheap 'crystal' wireless set at home, but the tuning of these sets was not precise since it involved probing the surface of the crystal with a fine wire, known as a 'cat's whisker'; consequently you could only guarantee to pick up the strongest radio signals which were not always those you wanted! Commercial valve sets with a built-in loudspeaker came in a square wooden box, one side of which had a nicely- patterned fretwork design to allow the sound to come through, but these were way above our means, even the cheaper ones for home construction.

Although we had no pay there was a little dole money, for which we had to sign on. I found drawing the dole very degrading, but to keep myself occupied I still used to come to the works and paint a few plates. Eric Owen had a key to the art school and during the strike he let me go in to continue my modelling. The head of the school, Gordon Forsyth, also took an interest in my work.

In my spare time my greatest pleasure was to wander through fields and woodland, perhaps with sketching equipment or with a book to read. I remember visiting Trentham Park in order to draw the interesting stable block there.

For some time I had been developing varicose veins in my legs which by now were quite pronounced. I refused to have surgery and wore elastic stockings instead. My parents had most likely worried for years about my health and it may have been for this reason that Mother, Hilda and her husband, took me for my first real holiday. I think it was the first time I had seen the railway station at Stoke and certainly the first journey I had ever made by train. It was a big adventure and I found the noise, bustle and smell of the steam engines very thrilling.

We went to Tenby where I loved the quietness, the fresh air blowing in from the sea, and sitting and sketching to my heart's content. I still have a small water-colour painting which I did of a sunset above the cliffs. One of the lingering memories of Wales is of some lovely water-lily pools at Bosherston. At a much later date I visited Wales again and saw Epstein's crucifix after it had been installed in St. David's cathedral.

When I was about twenty-one I decided to become a vegetarian as I had never liked meat particularly. My mother was alarmed, thinking I would not survive without meat, but the fact is that my health began to improve considerably; I had much more energy and an unexpected bonus was that after a few years I was able to dispense with the elastic stockings. (Now, in old age, my legs are completely free from this complaint.) For decades vegetarians have been considered cranks, but my body seemed to dictate that I should give up meat and I had the good sense to take its advice. Later, in a herbal shop in Newcastle-under-Lyme, I met Edmund and Anna Hart who were also vegetarians and we formed a lasting friendship.

After the strike, work resumed at the factory, but underneath the usual jokes and banter there was a general air of unease. One day the manager brought a plate for me to look at, painted by a man named Chivers who had been working for Worcester China but was now unemployed. He had brought a sample of his work, which was quite individual, to try to get a job; but the manager knew that my pay was a lot less than they would have to pay Chivers and it was suggested that if I could do the work satisfactorily, they would not need to employ him. Although I said nothing at the time I was horribly disillusioned by this attitude, which created a great sense of insecurity for my own future.

I began looking for vacancies advertised in the Staffordshire Sentinel and one day I saw that the old King Street China Works in Derby was advertising for painters and gilders. A decision to leave Minton was not easy so the next day I decided to ask the advice of Alboin Birks who worked in the studio next to ours. He was the last pupil of Solon to be employed as a pâte-sur-pâte artist and by this time was nearing his eightieth year, so that I thought he would be wise enough to give me sound advice. When told there was a chance of going to the Derby factory, without any hesitation he said, "Take it!" and so I applied.

As a family we had always avoided dentists and doctors because of what we considered an unnecessary expense, but now I was compelled by the inspector at the new factory to be X-rayed. I was offered a job and it wasn't until later that my new boss told me that I hadn't passed my medical examination, but they had decided to say nothing.

At this time there were other moves being made at home. My sister Hilda and Charlie Hudson, who had given me the treasured wristwatch as a small boy, had married just at the time when there was a lot of modern building being done at Clayton. They had bought a house there in what was rather nice countryside and Hilda persuaded our parents – or rather, Mother – that they should leave Trent Vale and move in the same direction. Alboin Birks lived not far away and I used to visit him from time to time. Before he died he gave me three reduced plaster copies of antique figures, including Venus, which he told me his wife had always insisted should face the wall! I have an example of his work in my collection.

I left Minton with mixed feelings. It had been my life and I was devoted to it. It had been my training ground during my adolescent years; I had learned the discipline of steady and careful work, had made some good friends and my vision had been broadened by study at the art school and library. Now, in my early twenties, I was to leave home for the first time to work in a new area. Who knew what experiences were waiting for me over the horizon?

5

My brother, Percy, was living with his wife at Shardlow on the outskirts of Derby at this time and working for Royal Crown Derby, so to begin with I stayed with them. The china factory where I was employed was owned by Paget the racehorse owner and was situated in King Street opposite Derby school with its impressive façade. The factory was not large, having only one small oven for firing the biscuit and glaze processes and a small kiln to fire the ware after it was decorated. They had, however, a fine collection of moulds, figures and shapes dating from the first china factory set up in Derby in the eighteenth century. The modelling of the figures was of a very high standard and included a set of 'Four Seasons': a girl with Spring flowers, another with roses for Summer, a girl with a sheaf of wheat for Autumn and to represent Winter, 'The Skater'. This was a girl, taken from life, who was wearing elegant eighteenth century costume, furred round the neck and the effect was one of romantic realism. They were as finely moulded and as beautiful as anything I had ever seen. There was also 'The Tithe Group', representing the period when farmers had to donate ten-per-cent of their produce to the church each year; this particular group showed a farmer presenting his tenth child to the parson.

Four painters from the Potteries had answered the advertisement, including two apprentices from Minton, and quite a number of operatives from the Royal Crown Derby works in Osmaston Road. Besides these the workforce consisted of a gilder – Mr.Haddock, a deaf painter – Mr.Jessop, the foreman of the shop who was also a painter – Mr.Mosely, and a number of paintresses and women gilders. There was a self-trained paintress, Miss Bailey, who had always worked at this factory so that her style was in the early Derby tradition. Her speciality was the painting of delicately moulded flowers and basketwork patterns. I was amazed by the refinement of work done by a previous woman modeller, in particular fragile flowers with very fine stamens. In my opinion, the best of Derby china is as fine as anything that has ever been made. Another of the original employees, Teddy Swainson, was very badly crippled and needed help to put on his coat and to get on to the bus. He was a modeller and a caster of figures which often were so complicated that they had to be cut into several pieces, each moulded separately. Teddy had the job of reassembling these when they were taken from the moulds and joining them together.

At the factory they still used an old traditional 'turning wheel'. A woman, often the wife of the operator, would work the potter's wheel by pulling a rope on a great wheel while the man did the potting. (There is an example of this wheel in the Gladstone Pottery Museum at Longton, Stoke-on-Trent, and also of the original 'bottle' ovens which at one time were such a feature of the Potteries' landscape.) There was a shop window at the front of the building, facing the old Derby school, with the wares for sale on display.

In the early days of china making at Derby, it was so expensive to produce that they could not afford to throw anything away. Sometimes a small blister of iron from the kiln or some other blemish might mar a piece of ware, so patterns were devised to disguise these imperfections. Perhaps they would be hidden by a spray of flowers and leaves, or the blister transformed into a ladybird. Very often this means of camouflage produced more lively and varied results than would be the case if each piece was flawless. Interestingly, when the Derby factory produced an absolutely perfect piece of ware it was left undecorated and kept for display only.

If you were to look at ceramics with a more critical eye and with a knowledge of the manufacturing processes, you would realise that many designs thought to be purely decorative came into being out of necessity. For instance, fluted ware was developed to prevent the rims of plates from sagging when being fired for the glazing process, for at this time the temperature is so high that the clay body is almost at the point of melting. Also, when the plates were stacked, this scalloped edge would make any slight sagging less noticeable. Another example is the Leaf Ware designed by Wedgwood. The first Josiah Wedgwood invented a rich dark green colour made up of copper and lead which produced a brilliant glaze, but it was so fluid when fired that it ran straight down a vertical pot and collected on the base on which it was fired; so he created designs of embossed leaf patterns with very strongly-marked veins, one of which was the cauliflower; the firm ribs could not hold the glaze but it ran down into the hollows of the leaves filling them with strong colour and leaving the ribs lighter. This variation showed off the new green glaze to its best advantage and was extremely effective.

I decided to enrol for evening classes at the Derby School of Art in Green Lane, going there every night after work. It was a purpose-built Victorian edifice of stone in Gothic design with the main painting and drawing studios at the top of the building, lit by large curved windows across the roof. I drew mainly from models in the life class, but also worked from antique figures arranged round the corridors.

It was here that I met Miss Thompson, who was learning water-colour painting and embroidery. She was getting on in years but was anxious to become proficient in whatever she did. Her embroidery was remarkable, not only in design but in its intricacy of stitching: so much so that she once received a machine-embroidery prize for work which she had done by hand. She also came to work at the King Street factory to help Teddy Swainson in the casting of china figurines, so that I got to know her quite well.

'Tommy' Thompson lived alone in a large Victorian house in Hayworth Street, about half-a-mile from the art school and half that distance from the factory. Eventually, she offered to let me a room, which I gladly accepted as I had found it a very long way to travel from Shardlow. I found her to be a bit above the ordinary. For one thing, she never threw anything away in case she could find a use for it, decorating boxes of various sizes, inside and out, with oil paints and using them for storage containers. She kept her brothers' straw hats and carpentry set; although she *did* give me a little steam engine which worked a fountain. She enjoyed clay modelling and tray decoration. Amongst her possessions was one of 'The Four Seasons' Derby figurines which I so admired, this one being 'The Skater'.

'Tommy' used to cycle about the town and one evening she came out of a side road too soon and hit a bus. I can see her now, sliding along the road and her head striking the pavement but, amazingly she recovered. She owned another house at the top of the street, with a Pugin gateway. The Thompsons were an intriguing family: their father had written educational books; one brother had been a carpenter but had been killed in the Great War; another, who lived in Cambridge, was almost blind, and a sister living in Kent was a teacher. Tommy hated her to visit because she was so demanding and 'took over' when she came to stay. This sister was rather gross and had to have someone to help her get up in the morning. I remember that she was very fond of fried onions, frying herself a great panful for breakfast and then 'exploding' all day in consequence. She was very religious and regularly attended the church down the road; but I was also impressed because she wrote books for small children. On one occasion Tommy was caring for a nestling bird which we fed with a straw and her sister eventually turned this into a story. Tommy's sister had a little cottage at Horsmonden where she lived alone like a gypsy, but she also owned land where she kept a caravan and, when she got to know me better, she invited me to use it for a holiday now and again. I was staying there on one such occasion during the Second World War when I saw a great flight of German bombers coming over, and shortly afterwards, the authorities visited me because someone had reported seeing me and had thought that I was a spy.

After I had been at the china works for about two years, when Paget was employing about thirty people, he advertised it for sale, realising that some firm in the Potteries might be interested in acquiring some of the original Derby figure moulds. I believe he had only made it into a going concern in order to get a high price for it – otherwise, during a slump, it would not have been worth much. When it came on to the market it caused great anxiety amongst the Royal Crown Derby management, who were concerned that the moulds for the Derby figurines might go to a rival firm in the Potteries. Consequently they paid an enormous amount to buy it themselves but, having obtained the moulds, they dismissed the workforce and demolished the factory.

I was now unemployed again and had to draw the dole, but what appeared disastrous in the first instance turned out to be very fortunate for me. I had begun a Ministry of Education art course during my evening classes and the principal of the art school, Mr.Hounsell, being impressed by the work I was doing, offered to take me on as a full-time student with a view to eventually taking the Ministry examinations. Naturally I was delighted to accept and he took the trouble to arrange special times for me to collect my dole money from the Labour Exchange so that my studies were not interrupted. The course included life drawing, drawing from the antique, perspective, architecture, memory drawing and creative design, and we were also expected to take an interest in one of the crafts such as carpentry or jewellery. I was very keen to do sculpture and Mr.Hounsell very kindly set up a class specially for my benefit, taking it himself and managing to get one or two more students interested so that he could run a life class specifically for modelling. What a wonderful opportunity for me! I could hardly believe my good fortune.

I found Derby to be a most interesting city. The old prison, where I believe John Bunyan had once been imprisoned, had been converted into houses with the old cells still in the basements. The newer prison was in a street which links with Friargate and I was told that, when a gentleman of some importance who had a house there lay dying, the road was covered with thick layers of straw to deaden the sound of passing traffic. In Friargate there was also an interesting cast-iron railway bridge crossing the road, and nearby the premises of the famous clock maker, Whitehurst, a local man.

The hospital where Florence Nightingale began her nursing career was still there and a statue had been erected to commemorate her. Beyond was the Market Square with its Assembly Rooms – a fine piece of architecture which had a pediment carved with musical instruments. I recall that I made a drawing of a splendid Elizabethan building nearby called 'The Mayor's Parlour', but this has since been pulled down. Beyond the lovely cathedral is Full Street where the artist Townsend had his studio, and the 18th century artist, Joseph Wright ARA, had also lived in this vicinity.

Down by the River Derwent was a Shot Tower where lead shot was once made, and lower down came St.Mary's Bridge, an ancient bridge with a chapel built on it. The chapel is attached ecclesiastically to the cathedral and is one of only four Bridge Chapels remaining in England. (I have heard that services are still held there occasionally). Amongst other things we had to go out and study buildings – the cathedral and various churches, but also modern architecture. There were two of the latter listed for us to examine: a private house and a concrete power station – a monstrous building on the river, not far from the cathedral. I thought it quite an eyesore, although we were compelled to draw it as a very fine example of modern architecture. A few years after my leaving Derby it was condemned and demolished!

These were exciting times and I enjoyed every minute. When I was not working in school I was out painting and drawing in the Derbyshire countryside. During the weekends and in the summer holidays I spent many hours drawing in the beech woods on the hill behind Kedleston Hall; also at a most interesting place called Kings Mills on the River Trent. This was frequented by a very skilful watercolourist, Harold Gresley, the art master at Repton School. His brother Cuthbert worked as a china painter at Royal Crown Derby and was friendly with my brother Percy. Percy introduced me to Cuthbert, who subsequently took me to see Harold's work.

The Gresleys were a famous family of Derby painters. Their father was a well-established water-colourist and their grandfather, the most gifted of them all, was a friend of Birket Foster, well-known for his romantic rural scenes which often included children picking blackberries or wildflowers. He painted exquisite little miniatures which commanded high prices and which can still be seen in the Victoria and Albert Museum. His work was never particularly valued by the art world, but many people still treasure them.

Cuthbert and Harold Gresley lived in Chellaston, not far from the alabaster quarry where all the stone was quarried for the famous School of Alabaster, working in Nottingham in the Middle Ages. Many of the churches in Nottinghamshire, Derbyshire and Staffordshire have wonderful memorials to knights and their ladies carved in this attractive stone. Alabaster is a soft marble, veined with iron stains, and very fine detail can be worked in it so that, for instance, the chain mail could be accurately reproduced. Generally speaking the carving of that period was very refined and of a remarkably high quality. A knight would be portrayed with his head resting on his helm, with weeping angels each side and sometimes a dog or a lion at his feet. On one or two female effigies the carver employed an endearing device of a small dog pulling the hem of the gown with his teeth. I am always fascinated to see how skilfully the carver twisted the drapery in a realistic yet formalised manner, like all first-rate sculpture.

We do not know how privileged we are, still to be able to look at these works of art in their original setting and usually having the place entirely to ourselves into the bargain. I was most impressed by St.Oswald's church at Ashbourne, which George Eliot called 'The finest Church in the Kingdom'. The churchyard is entered by magnificent wrought-iron gates whose stone piers are capped by skulls. On the south side is a very interesting window by Christopher Whall, depicting Saint Cecilia with Saint Dorothy and Saint Barbara on either side, commemorating two sisters who were burnt to death in their home. It is a brilliant window, using the clear glass to dazzling effect, unlike mediæval glass.

The north transept contains the Cockayne tombs. John Cockayne was steward to John of Gaunt whose wife, Blanche, was a daughter of the Earl of Derby. The Cockaynes were active in national politics throughout the Wars of the Roses, remaining at Ashbourne Hall until the 1670s when debts forced them to sell to the Boothby family. Most of the tombs are mediæval or Renaissance, but the exception is the remarkable tomb in white Carrara marble of five-year-old Penelope Boothby, carved by a local sculptor, Thomas Banks RA, with extraordinarily tender feeling and refinement. It is astonishingly realistic with the small figure well-defined beneath the drapery. It is said that Queen Charlotte was moved to tears when she saw it exhibited at the Royal Academy of Arts. There is a tragic inscription on the little tomb which reads:

To Penelope
Only child of Sir Brooke and Dame Susanna Boothby
Born April 11th 1785
Died March 13th 1791
'She was in form and intellect most exquisite
The unfortunate parents ventured their all
On this frail bark and the wreck was total'

The wreck was indeed total, for the distraught mother left home and never returned. The inscription is said to have been composed by Edmund Burke, the eminent 18th century politician and writer. Penelope was a remarkable child who already spoke a little French, Italian and Latin and inscriptions in these languages, as well as English, are on her beautiful memorial.

A friend of mine, visiting St.Oswald's recently, was chatting to an embroideress repairing an altar cloth who told her that she sometimes brings her tiny grand-daughter with her to the church. This little girl always goes to visit Penelope but says sadly: "I've stroked her hand Granny, but she won't talk to me."

Another poignant marble, 'The Sleeping Children', can be seen in Lichfield Cathedral. It depicts two little sisters, Ellen Jane and Marianne who died in 1812 and were daughters of Prebendary Robinson. Carved by Sir Francis Chantrey, who was a pupil of Thomas Banks, this particular work shows that he was strongly influenced by the Penelope Boothby effigy. Sir Francis became very wealthy and eventually left the valuable Chantrey Bequest to the Royal Academy. This enabled the Academy to purchase 'Works of Fine Art of the highest merit in painting and sculpture that can be obtained' provided that they have been 'entirely executed within the shores of Great Britain.'

I well remember the joy and exhilaration of discovering the magnificent scenery of Derbyshire and the more remote parts of Staffordshire. Now that I was an art student, the possibility in the future of becoming an artist gave added zest to my explorations. I travelled about on a bicycle, always carrying with me pencils and watercolours. How rewarding it was to return from these travels with a record of something that had interested me – maybe a church, a woodland, a rainbow, or a sunset. Sometimes if there was anything I was specially interested in I would return again and again until I was satisfied with the amount of information I had recorded.

It was a new experience to wander through the Derbyshire dales: Monsal Dale, Beresford Dale and over the stepping-stones in Dovedale – the lovely river Dove being the dividing line with Staffordshire. It was here that Izaak Walton, perhaps the most famous angler ever known, fished these waters with his friend Charles Cotton. Cotton had a fishing lodge in Beresford Dale with an intriguing high-arched doorway enabling their long, solid, 17th century rods to be accommodated.

Stafford is proud of its best-loved son, author of 'The Compleat Angler' who, in his will, bequeathed to the people of the county town a small farmstead at Shallowford (not far from where I now live) where he used to stay when fishing the rivers Meece and Sow. He also left a legacy:

> *to buie coles for some pore people… in the last weike of Janewary or in every first weike in Febrewary… the hardest and most pincing times.*

The farm was eventually sold and the trustees bought a tiny thatched house nearby which is now a museum where fishermen world-wide come to pay homage to this humble English gentleman.

Walton's life-history is a fascinating one. He was born, the son of an alehouse keeper, in Eastgate Street, Stafford, and baptised in 1593 at the church of St.Mary in the centre of the county town. Later he was apprenticed to a relative who was a wealthy draper in London and eventually Izaak had a business of his own in Fleet Street. He was serving as a vestryman at the church of St.Dunstan's-in-the-West when John Donne became vicar of that church and the two developed a lasting friendship; in fact Donne gave his friend one of his personal seals which was to be used later by both Walton and his son Isaac to seal their wills. I have always enjoyed reading Donne's impressive poetry and whenever I think of him I am reminded of his strange sculptured effigy, swathed in burial clothes, in Westminster Abbey. In spite of his lowly upbringing Walton became an accomplished author publishing, between his mid-forties and mid-eighties, five highly acclaimed biographies of Anglican clergymen, the first of whom was John Donne.

This was the period of the Cromwellian Civil War when the Anglican church was being forced underground and Walton, no doubt thinking it wiser, turned his writing abilities to the less controversial subject of his favourite pastime – fishing. In 1653 came the publication of 'The Compleat Angler or the Contemplative Man's Recreation', to give it its full title: a fascinating book which contains much information on country lore apart from river-fishing techniques. In it is a poem by Walton in which he affectionately refers to his wife, Anne Ken, as 'my Kenna'. She was his second wife and the half-sister of Bishop Thomas Ken, himself well-known for the hymns he wrote.

The family had quite likely returned to Stafford during this troubled period, as a place of greater safety than London, and here an exciting event occurred which they could not possibly have foreseen. After the battle of Worcester, one of Prince Charles's Garter Jewels had been hidden near to Stafford. It was imperative that it should be returned, secretly, to its custodian, one of the King's officers imprisoned in the tower of London. As a staunch Royalist, but also as a much-respected citizen with a business in the City, Walton was the obvious choice to serve his future king in this way. He set off on horseback, conveying the jewel safely and doubtless unassumingly.

Monsal Dale, unlike the other Derbyshire valleys, has a great railway viaduct striding across it. This must have upset many people when it was first built, but to many railway enthusiasts and to those who appreciate architecture, like myself, it is an exciting construction. It was a stupid and short-sighted act to close that section of the railway in the 1960s, it would have been an enormous attraction for today's tourists.

I had never been before to the Manifold Valley in Staffordshire. I discovered that Thomas Wardle, the silk manufacturer, had bought a weekend retreat there at Swainsley Hall, at the time when William Morris was using the Wardle dyeing technique for some of his designs, and the two men became good friends. The first contact that Morris made with the family was when he commissioned George Wardle to provide drawings of mediæval tiles, wall-paintings and carvings from country churches. He was also asked to make wood-blocks of drawings by Burne-Jones. Morris must have been impressed by George because he eventually asked him to join his firm as business manager. When Morris became interested in silk dyeing, George introduced him to his brother Thomas at Leek and Morris spent a lot of time there experimenting with dyes. Who could possibly imagine that in this remote valley you could find a house with one of its rooms known as 'The Rossetti Room' and containing about fifty pictures by The Master! The house also had a fine organ whose bellows were operated by water power, lifted by an hydraulic ram.

The neighbouring churches of Warslow and Cheddleton have several stained-glass windows done by Burne-Jones. When Morris became ill, Wardle invited him to Swainsley, suggesting that the peaceful surroundings would do him good; but Morris, unable to accept, wrote to his friend:

> My dear Wardle,
> It is very kind of you to invite me to share in your paradise and I am absolutely delighted to find another beautiful place which is still in its untouched loveliness. I should certainly have accepted your invitation but am quite unable to do so, for at present I cannot walk over the threshold, being so weak. The Manifold is the same river, is it not, which

> you carried me across on your back, which situation tickled us so much that owing to inextinguishable laughter you very nearly dropped me in.
> What pleasant times those were.
> With all good wishes and renewed thanks I am, yours truly
> William Morris.

Morris died six weeks later.

I remember on one of my trips in the High Peak, near the Blue John mines, I climbed a small mountain called Mam Tor. A terrific storm developed and it became so dark that I dared not move because on one side there was a sheer drop for some hundreds of feet; bits of shale were continually sliding down the steep slope, creating such an effect that someone had been inspired to name it 'The Shivering Mountain'. I was forced to shelter behind a wall with the sheep until the storm abated. When I eventually managed to climb down, with clothes absolutely wet through, I was fortunate to find a small hotel where I could get a bath, an appetising meal, and stay the night while my clothes were dried. I always remember the bath which was carved out of a solid block of marble. In that fascinating area the roadside verges were thick with lily-of-the-valley flowers and I found a place called Via Gellia, probably named by the Romans who mined for lead in that part of Derbyshire.

My ten years in the china industry set me apart in many ways. I suppose that today I would be called 'a mature student'. For one thing I did not find it easy to accept some of the ideas and opinions of my teachers. I had been trained to appreciate work done by past masters in art and I could not understand why we were not taken to see the magnificent display of paintings in the local art gallery done by Wright of Derby; nor why we were being taught in our History of Art class that Gaugin and Van Gogh were infinitely superior to the old painters. I thought it madness that educationalists could be so narrow-minded as to exclude us entirely from wonderful works of art. However, when we were studying the French Impressionists, my own experience as a china painter helped me to understand Renoir's flesh painting; he himself had been a china painter where, when painting shadows on flesh, it was necessary to use greens and blues rather than greys, which would look dirty on fine translucent china.

The head of painting and drawing at the art school was Alfred Bladen who was a fine draughtsman and helped me a great deal with life drawing and anatomy. His knowledge of anatomy was so thorough that he could show us immediately where we had gone wrong, drawing brilliant little demonstrations at the side of our work. He became a good friend and I was very fond of him, but he was a rather melancholy figure who seemed to attract disasters. I recall one or two instances when, in later years, students with whom he had kept in touch were involved with unhappy events, including one who hanged himself.

Roy Morris was tall, thin and subdued and had, so I heard, a huge family. He was a very good painter – one of the old school, who had trained at the Slade. He was about the only tutor who studied the Old Masters, and certainly the only one to enjoy Wright's wonderful paintings. The others tended to ridicule him a little, but he had a vast amount of knowledge. He had taught in Rome and whilst there had done some fine works of Vesuvius in moonlight. For some reason he came back to Derby and set up a studio where he taught very well and also enjoyed painting the locals.

The Principal, Mr.Hounsell, ran a series of lectures on the History of Art and, specially for my benefit, he included one on sculpture – only, for some reason which I have forgotten, I wasn't there and he was extremely cross with me! He was a rather clever water-colourist and I remember in particular a painting of a figure on a beach in which he had painted every pebble meticulously. He had been in the Great War and was very upright with a military bearing. Once I remember he showed us a photo of himself riding on a camel in Egypt with his brother officers. I liked him very much, and he was marvellous to me, giving me every encouragement.

One of our models was a middle-aged Italian named della Questa who was rather like a pyramid in shape as she spread herself out on the box. Her hips were very wide, she had small, sloping shoulders and a bun on top of her head. The college carpentry instructor, named Hawkesworth, was always interested in the models and seemed to spend his life planning excuses to come into the Life room to speak to them. At one time he was carving a wooden figure and came in for measurements, which involved careful measuring of the model who was quite a young girl. Della Questa, however, was more worldly. She had a flat in London where she did 'massage' and she must have chatted-up Hawkesworth and persuaded him to go down there one weekend. I believe he said that he was going to study figures in the V&A museum!

On the whole the other students were much younger than I was. There were two teenage sisters, Pamela and Patricia Newton, whom I considered to be real dazzlers: both had the most glorious raven hair, but although I found them attractive I spoke to them very little. For one thing they were way above me socially, living in a large house near Derby; and also my hair problems at Minton's had made me ill-at-ease with young women. I tended to be happiest concentrating on my course work and enjoying the solitude of exploring the Derbyshire countryside.

I got on very well with John Sanders, who lived locally and whose main subjects were graphics and wood engraving. John introduced me to the student organisation called 'The Graphics Club' and their newsletter, 'Art Herald', which he edited and for which he regularly wrote articles and an editorial column. The modelling room at the college contained the top half of a skeleton and John still remembers that he and I worked together making clay muscles to build up its body. We also went sketching together on our bicycles and John clearly recalls that my bike was hand-painted green and you could still see the brush strokes! On one occasion we cycled to Aston-on-Trent, went walking along the canal, and stopped to pluck a tiny flower from a waterside reed. It was one of a small cluster and we examined it with great intensity, agreeing on the miniscule beauty of its form and its subdued and somewhat sombre colouring. We decided that the government (probably Stanley Baldwin's) should establish a Department of Appreciation with paid appreciaters like ourselves to go around appraising the works of art and nature which meant nothing to anybody else!

At this time there was a great deal of talk and speculation amongst the students about the possibility of a second war with Germany. John was a pacifist, having done a lot of pioneering work in the Peace Movement and a number of the students agreed with him. After the horror stories I had heard from my own brothers of their experiences in the Great War I decided that there was little to be gained by further senseless slaughter, so that I myself was a natural conscientious objector. I had already decided that in the event of a war I would refuse to fight.

The course which I was taking normally took three years but I worked very hard and was able to take the examination after two years. The examinations themselves were very comprehensive, taking place over quite a long period of time.

In 'Drawing from the Antique', one exercise was to draw an antique cast from memory, so that one had previously to study a number of casts in great detail; also to study Anatomy pretty thoroughly in order to remember where all the muscles and bones lay and what they were called.

One exercise in Architecture was called 'measured drawing' and here one had to draw the plan and elevation of a classical building with columns, steps, water and a road, noting the position of the sun: this had to be set up in perspective showing all the shadows cast, and working out how the shadow fell on a curved column. An example of modern architecture also had to be drawn.

In Life drawing I knew that I would be expected to draw a model, and possibly a portrait. One was also asked to draw, from memory, some ordinary everyday object like a bicycle, a pram or a lamp-post and it was surprising how little one could remember without training oneself to be observant.

In the Sculpture examination I needed to know how tools were used and how the finished sculpture would be erected: for example, how an inscribed stone panel of enormous weight would be fixed on to a church. I had to model a sculpture in clay and then cast it in plaster. I was asked to design a panel for a certain purpose and I made a flat slab, weaving patterns into it in relief. Beforehand I had special metal tools made in oval and triangular shapes. There was also a paper on the History of Art. Looking back, it is astonishing that I completed the course in two years; but I was dedicated to art and worked night and day, and also I had some extremely good and helpful tutors.

I won a scholarship to the Royal College of Art in London for three years, to study sculpture, with a prize of £100 a year to live on. This was a stimulating time for me, but I cannot remember that I told my parents much about it. As a family we are reticent and discreet about our attainments and I don't think they realised the importance of what I had achieved.

Before starting my course I made a trip to London and visited the Central School of Arts and Crafts where John Skeaping was Master of Sculpture. He was married to the sculptor, Barbara Hepworth. He was particularly interested in the Modern Art movement and I recall watching one of his students twisting a piece of lead piping into the shape of a monkey. Skeaping himself was a leading sculptor of horses and also made realistic models of racing greyhounds, as these were two of his passions. During his career he made many lifesize bronzes of racehorses, in Britain and in the USA.

While I was up there I made enquiries about accommodation. The thirties of course was a bad time for business of all kinds and so there was no shortage of rooms to rent. There were a number of studios vacant and students would take these and share them. However, knowing no one and with very little money, I took a small room in a rather sleazy house in Redcliffe Gardens which cost me ten shillings a week. So, with mounting excitement, I said goodbye to my family and friends and travelled to London by train to continue my training at the RCA.

6

The Sculpture School, which I was to attend during the next three years, was directed by Professor Garbe – a very skilled stone and woodworker – who had himself trained at the Central School of Arts and Crafts under Professor Letharby. Garbe was quite a prominent figure in the arts and crafts movement. Each term a timetable was arranged by him and I realised that my days were to be very full, with a three hour morning session, two hours in the afternoon and a further two hours in the evening every Monday, Tuesday,Thursday and Friday. Wednesday afternoons were free, (or, as it said on the printed time table, 'Half Holiday'), as were the weekends. I was to study drawing and modelling from life, design and carving. The work I saw at the RCA impressed me very much as I had no idea what really large sculpture was like.

John Sanders and I corresponded regularly. I wrote to him:

> Thanks for your letter and the Art Heralds, I am looking forward to further editions. It's surprising how one begins to thirst for scraps of news coming from the place you have just left, especially here in London as newspaper is now a luxury ...I still can't get going yet I don't know why, I seem to work hard but don't get anything done. I think it is partly due to the fact that I am not very settled in these digs ... There is a lot of bad feeling between the Sculpture School and the rest of the college, the master just swoops on us and tells us sculptors never could draw, they are conceited, no humility etc... Professor Garbe of the Sculpture School is very sound and under-standing and would do a lot for us if he could, but I understand that he can't do much because they are trying to do away with the sculptors altogether. I advise you to make the best of the opportunities offered at Derby, it is not such a bad school after all.

Later on I wrote:

> My new digs are a tremendous improvement on the last. I have a small balcony overlooking a small garden ... one or two trees are visible from my window for which I am extremely grateful. One learns to appreciate every blade of grass down here, any sort of plant life seems so refreshing amongst so much artificiality.

I walked everywhere with my sketch books, for in this way I not only conserved my precious grant but got to know this bustling capital city, some of its people and its secret and quieter parts. I was determined to make the most of every minute whilst living there and I discovered Lyons Corner Houses where I sometimes treated myself to a reasonably priced meal. I didn't go to parties or the theatre, as the former didn't interest me very much and I had no spare money for the latter. Many students went regularly to the opera, sitting cheaply in the gallery and later talking animatedly about operas and plays which they had seen.

I missed the countryside a great deal, but it was easy to get down to Putney, walk across Wimbledon Common or Richmond Park, which had a country feel about them, and eventually reach Hampton Court. On Sundays, when it was quiet, I wandered round the city, sketching everything which interested me, in particular the wealth of monuments in parks, churches and cemeteries. I found Brompton cemetery quite exciting as it was full of monuments and mausoleums, some well-cared for, some derelict so that it was possible to peer through the doors and see the bones inside. Redcliffe Gardens where I was living, in a rather doubtful neighbourhood, had sinister-looking blue street lights and at the end quite a sizeable cemetery, so that I often wandered there. These places had attendants but on the whole they were very neglected; however, in such large areas there were always trees growing and I have always loved trees.

On one occasion I took a bus trip to St.Albans to see and sketch an interesting church there; Westminster Abbey intrigued me, but I did sketches of monuments rather than buildings because these were more relevant to my work in sculpture. I had been told about an interesting area not far from Shadwell Docks where there was a lovely Wren church in its own eighteenth century close, and nearby a pub called 'Paddy's Goose'. Inside the pub I found a small theatre with a proscenium arch painted by Rex Whistler; what an exciting discovery!

I never spent unnecessarily and kept a careful note of my expenditure. However, when I found that I couldn't live on my grant I stopped making notes! I seemed to manage by doing odd bits of work for people, especially during the holidays. Our Master of Woodcarving was Alan Dearst, who himself preferred the more modern approach to carving. An architect friend of his was designing a retreat house for old horses which had its own chapel with a wood-panelled door. The series of panels was to be filled with angels and Dearst got one or two students, including myself, to design and carve the angels. In my spare time I remember that I made a small wooden spoon, carving an angel on the handle. I also invented a coat-of-arms which I carved in wood. I was particularly fond of the plane trees with their unusual pinkish bark, enhancing the London colleges and parks. Once, when those at Kensington were being rather severely pruned, I rummaged around amongst the sawn-off branches until I found a piece with two smaller branches that seemed to have potential for carving a pig. Plane smooths up very well so I enjoyed working with it. The shape of the wood suggested a sloping back with a snout; I formed the smaller prongs into two front legs and then added two back legs: it was about 18 inches long when completed. Alan Dearst thought it was brilliant, which pleased me.

One of Richard Garbe's old students was Cecil Thomas who had a studio in Brompton Road. He had received an excellent commission from the USA to do the history of England in heraldry which meant modelling all the coats-of-arms. He obviously had to take on sculptors to assist in this work and I was fortunate enough to be employed by him for some weeks during college holidays. Amongst other things he did a great deal of coinage designing, so that while I was working in his studio I was able to observe the techniques involved. It is strange that in later years, when he was quite elderly, we were to compete in a design for adapting a special relief of The Queen's head on coin.

Cecil Thomas was a good mixer and enjoyed parties. Richard Garbe once met him in the street and Thomas said, "I can't stop Garbe, I'm off to lunch!" He certainly had a very different personality from his rather retiring old tutor; but he had great generosity and subsequently, when he died, left his studio – which was quite a valuable property in Kensington – to the Royal Society of British Sculptors, and it is now their meeting place and also where they display their sculptures.

Richard Garbe's brother was an importer of ivories which came packed in ground-up cork. One box arrived soaking wet – it could well have been recovered from a sunken ship – and sea water had mixed with the cork and penetrated the ivories, discolouring them and 'eating away' the finer parts. I remember that Professor Garbe helped his brother to restore them. This was the beginning of the period when awful thrusting modernism was beginning to take over and it was a terrible age for traditional workers. Garbe, who did exquisite ivory carving and bronze work, was very much ostracized by Modern thinkers. Because of this, like many skilled people, he himself was short of work. I recall that he made a figure for Doulton based on one of his brother's ivories.

I was very fortunate to have Richard Garbe as my Professor. He was the gentlest of people and I found that our attitude to the influences of the past and the need for wholehearted commitment to our craft was very similar. The previous Professor of Sculpture at the college had been Henry Moore, whose modern ideas of sculpture did not meet with everyone's approval, certainly not when the careful training of students had to be considered. He was eventually replaced by Garbe, who told me later that when he came to teach Moore's students, 'They just sat there rubbing two pebbles together and doing very boring work'. Garbe invited me down to his home in Kent a few times where I met his wife and daughter. The property had been a small farm and he had converted the buildings into a house and studio to his own design. I remember that one room had panels on the ceiling decorated with interesting ornamentation of birds and flowers. There was also a rather nice pool with a high wall surrounding it. I had the impression that Garbe was trying to bring me and his daughter together as he asked me to give her a lift back to London on one occasion.

I was about five years older than the majority of students because of my previous work in industry, but I made one or two good friends at the college and we made our own fun as students always do. A number of them came from India and included Bassubendranath Tagore and a Parsee girl named Shirin who, at a party arranged by the students, brought an Indian dish containing chillies which nearly killed Professor Garbe! The Indians found the damp heat of London unbearable and Shirin became quite ill one summer because of it. There was a student of design named Rene Hetherington, whose father was a clergyman in Workington. I became very fond of her, but she was not contemplating a serious relationship.

I was friendly with Andy Tittensor, another Midlander, and I made sketches and clay models of him. Sometimes he and I would go out sketching together. Eventually he became a teacher at Kingston School of Art. Andy had previously attended the very good sculpture school in Wolverhampton under an excellent tutor named Emmerson. Emmerson was a friend of the editor of the Wolverhampton Telegraph who provided him with a studio in their offices. He had a reputation for producing first-rate sculptors, almost all his students were able to obtain places at the Royal College of Art and many of them went on to gain the coveted Rome Scholarship, entitling them to three or four years study in Rome. One of them, Charles Wheeler, was later to become President of the Royal Academy.

From time to time I would take the train to Stoke and have a few days with my parents at their new house in Clayton. From the very beginning of their move Father had hated it, partly because he had another three miles to walk to work and the path which he used, called Bankeyfields, meant a very steep climb for him on his way home. Furthermore it was two miles further to his favourite pub and he missed meeting up with his friends regularly – another good reason for loathing it; but added to this I believe there were money worries. Their previous homes had been rented, but this one they were buying and Father most likely knew that they couldn't afford it and he went very much against his will. At this stage my parents had terrible rows which I found unbearable, so that my visits home were not always enjoyable. Mother was jealous if my father took notice of other women and on one occasion, when she saw him giving the widow next door a bottle of beer over the hedge, she went for him tooth and nail.

One day, when my mother had been out, she returned home in the evening to a strong smell of gas in the house and found my father with his head in the gas oven. He was dead. The family was very worried because there was a stigma attached to suicide: my brother William tried to make things sound better by saying that Father had an incurable disease and had no alternative but to take his own life. My mother never forgave him and, even when she was dying, was adamant that she didn't want to be buried in the same grave, although of course she was. They were buried in Hartshill Cemetery in Stoke. It was most distressing for me to lose my father whom I had loved and admired so much. As I worked I often recollected the time I had spent with him and Will in the old shed, learning to make small clay figures and to become more dexterous with the tiny handmade tools which they used. They taught me, amongst other things, that it helps enormously to have the right tools.

Since childhood I had loved the feel of clay in my hands and when I was at Derby I began to use it in earnest. Now, at the RCA, it became my medium and I dropped woodcarving and sculpture in marble to develop work in terracotta. The animals in the London Zoo interested me and I remember sketching and making models of a camel, zebra and bear.

Terracotta is a certain type of clay found near to ironstone and it can be buff-coloured or white, but when fired to a very high temperature it has a characteristic pinky colour. The Romans used this 'baked earth' extensively, probably because they had discovered that after firing it becomes virtually indestructible, being stronger than bronze. The Romans used clay dug from the ground which contained impurities and it was these which added to its strength. In the Pottery industry this type of clay is used to make 'saggars', the strong containers in which fragile china is stacked and fired. Its qualities have been recognised worldwide for centuries. The amazing army of sculptured soldiers found at Shanxi in the North-West Province of China was modelled in terracotta two hundred years BC., and is known as 'The Terracotta Army'. The Natural History Museum and the Wedgwood Factory buildings are built of terracotta bricks. In the fifteenth century the famous Florentine family of della Robbia perfected the technique of glazing terracotta reliefs with an opaque tin glaze. Today terracotta is refined to such an extent that it is unsuitable for saggar-making and sculpture, so old saggars are coarsely ground (a substance known in the trade as 'grog') and added to the clay before use.

John Sanders had come up to London after me, to the Central School of Arts and Crafts. One of the first things that he noticed, with the threat of war growing even more intense, was that trenches were being dug in Hyde Park. One year later, on 3rd September 1939, war was declared between Britain and Germany and I wrote to John:

> What do you think about this terrible business? It has upset things completely. I don't know what to do yet, have you made up your mind? I wish we could see each other so that we might talk things over. Is there any possibility of this do you think? ... I don't suppose for a minute that we will go back to college. I have been expecting to hear from the authorities. Have you heard anything?

However, college resumed that autumn. I had worked very hard during my course and 1940 was Diploma year. Every year Professor Garbe chose a different theme and the special subject set for us was a sculpture to represent the musician, William Byrd, born in the sixteenth century and well-known for his religious music. In the studios alcoves were built of plywood and each student had his own in which to exhibit his work. My chief influence was mediæval work and I made a model of a Madonna and Angels. All our best work was on show of course and a well-known critic thought that mine was the finest work in the entire college. A visiting sculptor, Charles Wheeler RA, bought one of my terracottas of a Mother and Child and paid me £15 which was quite a good amount at that time.

On the day that we finally qualified and were presented with our diplomas I hated the thought of wearing cap and gown, finally having to be persuaded to do so. I suppose that I was socialistic and somewhat aggressive, for I disliked ostentation of any kind and to me the 'Parents coming down to Col.' attitude of the other students seemed a superficiality which I couldn't stand. It was then, and still is, the *work* which matters to me; compared with the artists of old, like Michelangelo whose works have always been my inspiration, groups of people in gowns having their photographs taken seem an irrelevance. I had been awarded the Silver Medal, which was the top award of the Royal College of Art, and this included a travelling scholarship. Unfortunately I was unable to take this up because of the outbreak of war, so I went back home to Clayton where I stayed with Mother, but I urgently needed employment.

During the years since I had left Minton I had kept in touch with Gordon Forsyth who was now the Superintendent of Art Instruction for Stoke on Trent, and during the summer of 1940 he asked me to go and see him and offered me a job as Head of Stoke Art School. The school gave classes in drawing, painting and sculpture and, interestingly, in decoration and lettering for shop windows. It had a pottery and a small kiln. Here I met 'Tim' Timmis who used to come in the evenings for drawing lessons. He was co-director of the Pallissy Pottery and he asked me if I would advise him about design for his pottery production, which I did, little knowing that our paths were to cross again in later years.

I was in a difficult position, since others of my age were being drafted into the forces but I myself was a conscientious objector. I had been at Stoke Art School for only a very short time when someone reported me to the authorities and this information was passed on to Gordon Forsyth. He asked me if this were true and, on my replying in the affirmative said, "I am afraid that I have to ask you to resign. I have no alternative".

Professor Garbe and Mr. Jowett, the Principal of the RCA, had both been very impressed with my work as a student and realised that I was rather desperate financially. Jowett knew Josiah Wedgwood quite well, as the latter had an interest in art education and was on the board of governors of the RCA, and I think it may have been through his recommendation that Wedgwood engaged me to do a small amount of work for him, but this had now been completed. However, knowing that I had worked for them, Gordon Forsyth got in touch with Josiah to tell him the situation. He was sympathetic, possibly because the first Josiah had always been keen to employ those other ardent conscientious objectors, the Quakers, knowing them to be very reliable employees. I was asked to see Victor Skellern, Wedgwood's Art Director, and he employed me as a designer. At this time the Wedgwood factory at Etruria was in process of being moved from the original old buildings to a splendid new site at Barlaston, a country estate on the very outskirts of Stoke. The office block had already been built and I was put there, working on my own and more or less left to my own devices.

Victor Skellern had the job of sorting things out as the factory continued its removal process, but he was not always very discerning with the objects he was dealing with. I remember that they had an ordinary works' clock designed by an eighteenth century Quaker named Thomas Wagstaffe and beautifully made of mahogany and brass: but because this was the era of modernity he had it painted white – what sacrilege! Eventually it came into the possession of an employee who worked with Skellern, and he had this now historic clock stripped and restored.

The architect of the new Wedgwood factory, Keith Murray, used to stay at Tom Wedgwood's family home, 'The Lea' at Barlaston, while he was working on the plans. I often met Keith during this period and we became friends. Tom was Josiah's cousin and one of the directors of the factory. After his marriage in 1935, he and his wife Sally moved to Greatwood House near Eccleshall (coincidentally the farm which I had visited as a boy with the Capewells). However, in 1940 they moved to 'The Lea' with their two young children, Alan and Susan. Tom's sisters, Star and Joy, lived there until their marriages – Star to Maitland Wright in 1939, and Joy to Jack Fynn in 1942. Star was a designer for Wedgwood and Joy the Welfare Manager. In the late nineteenth century a very nice wooden annexe had been built on the house for use a a billiard room, now called 'the games room', and here the sisters jointly ran the local Girl Guides until the outbreak of war and Star's marriage.

Tom Wedgwood very kindly let me have the annexe as a studio where I could also sleep if I wished, with a curtained-off area for sleeping and cooking. His children found this most intriguing and used to come in from time to time since, until then, they had used it as a playroom. I showed them how to make little models in plasticene and then clay, as I had done myself at a similar age when my father and Will were busy sculpting. When Alan was three and Susan seven, I made busts of them in terracotta, and also a model of an angel for Susan which she thought was beautiful and still possesses. As well as doing designs for Wedgwood I was free to do my own terractottas which they generously fired for me and stored at the factory. Sally

(left) *"Father made a wooden scooter for us to play with"*. (ch 1) photo ©Machin Archive
(right) *"When I was about three or four my sisters made a Pierrot costume for me to wear"*. (ch 1) photo ©Machin Archive
(lower) **'The Child Fishing',**
Arnold Machin, early watercolour, 1916.
"I must have been born with a pencil in my hand, for I was drawing from the earliest days". (ch 1) (RA Sch 2001 Ex Cat No. 1) ©Machin Archive

Vase of Flowers. Arnold Machin, watercolour, 1925.
Inscribed, 'Drawing done at Trent Vale school and taken to Minton's to get my first job to train as a china painter'.
"During my last few weeks at school, I was allowed to draw and paint the whole time, much to my delight. The teacher who had a special interest in art gave me help and encouragement, one day bringing in a bunch of flowers for me to paint". (ch 3)
(RA Sch 2001 Ex Cat No. 3) ©Machin Archive

View of Minton's factory with flint mill, Stoke-on-Trent.
Arnold Machin, watercolour, 1926.
Inscribed on reverse, 'A view of Stoke with the flint mill and canal which went under the centre of town. This sketch was made in 1926 from the upper floor of the old Minton factory, which had its front on London Road with the canal forming the boundary at the rear of the factory'.
(RA Sch 2001 Ex Cat No. 4) ©Machin Archive

(Upper) **Four Minton plates decorated by Arnold Machin,** including (lower right) 1926 apprentice plate.
(RA Sch 2001 Ex Cat No. 46, 47, 49) ©Machin Archive
(Lower left) Design for teapot , early 1940s. ©Machin Archive
(Lower right) Design for plate, ©Machin Archive

Beechwoods behind Kedleston Hall.
Watercolour painted by Arnold Machin while at Derby Art School.
"When I was not working in school I was out painting and drawing in the Derbyshire countryside. During the weekends and in the summer holidays I spent many hours drawing in the beech woods on the hill behind Kedleston Hall". (ch.5)
(RA Sch 2001 Ex Cat No. 8) ©Machin Archive

LEGRAPH, WEDNESDAY, SEPTEMBER 1, 1937.

DERBY STUDENT'S SCHOLARSHIP

Mr. Arnold Machin, of Derby, who has won a Royal Exhibition Scholarship at the Royal College of Art, South Kensington, at work yesterday on one of his models. He is a student at the Derby School of Art.

(Upper) **Arnold Machin at Derby Art School** – on the occasion of his winning a Royal Exhibition Scholarship to the Royal College of Art in London.
Daily Telegraph, 1st September, 1937.
(Lower) **At the Royal College of Art, 1937-1940.**
Arnold Machin (centre) with fellow students including Andy Tittensor and Professor Garbe, Director of Sculpture.

Working in the RCA, (Arnold Machin centre/rear).
"The sculpture school which I was to attend was directed by Professor Garbe – a very skilled stone and woodworker. Each term a timetable was arranged by him… I was to study drawing and modelling from Life, design and carving. The work I saw at the RCA impressed me very much as I had no idea what really large sculpture was like".
(ch. 6)

Bust of fellow student at RCA, Andy Tittensor.
Arnold Machin, 1937-40, terracotta, height 20.5 inches.
(RA Sch 2001 Ex Cat No. 24) photo ©Machin Archive.

Animal figures.
Arnold Machin, terracotta, 1937-40
"The animals in London Zoo interested me, and I remember sketching and making models of a giraffe, zebra and two bears".(ch. 6)
(RA Sch 2001 Ex Cat No. 26, 27) photo ©Machin Archive.

Life Study of Reclining Figure.
Arnold Machin, pencil and colour wash, 1937-40.
(RA Sch 2001 Ex Cat No. 32) ©Machin Archive.

(Left) **Bust of Heather.**
Arnold Machin, terracotta, 1937-1940
(RA Sch 2001 Ex Cat No. 28) photo ©Machin Archive.
(Right) **Bust of fellow student.**
Arnold Machin, terracotta, 1937-1940
(RA Sch 2001 Ex Cat No. 33) photo ©Machin Archive.

(Upper) **Madonna & Child with Adoring Angels.**
R.C.A Diploma work, exhibited later at Royal Academy.
Arnold Machin, 1938, terracotta, height 25. 5 inches.
(RA Sch 2001 Ex Cat No. 77) photo ©Machin Archive.
(Lower Left) **RCA Silver Medal,** obverse
(Lower Right) **RCA Silver Medal,** reverse

(Upper) **A corner of the studio at 'The Lea', Barlaston.**
(Lower) **Adam & Eve: 'The Expulsion from Paradise'.**
Modelled at 'The Lea'. Saltglazed earthenware, height 23 inches,
RA Summer Exhibition 1951
(RA Sch 2001 Ex Cat No. 35) photo ©Machin Archive.

Bust of St. John the Baptist.
Arnold Machin, terracotta , height 21 inches,
purchased by trustees of the Tate Gallery, 1944.
(RA Sch 2001 Ex Cat No. 73) photo ©Machin Archive.

Europa and the Bull, early 1940s.
Arnold Machin, slipglazed terracotta, height 17 inches.
(RA Sch 2001 Ex Cat No. 41) photo ©Machin Archive.

Busts of Susan Wedgwood and Alan Wedgwood, 1941. Arnold Machin, terracotta. photos ©2002 J. J Wedgwood.
The wooden pig which Susan and Alan used to play with.
"Once, when the plane trees in Kensington were being pruned, I rummaged around amongst the sawn-off branches until I found a piece with two smaller branches that seemed to have the potential for carving a pig". (ch. 6) photo ©2002 J. J Wedgwood

Wedgwood recalls that about this time I was modelling a series of tortured figures of Christ and associates them with my troubled mind over conscientious objection.

The Wedgwoods were a fascinating family: they had a natural dignity and refinement which is not exclusive to their class, for Mrs Capewell had the same dignified detachment which is, nevertheless, kindly and caring towards anyone with whom they have contact. I suppose it can be described as classlessness since they were at ease with, and interested in, people from all walks of life. As there were so many of them connected with the factory they were known by their Christian names as, for instance, 'Mr.Tom' and 'Mr. Josiah'. The latter was often abbreviated by the workforce to 'Messiah'. Josiah took an interest in me and my work and eventually became a very good friend. When these younger members of the Wedgwood family came into the business they were expected to 'work their way through' the factory in order to thoroughly understand the manufacture of pottery. They were very much liked as employers and attracted great loyalty from their workforce; 'Mr.Tom' was particularly popular and was sometimes mistaken for one of the labourers as he shovelled clay in shirtsleeves and old trousers.

Josiah's father, Lord Wedgwood, had a brother – Sir Ralph – whose main interest was the Great Western Railway, and he came to sit for me at Barlaston so that I could make a model of him in clay. I had him perched upon a chair and one day the chair was a little unstable and he slipped, but fortunately didn't fall. This incident brought back a number of memories for him and, as I worked, he talked to me about them in the easy, interesting way which I found to be a hallmark of all the Wedgwoods.

Lord Wedgwood himself had a distinguished career. After working as a naval architect in Newcastle-upon-Tyne, he served in the South African war, returning there later to serve as a resident magistrate. He then served with distinction in the 1914-18 war. As well as this he sat as a Liberal MP, changing his allegiance to the Labour party in 1919. Lord Wedgwood was particularly fond of South Africa and he built a long, low, wooden house designed like an African farmhouse, at Moddershall in the Staffordshire countryside. Here he entertained early members of the Labour party, including Annie Besant, who was an indefatigable worker for the downtrodden.

She was particularly concerned about the women in Bryant and May's match factory where conditions left a lot to be desired; but of course, if you become interested in one group of people, your thoughts inevitably turn to others suffering hardship at home and abroad – and where does it end? Eventually she realised that the problem of purely physical hardship was endless and impossible to contemplate, so she turned her attention to solving the situation by other means. She met the Russian mystic, Madam Blavatsky, and her life completely changed. She concluded that, although one must continue to alleviate physical difficulties whenever possible, they could only be effectively dealt with by a spiritual solution.

Not long after the outbreak of the Second World War, the Minister of Labour, Ernest Bevin, came to speak in the Potteries, and Josiah took me with him to the meeting. We sat on the front row – I with a sketch-pad and pencil. During the talk I sketched a portrait of Bevin, rushed off to the factory immediately afterwards and spent all night there producing a clay model of him. Josiah presented this to Bevin next morning when he came to visit the factory. I think he was astonished. He certainly seemed very pleased with the model, copies of which were later produced in ceramic at the factory.

I produced terracotta busts of members of the Wedgwood family and of allegorical figures, and then developed portraits in bas relief which became very popular. Two of the most successful were of Winston Churchill and Franklin Roosevelt and in 1942 these were incorporated as lavender-embossed designs on white Queen's ware mugs. The cameo of Churchill was accompanied by one of his famous wartime sayings: 'Give us the tools and we will finish the job', and that of Roosevelt by: 'It can be done, it must be done, it shall be done'.

My brother Henry, who still worked at Trent Vale Brick and Tile Works, had done quite well and by now had a keen interest in cars. The first man in Trent Vale to possess a motor car had been the local grocer. It was a 'Trojan', chain-driven, and caused a great deal of excitement. For some time Henry had owned a car of his own, a Morris which he had bought for £100 and not only that, he intended to buy a more up-to-date model and offered to sell me his old one. I had very few savings, but he sold it to me very reasonably. I was intrigued by the fact that when the bonnet was lifted there was a handle to work an hydraulic lift to jack-up the car. It was a marvellous device but very simple and I am astonished that no one developed the idea.

Now that I had my own car I decided to rent a small place where I could work quietly on my own from time to time, although sometimes I stayed at Clayton with my mother. Father's death had upset us all and we visited her when we could. I found a small cottage, Sheepfold Cottage, belonging to Harleythorne Farm at Hanchurch. It was not too far from Clayton, nor from Barlaston; in fact I often walked there after I had been working. There was water laid on at the cottage which was most unusual. The previous occupant had been an elderly farm worker, living alone, who had not many worldly goods but who possessed a rather special brass fender and fire-irons. In the evening he did nothing but sit by the fire smoking his pipe and watching the reflections of the fire glinting in the brasswork. It was said that an interfering woman persuaded him to modernise and get rid of the brass fender, and this began his decline. He became very restless, went to local pubs for company, drank too much and died soon afterwards. I believe that there is a very therapeutic effect from firelight playing on brass.

The cottage was on the edge of woodland with a small garden and, as I enjoy constructing things, I made steps going up for three or four feet into the wood which was at a higher level. Here there were low mounds on which bilberries grew and distorted oaks, neglected after their original cutting. One year the trees were infested with a species of moth which festoons the branches with webs – an amazing sight. I found it most restful to walk through the wood and I also enjoyed growing my own vegetables. I had been a vegetarian for some years now and I still kept in contact with Edmund and Anna Hart, the friends I had made in the Healthfood shop in Newcastle-under-Lyme.

Edmund's father, Samuel Hopgood Hart was also a vegetarian and helped to establish the Vegetarian Society in this country. He was a solicitor but also intrigued by mysticism and he became friendly with a very interesting woman, Anna Kingsford, also a vegetarian. To justify her beliefs and in order to be able to argue her case for refusing to eat meat, Anna Kingsford trained as a doctor which enabled her to lecture and write with authority on this subject. She wrote a number of fascinating and very popular books on religion: 'Clothed with the Sun', 'The Perfect Way' and 'The Credo of Christendom' amongst them. Edmund's father edited these and helped her to find a publisher. Anna Hart was Edmund's second wife, a gifted painter, who had been a student at Glasgow School of Art – that remarkable building, designed by Charles Rennie Mackintosh, which I was to know quite well in years to come.

During the war the Royal College of Art had been evacuated to Ambleside in the Lake District where two large hotels had been commandeered for its use and, as I was given a small petrol allowance with my Wedgwood job, I occasionally took the opportunity to drive up there to visit Professor Garbe. We enjoyed catching up with one another's news. He was interested to hear of the work I had done for Wedgwood, especially the relief portraits of Churchill and Roosevelt. However, he found the times depressing but, on top of this, he sensed that the cultural side of life was moving in the wrong direction and the growing trend towards Modern Art made him feel very down at times. He also hated being away from London.

With the war in progress I was very unsettled, feeling that I should be doing something of use for the country: consequently I decided to go back to London and join the International Voluntary Service for Peace. We were provided with food and accommodation, though sometimes we found ourselves sleeping in Air Raid shelters. One of our jobs was to erect Anderson shelters in back gardens in the East End as protection for the householders. We would dig a hole, build up a retaining wall and then erect the shelter with corrugated sheets designed to be bolted together. The shelter was then covered with soil, leaving only the entrance visible.

London has always had its 'down-and-outs', sleeping rough in doorways, on park benches and on seats along the Embankment. During the war, hot soup and air-raid shelters were provided for them, some under the railway arches at Charing Cross. Sometimes I was sent there to help. Although some of these people were out of work and unable to afford accommodation, many were psychologically ill-equipped to live a normal life, and no matter how they were helped, would always remain outsiders in society. I remember one man lifting the sheet during the night, urinating on the floor and then covering himself over again, as he was used to doing when living rough. Some refused to sleep in beds, preferring to curl up in a corner somewhere. Many had their chosen doorways in which to sleep and I have a lasting memory of one elderly woman who always slept in the same place near South Kensington Underground Station. Her figure was completely obliterated with numerous coats and wrappings, her only possessions several paper bags full of heaven-knows-what, apart from scraps of bread. I used to watch her sometimes, settling down for the night. After endless adjustments whilst standing in the doorway she would finally arrange her bags round her feet, lean back in the corner and simply slide down into a sitting position until her chin was resting on her knees. There she would stay, never moving until daylight. What do these social misfits think about I wonder – do they have treasured memories of childhood or their families?

One of our jobs was to wash people who had lice or scabies, and we gave them hot baths, provided at the local swimming baths. The Service was run on military lines, with a very pompous fellow in charge who behaved like a Major-General. He and some of the others wore white overalls, and I recall that he walked around with self-imposed authority, imagining himself a doctor and attempting to diagnose ailments. Sometimes we were sent out to put bolts on doors of houses and other buildings, or we might be given boxes on which to fix handles and wheels to provide makeshift trolleys. One small boy wanted a little trolley and I was assigned to put handles on it. I thought it would help if I also fixed on the wheels. However, this task had not been allotted to me and I was severely reprimanded. I grew very disillusioned and went off on my own to help at the soup kitchens.

There was little spare time but when I could I went to the National Gallery. Most of the pictures were in storage, but lunchtime concerts had been organised to keep up the morale of those still living and working in London. We would buy our lunch there and be entertained by some of the country's best classical musicians. I particularly remember Dame Myra Hess who played the piano marvellously, transporting us, for a short time, into another world.

John Sanders had managed to find work with friends who ran a Youth Hostel in Derbyshire, Derwent Hall (now submerged under Ladybower Reservoir). A girls' convent school had been sent there for the duration of the war and for a time he helped them with the running of it. I wrote to him:

> I hope you manage to get a job at farming or some such occupation. It must be lovely at Derwent Hall just now with this marvellous autumn weather… If it had not been for this war I might have been able to do something to earn a living by now but as it is I am back where I started. This is the third time in my short life that I have been left stranded after working hard to do something worthwhile and each time when this aim of more has seemed possible something comes along and destroys my visions. The repetition gets a bit tiring, but I suppose one gains some sort of experience from every kick, even though it be painful it encourages thoughts in other directions and in consequence broadens our outlook on life.

Before long, John moved to Sheffield to join a timber corps run by the Forestry Commission and employing conscientious objectors. He became a 'timber snigger', using a horse to pull felled trees. We continued to keep in touch and, after the war, John taught art at a Grammar School, eventually becoming Principal of Lichfield School of Art in Staffordshire.

I knew that eventually my call-up papers would arrive, and when they did, I refused to accept them. I still had very bad varicose veins so that I probably wouldn't have been accepted for military service anyway, but I felt very strongly that fighting was wrong. My refusal meant that I received the following summons from West Ham Police Court:

> … for that you, on the fifth day of November, 1942, in the Borough of West Ham aforesaid, being a person liable under the National Service (Armed Forces) Act, 1939, to be called up for service failed to comply with the requirements of a written notice in the prescribed form duly served on you requiring you to submit yourself to medical examination on the fifth day of November, 1942, by a medical board at the medical board centre situate at Portway, West Ham. E.15., contrary to section 3(4) of the National Service (Armed Forces) Act, 1939…
>
> You are hereby summoned to appear before the Court of Summary Jurisdiction, sitting at the POLICE COURT, WEST HAM LANE, STRATFORD, in the said County Borough on Tuesday the nineteenth day of January 1943 at the hour of half-past Ten o'clock in the forenoon, to answer to the said information.

In the dock before me was a married woman, who had three children. Her crime was petty thieving and a list of items was on display and was read out: two pairs of knickers, one pair of trousers for a boy, one bottle of Lightning Cough Mixture and six white earthenware plates. The defendant pleaded that she was drunk and did it without knowing, to which the hollow-eyed, beak-nosed old Magistrate remarked, 'But you did not break the crockery!' I suppose this was intended to be funny as little giggles ran round the court.

My prosecution followed. I was asked if I pleaded guilty or not guilty to the charge of refusing to appear for a medical examination as written out and, on my affirming this, I was asked if I still refused; I answered that I did. The prosecutor for the Ministry of Labour and National Service asked that I be remanded in custody before being taken to the medical centre and this was agreed. After leaving West Ham I was taken from court to court in a van, waiting to collect more prisoners, eventually setting off on a longer trip which took us along the Embankment. I managed to get a squinting view through the windscreen and was delighted to recognise the familiar Millbank. We turned away from the river and at the next stop six of us were herded together in one cell. A long bench extended the length of the wall, with a hole at the farthest end representing a lavatory. One of my companions was a Chinaman who had been in a fight with knives; there was a Scottish jewel thief, remanded for housebreaking until his case came up at the Old Bailey (he was expecting to get about three years); another was a drunk and disorderly Irishman; one was in for the same reason as myself; the other was a slick looking chap who had been caught stealing. We were kept in the cell for a while and became friendly – a strange brotherhood.

Our final stop was Brixton prison and I heard the great gates open and clang behind us. As we left the van I noticed that the clock in the tower showed it was ten minutes to six. We were pushed into reception cells, which looked very similar to antiquated lavatories, though admittedly they did not smell so bad and the door was left unlocked. Shortly I received a good cup of cocoa and three small, thick chunks of bread with some sort of grease on them. I was ready for something to eat as I had been from cell to cell since 10 a.m., during which time I had only eaten a slice of bread with a mug of tea. After this, a warder at a desk at the end of the corridor took our age and all the usual particulars. We were searched and the contents of our pockets entered in a book. Cigarettes and matches were given back but they kept books, money, paper and letters. We were then ordered to take off jacket and shoes and stand on the weighing machine; our height was also measured, after which we went off for a bath. I found this very enjoyable after being pushed around all day. Wearing only shirts and trousers, our bawling warder instructed us to line up to see the medical officer being told that, when our turn came, we must toe the white line, drop our trousers and look at the star painted on the wall to the right. I did as ordered, a warder had a close look at my penis and the doctor tested lungs and heart and looked in my mouth, the whole seeming to take about half a minute. We then dressed and each received a pillowslip containing two sheets and a night-shirt, and were trooped off, each carrying his white bundle through a block of cells, a long corridor and outside to another block. This was a strange sight, a long line of us, dimly lit by the warder's torch, resembling ants carrying their eggs, except that there is rather more purpose to an ant's existence.

Our dormitory was a long, high, rectangular structure with cells all round the walls four storeys high. Each deck was reached by a flight of iron steps in the centre of the building and the approach to the cells was by long galleries running the whole way round the building. It looked rather like a ship. I was taken up to the second block, after being given a bible and a prayer book. The cell was not at all unpleasant, covering an area of about eighteen square feet and about ten feet high. The walls were painted with a dark green band at the bottom, one foot deep, and one third of the way up with cream, finishing with a thin green line; above that the rest was whitewashed. A bed made of wooden boards was raised about three inches from the floor by transverse members. A very lumpy mattress, three rather dirty and decaying blankets, an over-cover and a pillow completed the bed. One wooden chair, a small table, a two-tier corner structure with washbowl, water jug, soap tray and towel rail, and a corner shelf which I presumed was for books completed the furnishings. There was also a plate, mug, jerry, dustpan and small hemp brush, shaped rather like a tassel with no handle. We were allowed to use the lavatory and fill our water jug on the landing before being locked up for the night. By this time it was about 7.45pm. At eight the warder came round, lifted the cover of the spyhole in the door and announced that it was bedtime. I had been allowed to keep cigarettes and matches so I smoked and read the Bible for a while, then lay awake for quite some time on my uncomfortable bed. They forgot to switch off my light and as I had a pencil and a few scraps of paper, given to me by another conscientious objector whilst waiting for the medical, I decided to put down my experiences of the day in verse, in minute writing, before dropping off to sleep.

The next I remember was hearing, or rather I thought I heard, a warder calling five-thirty. I lay for some time before getting up and dressing. It was January 20th 1943. Just after 6.30 I heard a warder going round asking who was going out. The cells were unlocked and prisoners filed out to empty slops and get fresh water. He grumbled when discovering that my light had been switched on all night! I packed up my sheets and night-shirt in the pillowslip and trudged off to the ground floor with my white pack on my back. We were lined up and checked and replaced our bibles. While standing there I noticed the incongruous posters on the walls such as, 'Watch that fuel target' and, 'Turn that gas down', with appropriate illustrations. After retracing last night's steps we put our bundles on a rack with a tie-on identification label in case we returned. Then we stood to be searched, though God knows what one might pinch from a prison. The warder doing this operation remarked, "Are you a CO?" "Yes". "Cor lumme", he said, "It's funny how I can always pick 'em out", and laughed heartily. It was quite funny to him but it did not require much intelligence or knowledge of psychology to separate us from the old lags. After collecting the items deposited on the previous day, we sat in the corridor on a long bench to eat a breakfast of a huge plate of porridge, without milk or sugar, two thick slices of bread and marge and a mug of tea. I couldn't eat much of mine, although this simple fare appealed to me. The corridor was clean with a red and cream tiled floor, suggesting the atmosphere of a monastery. The only objectionable thing was the smell from a dumb and deaf half-breed with tattered clothes and jerky, nervous movements. We were checked out of the building and into the prison van which soon began to reek after the poor mute entered, and I had run out of cigarettes. It was quite dark when we left Brixton at 7.15 a.m. and again we travelled all over London picking up prisoners from various prisons for trial later in the day. This most depressing journey lasted for about three hours until the van reached West Ham Police Court and I was again in the custody of Detective Bond, the officer in charge of my summons. After being presented with my razor and other items which had been confiscated the day before, I was driven about five miles to the Medical Centre at Ilford where I was presented to the chairman of the Medical Board. He asked if I would submit to an examination and, upon my refusal, I was taken to Stratford Police Court and my case heard about 11a.m.

The trial was conducted by a Magistrate and about five J.Ps, including two women. After reading my offence I was asked if I had anything to say. I had not but I handed over two letters, one from Josiah Wedgwood and the other from P.H. Jowett, my old Principal at the Royal College of Art.

The presiding officials read them and muttered something about a very good artist and fine character. Then the prosecutor from the Ministry of Labour stood up and said, "It is obvious that he is a very fine character and a fine artist and craftsman, but that is not the point". The Magistrate, who looked rather like a successful butcher, pronounced in a cheery voice, "I shall have to send you to prison for twelve months". There was a heavy sigh behind me from a female. She was no one that I knew, since the only friends present were Dennis Allen and Charles Kindsay. I was led from the dock to a cell. The shock of twelve months was a bit rattling and I was relieved when, after quite a while, I was called out to talk to Dennis. At that moment however, bombs began to fall, although I had not heard the siren. The policeman on duty seemed quite frightened and rushed me back into the cell. Strangely enough I felt nothing, only cold as there wasn't much heat. Dennis departed to find food and cigarettes for me, but while he was away the officer brought tea and bread and I thought I was doomed to a repetition of my four previous meals. I had just begun to chew the bread when Dennis returned with a very welcome lunch of beans, carrots and potatoes with mincemeat tart to follow. He sat with me while I ate and I gave him my civilian clothes and sweet coupons and asked him to arrange for someone to organise my appeal. I was ordered to Wormwood Scrubs prison and after a further prolonged drive in the offenders' van we were dumped in 'The Scrubs'. Charles very kindly agreed to arrange for my appeal and on January 29th I received a heartening letter from my staunch friend, Josiah Wedgwood:

> I am extremely sorry to hear your bad news, which I also learnt from Dennis Allen. I have written to Allen saying I will be glad to do what I

> can in connection with your appeal, and to ask your solicitor to get in touch with me and to give me all particulars. Certainly I will witness to your character and the sincerity of your convictions and appear in person when necessary... Meantime Tom joins me in sending you sympathy in your bad time and sincere wishes that your courage may enable you to face whatever must be faced. Your models at Barlaston are being kept carefully and you must look forward resolutely to the time when you can resume your profession and make more nice things.
> Your friends at the Lea and works and here send you their love and sympathy. Whenever you are allowed to write and feel like writing I shall be glad to hear from you.

Josiah came to my appeal but this was turned down. Josiah told me later that the appeal judge hated the name of Wedgwood, as he had once suffered a rebuff from Josiah's father.

It felt very strange to be in prison. One regular job, of course, was sewing mail bags, but I was surprised to find that the standard of work was not very high: if the stitches were five inches long that was accepted, providing the quantity was correct.

Twice a day, in the morning and again in the afternoon, we were marched round the yard for exercise, and there I met all kinds of people – murderers, rapists and a lot of Black Marketeers. One fellow, a Dutchman, was furious when I told him my 'offence'. "What are you in for then?" I asked him. "I was on a train, punched a woman in the stomach and snatched her bag", was his reply. Nearly every prisoner claimed to be innocent. I talked to one who was known by the police to have stolen goods but they could never prove it. He said that he and his cronies stole anything, sometimes just for the fun of it: once they took some plywood, which they didn't really want, off the back of a lorry simply to imagine the puzzled face of the driver. The police raided his house on one occasion and found a lamp from a Messerschmitt, but he had won it at a dance, so they couldn't get him for that. Eventually they found a stolen Army blanket and he was imprisoned on that evidence.

One thing which intrigued me as I studied my fellow prisoners was how, even within the constrictions of prison life, their basic personalities did not alter: the neat and tidy person polished his shoes well and tied his tie with care, managing to keep a smart appearance in spite of altered circumstances; caterers found work in the prison kitchens; Jews still continued to acquire things, somehow managing to get more bread than anyone else and then doing a deal with others for cigarettes.

Somehow we conscientious objectors managed to produce a monthly magazine which was surreptitiously passed round; much of the contents lampooned the warders. There was a library and also friends were allowed to send in books for us to read, but these had to be stamped with our prison number. I still have some of these books.

My mother wrote regularly. In March came the following letter:

> ... I hope you are keeping in good health. I am very pleased to hear they are giving you that privilege -to have the Books as you can study and it will keep your mind busy, for it is all you have wanted in life is work. That is what the Professor at the College said when I and Cath came to the Exhibition in London. He said Arnold only wants work and money does not bother him..... I have had a letter from Albert last week. He said 'let me know as soon as you get news about Arnold'. I am pleased you are making the best of it. I know you will be no trouble. It is your nature to be good and reserved. Will came up last week. He is not working as he was in a bit of explosion at his work. He was lucky it has only burnt his right hand. He had just gone to work after the flu. Oh what about your endowment? Should I see Ida Boulton if you are not going on with it? If you leave it too long you lose all you have paid over 10 yrs... I am glad you can have a visitor, also grateful you have got friends in London. By your letter it seems you did not get much chance. I really thought they would hear Wedgwood. To say what he wanted to... you have got a nice friend in J Wedgwood. There are not many men like him, few and far between. I am pleased to hear you say you are happy. I hope you will remain in the same spirits as you are now, right through until the finish. I hope your representatives can do something about it. All that we can do is wait.
>
> Well Arnold, good night and God Bless you. I wish you the Best of love and Luck
>
> Mother xxx

In prison I had a small copy of Dante which fitted neatly into the pocket of my prison uniform. One day, when we were exercising in the prison yard, one of the warders accosted me, "What have you got there, in your pocket?" I began to reach into the pocket containing my precious book ... "No, not there – the other one" Thankfully I reached into the other pocket which was stuffed with a large blue cotton handkerchief and pulled it out for his inspection!

I have always been fascinated by unusual literature, reading many of the works of Goethe and also 'Conversation with Goethe' written by his secretary, Eckermann. I had done a lot of drawings based on characters from his books, such as Margaret and Francesca. William Blake had been a favourite, ever since I had discovered his strangely illustrated books in the library at Stoke. Mystical things have always interested me. Later on in life, when I had the money to spare, I bought a reproduction of one of his books illustrated with engravings done by Blake and his wife – all rather dramatic and wonderfully executed.

The prison buildings were magnificent, having been purpose-built for high security with the minimum of effort. There was a great central hall with cells around it, one storey above another, and strong nets strung across to prevent prisoners from throwing themselves off. The skylight had to be painted during the war years because of blackout regulations, but for psychological reasons this was painted blue and it gave a most eerie glow to the large hall. There were narrow slate balconies marvellously supported by metal brackets. There was only room for one person at a time to walk along these so that no one could start a riot. I remember the inmates standing in their cell doorway each morning, holding their bowls and waiting for porridge.

Our uniform was entirely grey – jacket, trousers, shirt, tie – and everything was made in the prison including our shoes which were loosely sewn together. The exercise yard was also grey, with mud that spread everywhere – even the prisoners faces looked grey. For someone like me with an eye for beauty it was particularly depressing as we tramped round and I remember, in the Spring, how delighted I was to see a few irises growing in the cinders on the path and the top of a single green tree over the high wall: they were remarkable events in a drab existence. I maintain that, even without noticing it, the movement of live branches helps one spiritually.

Another extraordinary happening was the day we were given white bandages and red flannel to pack up, most likely to send to the troops abroad: the vivid contrast between the two colours was unbelievably startling to my eyes. I found the slightest bit of colour very stimulating.

The cells had one small window, quite high up, so that it was difficult to read easily. I used to put my chair on top of the table to be nearer to the light. I was lucky because I was always on my own. Some people liked sharing, but I did not. If one was known to be trustworthy, the door was left unlocked as a special privilege – not open, but unlocked. This did a great deal for one's morale. It was very disturbing to hear bombs dropping during air-raids and shrapnel peppering the roof, but fortunately I was of a philosophical nature.

On Sunday evenings we had visits by a prison visitor who came with his daughter to show very ancient films with religious themes such as 'The Good Samaritan'. He was really old-fashioned, like someone out of the past, but such a gentle, sweet-natured person. The prisoners found these film shows amusing and I think they went simply for something to do.

Letters from family and friends were eagerly awaited and helped enormously to bring the outside world into our monotonous existence. Victor Skellern addressed this letter to :

> Arnold Machin Esq. ARCA 18/3/43
> 4329 Wormwood Scrubs.
> I was very pleased to hear from you and learn the news. We had been wondering many times what had happened … Mr J.W. has mentioned you several times but never told me much, probably thinking I was fully acquainted with details. Yes, we had the models fired, through the Electric Oven. The figure subjects are tip-top and so too are the busts. The

slip decorated one is really good and I am sure you will agree that this method suggests great possibilities. I like it very much indeed. The large full figure came out intact but with cracks in several parts. I rather think that the clay composition was a little too fine and you will have to use a stronger grog for such subjects or a tougher body.

These models will make a magnificent display when we have the proper showroom and accessories. If it is possible I will have a photograph taken, but at the moment I simply have no idea how this is to be accomplished. Photographic film etc. is practically impossible to get.

I paid the rent of the cottage for the 3 months ending March 31st and will continue to keep this going as long as possible until you return once more to take up residence. I cycled over there yesterday (Sunday 21st) to see how things were and the general state of affairs after the Winter. The cutters have practically cleared the wood behind the cottage. Only a few large oaks remain. It is most unfortunate but it is still very lovely down those parts, it is certainly much lighter. Inside the cottage things were undisturbed although damp was beginning to affect things, particularly metal, and many things are getting rusty. There was some mould on the floor and woodwork, but not sufficient to cause damage to the latter. I gave the place a good cleaning out and had a big fire going, and I certainly think it did the place a lot of good... Walpamur is off the market, – would you object to a judicious use of whitewash around the place? It wants doing because of flies, upstairs one window was black with them...

Here at Barlaston we keep very busy and in spite of coughs, colds etc. production is being maintained at the highest possible level... It is strange that you should be using a pot stamped Barlaston. It's quite likely that you saw it being made or in the finished warehouse at the time. By the bye a Xmas card arrived this last week for you. I am enclosing it in this letter, it is from Shirin Jal Virgee. Apparently she is back home again and settled down.

Norman Makison came to visit me a few weeks ago. He has had some rather terrific experiences at sea in Russian convoys and North Africa...

Josiah and his parents were sympathetic and from time to time I had letters from Lady Wedgwood, who was herself a conscientious objector. In April I received the following:

Northumberland Hall Hotel
Brighton
Dear Mr.Machin

Owing to the fact that my husband, Lord Wedgwood, is ill here in Brighton, and his son "Mr. Josiah" has been visiting him, it happens that I have read your letter to the latter (& also his letter to Mr. Morrison asking that the question of your release may be re-considered). I felt I shd. like to send you a line of greeting from a fellow CO. I have been one ever since the Boer War; tho' I have never suffered persecution for my convictions, I have pained and angered a good many friends. It passes

my comprehension how anybody with reasoning powers and a sense of justice can approve of this method of settling disputes by the wholesale slaughter of innocent men – & women & children too in these days! But obviously they can! During the last Great War I was out in the back blocks of Northern Queensland during the greater part of the time; & afterwards in San Francisco, therefore I never came up against Government orders. In this war, I am too old to be conscripted, so it is not likely my sincerity will be put to the test which you (& many others) have successfully met. It is good to know that there are a great many more COs in this war than in the last, & their number will continue to increase as the world grows older & wiser!
You will be sorry, I know, to hear that Lord Wedgwood is seriously ill; but we have a good nurse & a good Dr, & I hope the sea air & complete rest will soon do him good. Mr. Josiah went back to Staffs. today, we shall miss his help & sympathy – & his music. He is determined to secure your release, & I only hope he will be successful; but as you know, if "the law is a hass", many Cabinet ministers are mules! With kind regards & warm admiration, Believe me,
Yours sincerely -
Florence Wedgwood.

I found her kindness in writing to me, and her alliance in my cause, most heartwarming. Mother wrote with great regularity, telling me news of family and friends to keep up my spirits:

Andy (Tittensor) he was over a few weeks ago. He said he had no news of you for a long time. He says he will try to see you before long. I gave him the letter to read that you sent me – he was pleased to read it and said that it rested his mind as he had been thinking a lot about you. He also said that your letter was very cheerful. Wilf he was over last week – he wishes to be remembered to you – he says try to keep OK, the time will soon pass by. Albert he wants your address to write. I will send it on. Have you heard from Miss Thompson lately. I have had a few nice letters from Miss Mary Butts – she seems nice by her letters…

By coincidence a letter from Miss Thompson arrived a few days later. She was my old friend 'Tommy', with whom I had lodged in Derby.

Dear Arnold,
I would have written before, but didn't know I was allowed to. How am I to tell? ….May I talk about myself for a bit? When you were here, I think in the summer, I told you of an experience I had with a child. Joe Dorrington's little girl, who though she had never seen me before, took my hand, and chattered away as if she had known, and loved me, all her life, and didn't want me to part with her. There was "something"that moved me very much. I hadn't seen or heard from Micky (*a tame robin*) for months until this week when I thought I heard him fly over making

> his little call. I answered, but didn't know whether he heard. Yesterday morn I was putting tomato plants in the greenhouse when I heard him call to me outside. I answered and went on with my job, but he kept on, so I went out and talked with him. I told him how sorry I was I hadn't been able to get seed for him this last two years. He said I wasn't to worry about that ....and whether there was seed or not he would come just to see and hear me in the garden, he was quite a long time talking away with marvellous expression. I was deeply moved... in the end he called his mate... and with a Cherio from him they both flew off. He told me he had brought a message of faith and somehow you were connected with it, and I remembered the time when you were there and he settled in my hair one evening and refused to be moved, then, the feel of his little body pressed against my head gave me new hope. Do you remember the time? ... This is not imagination, it is just that my senses were tuned to hear and receive something that no one else would understand. I wouldn't tell this to anyone but you, as I know they wouldn't understand and then I wonder – Do you? ... I pass on Micky's message to you, "Be of good courage, for I am with you, even unto the end of the world", that he brought and delivered so beautifully from his Creator. In your letter I read "I shall be pleased to hear all the good news from you and the birds."... Let me know if there is anything I can do for you. I come and see you very often in spirit, so don't think you are alone, stone walls don't keep me out ...other kinds don't either, distance no object, I'd come in the flesh, if you wish, so don't forget to smile if only for the sake of Tommy x

One event which stands out most clearly in my mind was the arrival of the composer, Michael Tippett, also a conscientious objector. He was on top of the world when he came in and had an irrepressible personality, as we were soon to discover. He was writing, 'A Child of Our Time' and being in prison gave him the opportunity to develop the theme of his music. Walking round together we became very friendly and I visited him when we were eventually released.

I remember the Governor well: he was a very silent man and never spoke to anyone as far as I could observe. His Deputy however, was much more relaxed and Tippett managed to persuade him to have some musical instruments brought in, which Tippett distributed and began to rehearse the men who had musical ability. He did a remarkable job and displayed great skill with them. If their playing didn't come up to his expectations he would say, 'If you can't do better than that I shall go *home*!', which of course caused great hilarity. He also persuaded the Governor to allow Cyril Smith, and his wife Phyllis Sellick, to come in and give us a piano recital. He was full of life and vitality with an absorbing love of music and through him our exceedingly drab lives were enriched.

In July came an unexpected letter from Keith Murray:

> Dear Arnold,
> I have just returned from a few days at The Barlaston Factory – The first serious visit I've done there for well over a year. Coming back to things with a fresh eye, I was enormously interested and pleased with those three pieces of yours in Skellern's studio – the armless woman, the black-haired bust, and the man's head– they are very good indeed, and I was so impressed with them that I am writing this note to encourage you not to lose heart or interest during your spell of isolation. I hope to see these pieces, together with some others from your Studio at the Lea, as a higher-plane section of the first Wedgwood show after the war. It is a great pity that your researches should have come to this temporary halt, and I only hope that your association with Wedgwood's will be renewed as soon as possible.
> Some months ago I collected all your Lea work into your studio, and looked at it again this week to see that it was intact. The door is locked, so there is no likelihood of intruders getting in. Can't you get permission from the Governor for you to be supplied with clay or other modelling materials, so that you can continue working. It is such a pity for all this time to be wasted.

It was extremely heartening for me to know that many friends in the outside world had my interests at heart and were keeping an eye on my possessions. In the same month I heard from Richard Garbe:

> I heard some time ago that you were an inmate of one of His Majesty's Institutions. I need hardly say how sorry I am; but man's actions one to another are difficult to understand, and I am sorry indeed to send these few lines to such an address. I have thought much about your wretched position in the scheme of things and will always remember your kindness and consideration to me when I was in hospital – I want to say to you be brave – despite being forced to move and have your being amongst criminals. The old values which we based our lives on, have indeed been shattered – and those, it seems, who based their principles of action on the old ethical law have to pay the price… I trust you will soon be set free to help the cultural side – it needs it badly. I feel very down at times but it's to no purpose – try to think of what you will do in the future. Miss Abbot the pottery student said I may write to you, she's clever and seems to know so much too of the science and technical side of pottery. I am sorry to say that Mr. Harding died after taking to bed for a fortnight (cancer of the stomach). He was a wit, and a clever man, 57 years of age. He died 2 weeks ago. Another tragedy was – a painter student, age 19, blew out his brains 2 months ago. It's Sunday and people are returning from church, having given thanks to their Deity – "from whom all blessings flow". I fear this letter is none too cheerful – but the world is out of joint – and may be for some time. I regret also if this letter is very short – It is difficult to write about things which are acceptable to

> the powers that control our lives. With very best wishes for a speedy release …

Our surroundings in prison were not very hygienic in my opinion, and the medical officer didn't seem to care whether or not our cells were properly cleaned. Providing you poured a bucket of water over the floor it was considered cleaned. The cells were like brick vaults, unplastered and with the bottom half of the walls painted dark green. By contrast the medical cells were plastered and painted white throughout, but the prisoners hated going into them, feeling that they were being shut up in a glazed box which would drive them mad.

Each day we were given a small bowl of water to wipe out our cells and for months I had painstakingly cleared mine of all the accumulations of grime so that at last I could spend my days and nights in reasonably hygienic surroundings. I had no sooner finished than they decided to change my cell and I was moved to another, equally filthy. I was absolutely incensed: so furious in fact that next morning when my door was unlocked I rushed out, down the steps, and insisted on speaking to the head warder. This was quite illegal of course, but being locked up makes one behave rather differently. I must admit that I expected a severe dressing-down but he was very sympathetic and, to my astonishment, said that he would allow another prisoner to clean it out for me. He realised that my behaviour was quite out of character. However, my conscience would not allow me to pass on the task to a fellow prisoner, so I did the work myself.

In August Mother wrote:

> … it will be a blessing for everyone when this war is over … it seems to be going on alright for us (*the Allies*) hoping it will be the last… When I told Percy where you were he was very surprised. I told him on the Saturday I went over and he wrote the letter to you on Sunday. So he was not long in writing to you. He asked me to read the letter (*which was suggesting a job which might be available for me on release*) but I know you would not want that kind of work. you have got something waiting for you much different to that. but still it was very nice of him to suggest it. I am pleased to hear Miss Thomson writes to you and she is saving you some fruit. I have got a nice few eating apples on our trees I must save you a few… I am pleased to hear you are doing a bit of painting also you are supplied with books… well Arnold keep your spirits up time is going by…

Time was indeed going quite quickly now. On the 4th September I wrote to my friend Mary Butts:

> It is more than a haircut and a shave since I had your last letter… It will not be long now before I am released. I hope to be out in just over a

night's lodging from now, it will be good to get out of jug after doing a stretch – No, I have not gone mad, I am still as sane as I ever was, these strange terms belong to a new and wonderful language I have been learning; I seem to get on much better with this than French. Most of the words are derived from the English – in fact they are English words with totally different meanings from those we are used to, as you may observe above. Three classical questions are: 1. Owlonyadooin? 2. Watchyerinfor? 3. Warejagettit? The first may be answered by: 'a night's lodging' or 'a shave' or 'haircut and shave', 'a carpet', 'a stretch', or 'lagging'. The most common answer to the second is, 'furnuffin' but occasionally it is, 'fursomeffin' and this might be 'fiddlin', 'blowing the gaff', 'hit and miss' etc. etc., and the third might be, 'the OwlBiley' etc. Another popular question is, 'arlongyergotnah?', to which the reply might be, 'a hundred and twenty one cocas', 'four visits', 'eight letters'. 'My flowery', 'My Peter' both refer to the cell. 'Flowery' is an abbreviation of 'flowery dell', 'snout' is tobacco and so on. Every morning we can hear something like this: 'ararmencomplaininsick- comeondownere, menforessesmo, menforadoctor, menforreddinggerrinside- outofit'. However, there is one English noun which up to the present cannot be translated into this language and it still remains as a sign which, though it may not have any mystical significance, reminds me of the 'Masons' or the 'Buffaloes', otherwise the English has to be used sandwiched between several violent adjectives.

As I cannot write the adjectives here I will try to describe the 'mystical' sign – Stand with arms hanging down, palms facing inwards. Raise the left arm and take the wings of the nose between the first finger and thumb of the left hand. Then raise the right hand, bending only at the elbow until the lower part of the arm is at right-angles to the upper part. Now press together the finger and thumb of the left hand so that the air passage of the nose is firmly sealed; simultaneously form the letter O with your lips, repeating several times without allowing any sound to escape, and move the right hand forward slowly, at the same time flexing and extending the fingers making a serpentine movement. If you can't guess what this sign means perform the action described in front of a mirror – you might find it funny if nothing else.

Now that I have rid myself of this nonsense at your expense, please tell how you are. Are you still farming? Have you done anything about a job for next term? I hope to be released in two weeks time. As yet I have not made any fixed plans except I hope to see Jane on Tuesday Sept.21st. She has to return to her unit the day after and then Tippett asked me to stay with him for a day or so. His piano sonata will be played at the National Gallery on the 24th. Perhaps you will be back by then, but I must wait until I am out and until I hear from you. I do not suppose I will be able to write again until I am free. I am looking forward to seeing you outside this place where there is no time limit.

I do hope you will be able to find suitable employment. You must try to get fixed up before the M.of L. become interested. There is no knowing what they will direct you to and I think it is well to keep free

> from them... How did the backcloth go and did Russell Flint inspire you!!? At the mention of his name I immediately have visions of seductive females lying about on some lovely beach, or a divan with pink and gold cushions, or maybe the Amazon variety, dramatic creatures, usually displayed either nude from the waist upwards or one full breast protruding through a torn garment as they stand defiantly between the hunted rebel and the brutal soldiers. Having made this observation I am thankful you will not be able to see my efforts at painting.
>
> We have not had any more concerts but we had a film show; one picture on Gray's Elegy was quite interesting – the lovely Stoke Poges and the surrounding country is marvellous, one of the spots I must visit sometime. We are due for another film tomorrow which I understand to be 'The Magnificent Obsession'. It is supposed to be a very good film...

On 9th September I received a letter from Michael Tippett:

> You're nearly out! This is just to confirm that you ring me on the day (or evening) after you come out. The 21st itself I shall have to be at Northampton I think. And will you come to the cottage here on the Thursday evening? That means you come to Morley College, Westminster Bridge Road – (Lambeth North Bakerloo Stn.) by 8.30pm & we will go down to Oxted together. The Sonata is being played at the Gallery on the Friday, 24th – so I shall come up to town again for that, & we can go together. OK? Looking forward to seeing you.

I didn't resent being sent to prison; it was the law of the land and I felt that they had a perfect right to imprison people who objected to fighting; consequently imprisonment never affected me. When you do what you know to be right for *you* and the consequences are inevitable, then do it and forget about it. In some ways I felt that my older brothers in the 1914-18 war had far worse things to put up with. My brother Percy, for instance, was sent to bury the dead. He had to find bodies and give a name to the corpse before burial. We younger children knew that there were hardships to be endured but we couldn't realise all that was going on. Maybe it was the stories which our brothers brought back which made me eventually realise the futility of fighting. Years later when I visited Arras it was terrible to see the graves of all those young men slaughtered by this wicked system.

7

I had been sentenced to twelve months' imprisonment but because of good behaviour I was released in nine. I was to find that treatment of conscientious objectors had improved since the Great War, for a Quaker visitor to the prison, Mr.Lord, told me that during that war he had been a CO and after release he and others were invariably 'picked up' and imprisoned again – some of them several times – having the indignity of being played with in a cat-and-mouse game.

I continued to receive and reply to letters from the friends I had made during my years in London and in prison. Charles Harding wrote, shortly after my release:

> Firstly greetings my friend, (if I may drag you down to my level) 'twas good to hear that you were 'free', or would it be more correct to say 'out on leave'! Vickery told me that you were suffering from after effects of the dehumanising process. I can therefore readily sympathise with you having been through the process myself, and I trust that you speedily return to your pre-prison habits and feelings. 'Vic' also told me that you have been reproaching yourself for not having made a more determined stand 'agin' the authorities inside, believe me when I say that in my humble opinion you have no need to reproach yourself on such an issue, you were one of the few COs whom it was possible to rely upon and your fearlessness in 'standing up' to the Governor and the 'Screws' in their attempts to robotise you was an inspiration to the few rebels among the CO movement in prison, among whom I count you. One good thing which one learns in prison is self discipline (or if you prefer 'self control'). You should be able to use your experience in the next few weeks and I would advise you to force yourself to take up as soon as possible your old ways, otherwise you will find your present mood of indecisiveness and restlessness lasting longer than needs be. I am not in the habit of corresponding so forgive me for such a short note. In the hope that some day we will renew an acquaintance which I am pleased to have made. My kindest personal wishes. Fraternally Yours…

Michael Tippett, in a very busy schedule, found time to write reassuringly:

> …it took me quite long enough to 'thaw out' after a bare 2 months inside, so I know how it was with you. Don't worry. I wish you'd manage to find

your own inner path – but it's a hell of a long road for a modern, the outer world being what it is.

Four welcome letters arrived during the Christmas period, which I was spending at Clayton with Mother. Firstly a brief communication from the Ministry of Labour :

National Service Acts 1939 – 41.
I am instructed to inform you that it has been decided not to proceed further with the question of your medical examination under the above Acts .

Secondly a letter from Richard Garbe at Grasmere:

...I was pleased to hear that you were out of that place. I can readily sympathise with you in your experience, although I have not had the misfortune of meeting my fellow humans? in the raw, as you have. I can well understand that your preconceived values of humanity, and all that goes with it, are upset. What I abhor are those who sit in comfort doling out what they consider justice, and those that make what they choose to call laws – those dirty time-serving politicians, and the hyenas – the opportunists who do their supposed 'bit' by proxy. In fact, 75 per cent of humanity, and not forgetting the bloody church dignitaries – the most loathsome creatures and hypocrites. I dislike journalists and liars – but there, if I go on like this it won't help you or I ... I normally say little- it's wisest – never mix in politics, keep my ears open and get on with my work. Don't try to reform – as Lutyens said to me – 'They would crucify Christ again'...
Forgive me the tone of this letter, it's not a helpful note, but it helps me to get something off my mind for I know you understand. It may seem strange to you that one of my age should write so, when silence is the cap of dignity. I want to confide in a fellow artist who I feel instinctively thinks as I do. I want to wish you peace of mind for the future, and a healthy New Year. Should you be up this way do call to see me. Don't be too critical of your own work – I know one can get like that and ask oneself is it important? It is – and more important than all the political jugglery etc. It's the thing by which the past civilisations are judged – and not by damned journalists. So be happy in the thought that you are one of the most important people, and are serving humanity. Be grateful that you have friends. Your day is coming, and your like, and the others will have been all forgotten. Give my love to Tittensor and those who remember me kindly. I sincerely hope that you will be allowed to do the work which nature has fitted you for, and to hear that such is the case...

The third was from Victor Skellern:

Today we have had Mr.John Rothenstein, the Director of the Tate Gallery,

> as a visitor. We showed him your works, terra-cottas etc., and he was very impressed, so much so that I took him up to The Lea to see some of your other works. Mrs.Tom (*Wedgwood*) very kindly took him around. He liked your St.John very much indeed and said that "subject to the approval of the Trustees" he would like to purchase it for the Tate. He is anxious to know a few sculptors who would be prepared to execute commissions for churches. Apparently the Ecclesiastical authorities, particularly the Roman Catholic, have begun to realise that their churches are full of the most appalling rubbish and think that it is high time that something was done about it. To help him to show what can be done Rothenstein would like, with your permission, to have some of your terracottas on show at the Tate… let me know as soon as possible and I can arrange for the packing. Furthermore he would very much like to see you at the Tate. Before calling however he would like you to drop him a postcard to fix an appointment, and also to tell you how to get at him. Owing to the bomb damage the entrance is through some mysterious ways… Mr. Josiah was very pleased indeed for your work to be recognised by the 'powers that be' and thinks that the proposition as outlined has distinct promise for you.

The fourth letter was from Lady Wedgwood:

> Your Christmas remembrance gave me great pleasure, and I think the design and colouring are beautiful. I have placed the card on a corner bracket in my room, it looks v. nice up there. I presume you are free again now? I must ask Mr.Josiah when I see him – probably next week. I have just been reading 'Prisoners' Guide', a pamphlet issued by the Prison Medical Reform Council. Do you know anything of their work? If you have any evidence to give after your experience in prison, of reform urgently needed, you ought to get in touch with them. Their address is 5 Lower Camden, Chislehurst, Kent. Apparently conditions are appalling in some prisons – including Stafford! Vera Brittain has written the Preface to this 1/- booklet. I shall be seeing her next Sat. & cd. pass on to her any evidence you might wish to give. I hope all goes well with you now? Good wishes for a happy New Year.

After my return to the Potteries I was delighted to be appointed as a full-time figure modeller at Wedgwood. This was a difficult time, with most of the skilled labourers going to the war, and Wedgwood did what so many businesses had to do and employed untrained women in the factory. It was therefore necessary to design items which could be produced mechanically and decorated without difficulty. I devised a simply-moulded wedding group based on old Staffordshire figures, which would be easy for them to deal with. Behind the figures was a tree with names carved into the bark, including 'Wedgwood.' I designed a bull which could be very simply moulded and then decorated with lithographs, so that all the girls in the factory had to do was to attach the decorations before firing. I designed the lithographs of zodiac symbols myself – a process which I had never done before. When I originally proposed the idea to Josiah Wedgwood he said, "I don't understand it Arnold – but *you* are the artist!" The bulls sold for about £10 each but now, I believe, are worth about £400. The model was also designed so that plate patterns could be used to decorate it, but this idea was never taken up by Wedgwood. 'Taurus' the bull was an enormous success and sold for well over thirty years: it also gave Wedgwood a great deal of publicity in all the magazines of the time. Later, on being awarded an OBE I received a complimentary note from Sir Hugh Casson (who was a visiting tutor at the RCA). Brief and very much to the point, he simply sketched a caricature of the bull and wrote beneath: '**O. B.**ravo **E.**xcellent. H.C.'

There is a model of 'Taurus' in the V&A Museum. Interestingly, in 1959, when the Labour Chancellor Hugh Gaitskell and his wife visited Moscow, Mrs Gaitskell selected one in gold and porphyry to present to Mrs Kruschev, the Russian leader's wife, and I noticed it on Kruschev's mantelpiece during a television programme.

I had given the little pig, carved from London plane, to Tom Wedgwood as a small gift, and it was probably about this time that he remarked to me, 'Your pig's quite all right – the children draw on it'. I wonder if they were decorating their own Taurus? The wooden pig was eventually to be passed on to Tom's wife, Sally Wedgwood.

I had managed to have photographs taken of some of my private work, including a chess set and these I sent to anyone who might be interested in commissioning work from me or who might advertise my sculpture. One such person was an old prison colleague, Arthur Vickery, who was an osteopath in Palmers Green. I also told him that I was concerned about my mother's deteriorating health, for she had had one or two slight strokes. In July 1944 I had a letter in reply:

> Your letter was most welcome, the knowledge of your present circumstances not so pleasing . I had no idea that your mother was either of that age or in that medical condition which makes the possibility of death a probable one; please do accept my most sincere sympathies. You would be wise either to move or get some woman to undertake chores for you, no artist can expect to create and domesticate at the same time. D.H. Lawrence was reputed to be a first rate cook and house decorator but his wife seems always to have been at hand. There is no doubt that the artist needs first and foremost time in which to reflect, an incompatible state with the minor irritations of running even the simplest of rooms. *(As it turned out, decisions were taken out of my hands with the death of my mother from a massive stroke shortly after this.).*
>
> ...This district has not so suffered to any extent with the flying bombs but South London is almost like a battlefield, the blast from them being terrific. I have seen them pass over whilst in Town. The past few days have seen some diminishment in their activity but you can never tell

> when there will be a fresh exacerbation. My work so occupies my life that there is no time left for worry and anxiety over these raids, for which I am thankful: neither has it made any appreciable difference to my practice. But life will be happier without them. I should discount many of the rumours you hear but should anyone suggest there is nothing in them, they lie. Such a method of warfare seems to be the inevitable development of man's madness and only the cessation of war can remove it. Some think that there are unfair wars but cannot see that all warfare is an abomination… I am returning your photos by registered post, for safety. Many thanks for their loan… I can assure you I enjoyed them and it is now one of my secret ambitions to have a piece of your terracottawork or modelling in my waiting room. Indeed I have always hankered after such work in the home… The chessmen and the animals please me, the bears in particular. … the two nudes mean little to me, I have never cared for naturalistic work and until one sees them you cannot judge the technical skill in them – but this is no criteria of their excellence, just a personal reflection… The modelled heads I should very much like to see first hand, it is so difficult to get their full power from photos … I think your finest work is the religious models … The model with the folded hands before her I admire and the group with Virgin and Angels; in the latter there is such a fine disposition of the lap and feet of the Virgin, I always like a firm base to which the eye may travel at any time. Perhaps I shall have the privilege of seeing them sometime.

In my reply to this letter I commented:

> I agree with you in your dislike of naturalistic art when you use the term to describe a mere copy of surface forms without reference to the animated, abstract something which I suppose is the life or spirit of a being or thing. In a sense Epstein's portraits are naturalistic, so is the work of Donatello, M. Angelo & Durer since they express themselves with natural forms. The immortal quality of their work however, is the result of a profound understanding of the hidden forms or abstractions of life, though they must use a language which is understandable in order to convey their ideas to others. The indefinable must be expressed in a concrete form. To quote from the Bible, 'the word must be made flesh', which I think is an extremely lucid phrase and describes what I mean admirably. Angelo, Durer and Donatello move most painstakingly in their study of natural forms & I think it is possibly due to their thorough and complete knowledge of the purely physical forms (both surface & deep seated muscles, also bone structure & vein system were studied minutely) that they were able to use the natural forms rather than being used *by* them. We only become slaves by ignorance and lack of wisdom – only the truly great are free, and it is this freedom which expresses itself and imparts a sense of pleasure and exhilaration to the observer of a great work of art. It triumphs over all the conventions of its time, and national prejudices & taste, speaking in a universal language for all people for all time. By this I mean that it is the concentrated effort of generations

> accumulated in the mind of a great artist and then directed to a comparatively small spot in the shape of a painting or carving. Sickert very aptly said 'a work must not be only one man deep but a thousand or a thousand thousands deep.' ... when someone commented on a portrait that Michelangelo was modelling, saying that it was not like the sitter, his reply was, 'no one will care whether it looks like him or not in a thousand years but they will care whether it is a good piece of work or not.' Similarly Rodin, when asked how he began a piece of sculpture – expecting him to go into a lengthy description of how he took careful measurements from a sketch model – said, 'Oh just get a piece of stone and knock off the lumps you don't want', but one could go on endlessly with such quotations. What most people have not yet learned is that each individual perceives things differently, that we are extremely alone and separate, not knowing our most intimate friends or even ourselves; even the words we use have subtle different meanings for each individual. All that we can hope to do in a work of art is to keep an open mind free from preconceived ideas and in this state of humility and receptiveness we may touch the greatness of the utterance without understanding the words. In this way I find it possible to get terrific joy and mental uplift from the obscure writings of Blake which, if you asked me to explain any particular phrase, I would not have the slightest idea how to put it into words and yet I feel that in some measure I understand Blake.

In 1944 the Tate Gallery bought two of my terracottas: St.John the Baptist and The Annunciation. This was extremely pleasing to me as well as being a good advertisement for my work. I had the following letter from Michael Tippett:

> Terribly pleased to get your letter & all its news. I did not see the Times – wish I had. May try to get a copy & then will send you. Also I'd like to send it to Curator of Leicester Museum – Trevor Thomas whom I know, just in case something came of it. I'd be wonderfully pleased to have you model my humble self – no one has done anything of the sort – & it would be for me a happy association. If you could make a trip to town to coincide with the enclosed I could find you the means to entry – i.e. a ticket or more than one. You might come down the evening after the concert perhaps? As for the modelling, it's for you to decide if it can be done down here or if I should come North, wh I wld & cld do by arrangement for a day or this week after Mar 19th. If you could suggest which is the better. If you come down unexpectedly & don't get an answer here, ring Schott & Co or the London Philharmonic Orchestra or Morley College – all in phone book. You see, I am probably in London at the time & these are the haunts.

I managed to persuade Tippett to come and give a talk to the Quakers, in their Meeting House in Stoke, which they found fascinating. Afterwards he returned the compliment and asked me to give the next talk! I must admit that I was concerned about speaking to them as I had never done anything like this before, but I prepared a talk on the poet and mystic William Blake, which began as follows:

> I have decided to begin the discussion this afternoon by a talk on William Blake the Mystic Poet and Painter who lived in the latter part of the 18th century. This remarkable genius was almost completely ignored in his own time – his great talents only recognised by a few kindred spirits – and even some of these enlightened admirers were inclined to share the opinion of the prosaic multitude and look upon him rather as an inspired madman. His contemporary Wordsworth said of his 'Songs of Innocence and Experience' which he openly admired, "Undoubtedly the work of an insane genius"; later qualifying this remark by adding, "The madness of this man interests me more than the sanity of Byron or Scott", which is no mean tribute from a man like Wordsworth who rarely eulogized brother poets. Flaxman, the eminent sculptor and subsequently Blake's best friend, said of his designs, "The time will come when they will be as much sought-after and treasured as those of Michelangelo are now, and his poems are as grand as his pictures", which I think you will agree was a remarkable prophecy.
>
> When I consider the indisputable supremacy of Michelangelo's Art compared with the unknown work of Blake which as yet had not withstood the test of time – and this imparts to all things their true relative values – I always admire Flaxman for this recognition of the truth of Blake; even more so when one realises that Flaxman's was not an original mind: accomplished, technically beyond reproach, yet uninspired and lacking in originality, imitating the Art of the Greeks and stealing his designs from Blake. Blake remarks on this in a couplet to Nancy Flaxman:
>
> How can I help thy husband's copying me?
> Should that make any difference twixt me and thee?
>
> However, time has now established the wisdom of Flaxman's remarks on Blake and his work is gradually gaining the recognition which it deserves; all books on his painting and poetry are eagerly sought and quickly disappear from the book shops.
>
> In an age of Academies and Associations, an age steeped in Newton and Bacon and Locke, there is really little to wonder at, I suppose, in the neglect of a solitary self-taught, semi-taught artist and dreamer such as Blake, with his unsophisticated, archaic, yet deeply spiritual manner. Even Gilchrist, his sympathetic biographer, did not fully understand him and likens him to Cimabue – of whom Ruskin said, "He delivered the burning message of prophecy by the stammering lips of infancy". He was most certainly delivering a burning message, but 'stammering lips of infancy' is a most unfortunate lack of understanding of Blake… I quote Blake's own words from a description of his vision of the last judgment:
>
> General knowledge is remote knowledge: it is in particulars that wisdom consists, and happiness too. Both in art and in life general

> masses are as much art as a pasteboard man is human. Every man has eyes, nose and mouth; this every idiot knows; but he who enters into and discriminates most minutely the manners and intentions, the characters in all their branches, is alone the sensible or wise man; and on this discrimination all Art is founded. As poetry admits not a letter that is insignificant, so painting admits not a grain of sand or a blade of grass insignificant – much less an insignificant blur or mark.

The clue to Blake's wisdom is, in his own words: 'I rest not from my great task: to open the eternal worlds: to open the immortal eyes of man inwards into the worlds of thought, into eternity ever expanding in the bosom of God'. The cornerstone of his philosophy is this, "All things exist in the human imagination" and to know Blake and understand him, amidst what at times appear to be a mass of contradictions, incoherencies and wild assertions, we must ever bear this in mind – that for him the conceptions of the mind are the realities, the human imagination an eternal world. That is the gateway to the storehouse of Blake's wisdom and we must return to this entrance for an understanding of his writings and paintings. As he says:

> See through the eye, not with it. I assert for myself that I do not behold the outward creation and that to me it is hindrance and not action. What! it will be questioned: when the sun rises do you not see a round disc of fire, somewhat like a guinea? No, no, I see an innumerable company of the heavenly host crying: Holy, Holy, Holy is the Lord God Almighty! Question not my corporeal eye any more than I question a window concerning the sight I see through it and not with it…

Another cardinal point of Blake's philosophy is that evil is not positive but only a lack of goodness. Of the angels he says that they are not holier than men or devils; they are angels because they do not expect holiness from one another, but only from God.

For some reason the relief portrait which I had hoped to do of Michael Tippett never materialised. He had an increasingly onerous schedule and I myself was kept ever busier with work at Wedgwood's and a growing number of commissions, so that it became impossible to find a date when our free time coincided. Arthur Vickery and I continued to correspond and towards the end of the war, I wrote:

> More and more I cling to the illuminating visions of Blake; he becomes more distinct as the world around grows more obscure and confused and I thank God for this 'fountain of life' where I can renew the hope and energy which is constantly being squeezed out of me by the 'mind-forged manacles'. I am much encouraged by Blake's words ' I know of no other Christianity and of no other Gospel than the liberty of both body and mind to exercise the Divine Art of imagination.' You must be tired of my Blake quotations but for me he symbolises 'The Ark of hope and life

sailing on the flood of materialism and despair'. I have done very little work during the past three months and though outwardly I appear bright, a great emptiness grows within. I can't quite put my finger on the spot that hurts – for one thing, when some of my works were exhibited in Hanley some time ago, an old councillor prevailed upon the gathering at the opening, 'not to pass lightly over the exhibits if they appeared strange at first'. I was rather cheered by this as I imagined my work to have somewhat of a sensual appeal – I thought perhaps my work had more depth since the beauty could not be comprehended at once – can you imagine my distress when several 'charming' women told me 'how lovely they are'. And then I am most inconveniently fixed with regard to my studio which is seven miles away and a not very good bus service. I found myself running to get the bus every morning with a little attaché case like the rest of the natives, and returning home with them with the usual 'Good morning, it's a nice day' or 'a beast of a day' as the case may be... when quite suddenly one day I was visited by a most fearful vision: I saw myself growing like these automatons – getting the same bus each morning for 40 years or so, coming home to devour the evening paper, listening to all the rubbish on the wireless, showing my interest in cultural pursuits, digging a bit in the garden, and trimming the hedges into fantastic and unnatural shapes to show my artistry and love of nature, rejoicing in wresting a few miserable cabbages from the unyielding earth, and eventually creeping into the grave to the echo of the usual remarks, expressed on such occasions by the local survivors secretly rejoicing in another soul swelling the vast ranks of 'human nonentities'.

When I was quite young I remember reading in the paper about a man who became so distressed because he missed the 8.30 once in 25 yrs that he took his own life, and the coroner expressed his regrets that there were not more such conscientious men in the world. It created a great impression on my mind – it seemed terrible even then, and more so now, that a human being should make a virtue out of a machine-like existence; and looking back now his self-destruction was, it seems, inevitable. It symbolizes the fate of those who voluntarily permit, or permit by compulsion, the mechanization of human life. The revolt against this type of existence became so strong in me that I was compelled to break the sequence of these events; for two months I have not been to the studio – I stayed up late and sometimes all night, reading and drawing. I had to do something like this to convince myself that I was free from this centripetal force driving with such voracity to the centre of vacuity. I made an attempt to do something last week but have not yet reached that absolute state of quietness within, which I seem to need. However, I am in a much happier frame of mind and wait patiently for some worthwhile thought to take shape. I have just had a rather tiresome time with a burst in the bathroom: water poured through the ceiling and flooded below and I have been several days without water. No, I have not written any articles for 'The Studio', but it may have been written by someone else on my work, though I have not seen it myself. 'The Studio' had an

> illustration of the 'St.John' which The Tate purchased. The art critic of 'The Times' said of this work and 'The Annunciation' that they were 'remarkable for their subdued tenderness' etc. I was most grateful for the adjective 'subdued' – it would have appeared commonplace otherwise.

The war in Europe ended on 7th May 1945 and on the 17th Arthur wrote to me:

> I have paid a visit to the Mansion of Mediocrity last Saturday. The Summer Show is worse this year than ever before; more and more do I feel that the Royal Academy exists to grind all art in England down to a common level and murder all creative genius – what Blake would label the Antichrist. Never before have I seen such an array of lifeless and uninspired pictures. The watercolours (my main interest in pictures) were terrible and more amazing too most of them sold!! Last Saturday I saw the worst watercolour that I have ever seen and this hanging on the Academy walls. I am wondering on what principles the Selection Committee choose a work for exhibition – none, I fear. The sculpture, on the whole, was an improvement on the oils and watercolours but still deadly dull. An artist friend and myself both, without consulting the catalogue, singled out ' Beatrice' as one of the few original and worthwhile pieces in the room: I was delighted to find your name as its first cause and sold as well. My first impression was of some influence from Indian Art but this probably arises from the essential decorative style in which the work appears to have been cast: there was a vitality, life and unity which I think comes from a most happy fusion of form and vision. The bust of Wedgwood did not move me so much as the statuette yet far more than the work of Woodford, the new RA. If you will forgive me may I add that Epstein in his modelling is the style I look for: I feel that you have yet much to express in this direction. I quite agree that your work is out of place at the Academy, being superior in every way. Why not a one man show soon? Much more satisfactory both for the artist and those who appreciate art. Would you very much mind my knowing the price of the statuette? Having been sold, the price was no longer available to the public...

After Gordon Forsyth retired as Superintendent of Art Instruction for Stoke-on-Trent his successor was Robert Baker who had also trained at the RCA, as a painter, but at the time when William Rothenstein was principal. (John Rothenstein was his son and director of the Tate Gallery and it was he who had recently bought my terracottas for the gallery). Like myself, Baker had deep admiration for the artists of the Renaissance period, believing that historical tradition and a firm foundation in drawing were essential for good craftsmanship of every kind. After leaving college he painted murals for various buildings before becoming a master at Wimbledon School of Art. During the war he worked for the Rural Industries Bureau and in 1945 took on Gordon Forsyth's job. At about this time I had thoughts of becoming a teacher of art myself and I taught a little part-time at Burslem School of Art, getting to know Baker very well.

Lord Wedgwood had died in 1943 and his 'African' house at Moddershall was on the market, so the Bakers decided to buy it as it was conveniently situated for reaching Stoke. Eve Baker was herself a talented artist, having also trained at the RCA. She was extremely interested in the restoration of mediaeval wall-paintings and became the leading authority in this field, working in many churches all over England. She had the job of conserving the church paintings that Professor Tristram had misguidedly 'restored'. He had covered these lime-based frescoes with wax, apparently to protect them from the damp atmosphere, but it had the reverse effect, held the damp within the plaster and ultimately darkened the frescoes. Eve conserved mediaeval wall paintings all her life and when she died the church authorities, in recognition of her work, held a memorial service in Westminster Abbey.

I was finding it increasingly difficult to cope with life alone in my mother's house, particularly since the burst pipe in the bathroom. I really needed somewhere where I could live and work in peace without the problems of maintenance. The Bakers very kindly invited me to share their house if I wished, as it had a number of spare rooms. They were expecting their second child, Rosalind, and as the little girl grew older she used to call me 'Arwa', and we became friends for life. She was very talented and eventually was to work as a conservator at the British Museum.

The house was a long, single storey, wooden structure built at the top of a small hill overlooking Moddershall pool and surrounded by thick woodland. Water was supplied by a ram-pump situated in a deep brick chamber at the bottom of the hill and beside a stream. The stream, falling by gravity into the chamber, provided the power to lift the valve in the pump and begin to raise the water; I believe it would lift thirty feet. I do not know when this marvellous pump was first invented, but it was used extensively during Victorian times; it is the nearest thing to perpetual motion.

I was still using the studio at 'The Lea' for my own sculptures, which Wedgwood continued to fire for me. I remember Tom telling me on one occasion that whilst they were living at Greatwood House there was a very severe winter when he skied over the hedge-tops to get to Barlaston. There was an old stone quarry near this house and here, as an officer in the Home Guard, he had taken his men for rifle practice. Unfortunately Tom Wedgwood later had a major disagreement with his co-directors at the factory and decided to take his family to South Africa; consequently 'The Lea' was let, but I was allowed to retain the use of the annexe as my studio. I was astounded to discover that the new tenant was Hulsie, the girl whose beauty had impressed me so much when I was a young lad. She was now married with a family and I saw them all quite often. She was still extraordinarily beautiful but I do not think she ever knew of my interest in her physical charms! How strangely events and lives interweave.

Gordon Forsyth had at one time introduced me to John Adams who was Managing Director of Poole Pottery. The Wedgwood archives have correspondence between John, Josiah and myself from this period, including the following letter which John sent to me after purchasing one of my figures:

> I got home safely with Penelope and feel I must write and tell you how well she looks in her new home. Pots of any kind always look so very much better away from the factory. One must isolate them to get their full value, and this piece of your work looks very fine indeed in this setting. Good luck to your plans. I feel sure that presently you will find the mood of the material that suits you best and then your work will leap forward. Personally I'm content with this fine white glaze which allows the form to tell its own story, as it does in the fine Rosenthal and Copenhagen specimens. My own feeling, for what it is worth, is that pattern superimposed cheapens it; the way out is probably research to give quiet colour and surface qualities that do not disturb, but only explain and intensify the form. This is too big a subject to discuss in a brief note. With best wishes…

Two people from my student days at the RCA with whom I corresponded were Rene Hetherington and Shirin Jal Virgee. During the war Rene had met and married a colonel in the British Army, named Siegfried, who was of German extraction. After the war Rene taught in Carlisle and rented a border-tower which she turned into a lovely home. I was invited to stay with them and was full of admiration for the beautiful garden which she had created, and also the old Rolls Royce which she had bought for herself.

Her husband had a brilliant brain when he talked normally, but during the night he had a habit of tramping through the nearby woods shouting loudly, which he did one night when I was staying. I wonder, in retrospect, whether he had worked for British Intelligence and his wartime experiences had affected him mentally. He certainly knew, long before it became public knowledge, that Anthony Blunt had been a spy for the Russians. Blunt, incidentally, was an Art historian who became Keeper of The Queen's Pictures and was knighted.

Shirin and I kept in touch for many years after her return to India and sometimes she would telephone me. It was a financial disaster when I once 'phoned her, because she talked for hours! She had a sister who was nursing and a cousin who was a doctor, both in Bristol. Sadly, when Shirin was aged about fifty, she developed cancer and came over to Bristol to be treated. Her sister contacted me to say that she had not long to live so I went down to visit her and it was quite obvious that she was in a very bad way. I sat with her all afternoon, holding her emaciated hand and chatting, and her sister was amazed to find her so animated. We had a happy day together but, as I turned at the door to say a final goodbye, she said: 'Arnold, will you pray for me?' I had promised to visit Shirin again but she died two days later.

I had travelled through Coventry soon after the horrific bombing by the Germans which destroyed so much of the city, including the cathedral, and the sight was one of devastation. Now the rebuilding was being considered and Gilbert Scott had produced designs for a new cathedral. I was asked if I would undertake the supervision of a team of craftsmen and carvers to carry out all the decorative work and figure-carving. The prospect was exciting and I had numerous interviews with the Bishop, the Dean, the City Architect and Lord Burstead. It was more-or-less settled when, out of the blue, the Dean asked me to see him and told me that the entire plan had been scrapped. It seems that modern architects who dominated the scene at the that time had become involved, deciding that they wanted a modern building and eventually they commissioned Basil Spence to carry out the work.

It was a disappointment to me, especially as I have no love for modern architecture, but only time can tell the opinion of future generations. I predict that the splendid cathedral by Gilbert Scott at Liverpool will be seen to be the last of fine cathedral building in this country.

I still saw and corresponded with Richard Garbe and in 1946 it was he who suggested that I enter a terracotta figure for possible inclusion in the Royal Academy Summer Exhibition and that I send a few samples to Frank Dobson RA for his opinion. Dobson's comment was: "They're all right but can he do anything bigger?" I immediately set to work in my studio at 'The Lea' to produce a terracotta in the classical Italian style, much larger than I had ever attempted before. It was to be a seated nude, about 5 feet high, with attendant cherubs and entitled 'Spring'. Every terracotta figure is an individual piece and no copies can be taken from it since there is no mould as there is with bronze. It doesn't take too long to start a head, but thinking about it and re-forming it takes time. Only in a terracotta head can you get the full effect of a mass of hair on a woman; in any other medium the weight of the material would make the piece top-heavy. The major difficulty is that the figures are hollow and have to be built up from the base, with the sculptor's fingers working inside and outside the clay simultaneously. There are no iron supports or leaden skeletons, although larger figures, like the one I was now making, are strengthened inside with clay 'ribs' – made as you go along.

I worked painstakingly on the figure for some months and eventually, when it was ready for firing, I arranged for it to be collected in a lorry and taken to Wedgwood. I was full of concern that the men might drop it, but they got it safely in position and set off. It was not very far to the factory and after a suitable interval I telephoned to make sure all was well – but it had not arrived. I rang again at intervals and at long last the answer was in the affirmative. It seemed that the men had driven all round the Potteries to collect other items before reaching Wedgwood. I thought it a pretty risky journey for my precious creation!

The most hazardous stage in making a clay model however, is in the firing process and if I had known what was to transpire next I would have gone in person to oversee the work. 'Spring' was to be fired in a bottle-necked oven together with saggars and because these can stand rougher usage the men in charge are less careful than those firing fine china. The item is placed in the kiln and a panel, or baffle, put in place to prevent air from entering: this is known as 'the bags'. The opening is then bricked up and firing commences. Their usual practice on the completion of firing is to knock down the door and remove the bags straight away whilst the interior of the oven is red-hot. This does not damage the tough saggars but for this large figure in a different material it was disastrous. This stage should have been done by degrees to allow the clay to cool slowly. In the event, the model had fired very well but the cold air rushed in and shattered it. They 'phoned me to tell me the disturbing news and to say that they had left it in the kiln.

I was distressed, to say the least, and hurried over to see what could be done. I still recall the horror I felt when I first saw the extent of the damage before the model was removed from the oven. Pieces had shaled off down the legs and body but the head had been completely blown off and was missing. I searched frantically amongst the rubble where I found it intact and miraculously undamaged, although the neck was in small bits which were quite useless.

The manager felt a little bit guilty and helped me to gather up the pieces, but I was heartbroken and really thought it was the finish of my project.

However, when I was a little calmer and able to think objectively, I realised that with care it *could* be repaired. It was moved into a workshop at Etruria where I spent time thinking out a plan of action and then set to work to see what could be done. The main problem was that there was no link between the head and body and it was difficult to gauge the correct distance between the shoulders and the chin without reference to the neck. I began by fixing an iron bar firstly into the head and then into the body with cement, taking a chance that the angle would be correct. I then constructed the neck round it. Pieces of clay can easily warp, but I had managed to find some fairly big pieces still intact and modelled them in again using cement and plaster. The rest of the restoration, although long and tedious, did not give me many problems as it was like fitting together a three-dimensional jigsaw puzzle.

If the head itself had been broken there would have been no chance of repairing the model, but I worked incessantly filling all the cracks and missing bits with cement and plaster and adjusting the colour to match the original until, eventually, it was almost impossible to see where it had been

Preliminary Drawing for 'Bridal Group', 1941.
(RA Sch 2001 Ex Cat No. 64a) ©Machin Archive.
Wedgwood 'Bridal Group', 1941.
Designed by Machin to be easily produced by untrained women during the war years.
Queen's ware, 11 inches.
(RA Sch 2001 Ex Cat No. 64) ©Machin Archive.

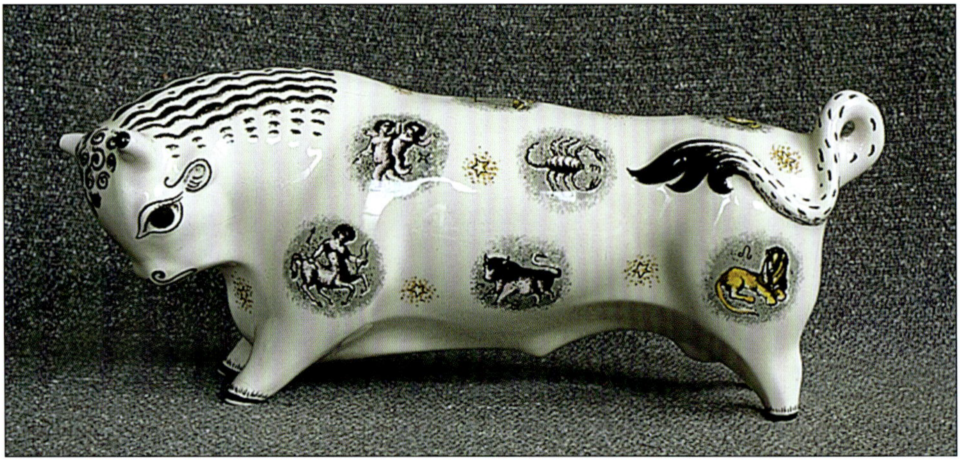

(upper) **Wedgwood figure of 'Taurus the Bull', 1945.**
Queen's ware decorated with lithograph of zodiac patterns.
"When I originally proposed the idea to Josiah Wedgwood, he said, "I don't understand it Arnold, but you are the artist!" Taurus the Bull was an enormous success and sold for well over 30 years." (Ch. 7). (RA Sch 2001 Ex Cat No. 71) photo ©Machin Archive.
(lower) **Wedgwood Chess pieces, 1940s.**
Arnold Machin, slipcast models. (RA Sch 2001 Ex Cat No. 62) photo ©Machin Archive.

Wedgwood Queen's ware figures of Pottery Workers, 1941.
Left to right -'The Thrower', 'The Placer' and 'The Paintress'.
Modelled by Arnold Machin, height of 'The Placer', 11.25 inches.
(RA Sch 2001 Ex Cat No. 66, 67, 68).
Image by Courtesy of the Wedgwood Museum Trust Limited, Barlaston, Staffordshire, England.

Wedgwood Queen's ware group , 'The Country Lovers', 1941.
Modelled by Arnold Machin, height 12 inches. (RA Sch 2001 Ex Cat No. 63).
Image by Courtesy of the Wedgwood Museum Trust Limited, Barlaston, Staffordshire, England.

Wedgwood Portrait Medallions of The Royal Family.
Blue and white jasper:
HM The Queen, 1950s; HM The Queen Mother, 1975;
HRH Princess Anne, 1973; HRH Prince Charles, late 1970s.
(RA Sch 2001 Ex Cat No. 57) photo ©Machin Archive.

Relief cameo of Patricia Machin, 1949.
Arnold Machin, terracotta. (RA Sch 2001 Ex Cat No. 42) photo ©Machin Archive.
(lower) **Wartime employee at Wedgwood holding Roosevelt and Churchill mugs.** Inscriptions at base: 'IT CAN BE DONE. IT MUST BE DONE. IT WILL BE DONE' and 'GIVE US THE TOOLS AND WE WILL FINISH THE JOB'. Relief portraits by Arnold Machin.
Image by Courtesy of the Wedgwood Museum Trust Limited, Barlaston, Staffordshire, England. (Original photo Fox Photos)

'Spring', 1947.

The statue won Arnold Machin the Royal Academy's Chantrey Bequest and was subsequently purchased by the Tate Gallery.

"I set to work in my studio at 'The Lea' to produce a terracotta in the Classical Italian style, much larger than anything I had attempted before. It was to be a seated nude, about 5 feet high, with attendant cherubs".(ch. 7).

(RA Sch 2001 Ex Cat No. 87) photo ©Machin Archive.

Arnold Machin in the studio at The Villas, Stoke on Trent, 1955,
modelling a bust of Patricia Machin with son, Francis, in doorway.
(RA Sch 2001 Ex Cat No. 175) photo ©Machin Archive.

The Fallen Angel', 1956. Arnold Machin, terracotta, height 33 inches. *"My Diploma Work, which I presented to the Royal Academy of Arts on my election, was a terracotta which I entitled The Fallen Angel and this was on display at the Summer Exhibition in 1957."* (ch. 7)
(RA Sch 2001 Ex Cat No. 75) photo ©Machin Archive.

Busts of Shirin Jal Virgee (left) and Susan Abraham (second from right) in the studio in Staffordshire. Arnold Machin, terracotta.
"Shirin was a fellow student at the RCA. At a party arranged by the students, she brought an Indian dish containing chillis which nearly killed Professor Garbe". (ch. 6)
photo ©Machin Archive.

Arnold and Pat Machin and the gas lamp protest, 1956.
Machin tried to save the gas lamp from being replaced by the council at The Villas, Stoke-on-Trent, 1956. The protest was reported in many national newspapers and letters of support were received from all over the world. These include those from the President of the Royal Academy, 'The Architectural Review', and Sir Hugh Casson and John Betjeman. (ch. 7)
(RA Sch 2001 Ex Cat No. 203) photo ©Machin Archive.

The Garden at Offley Rock, 1970, showing part of Elsie Key's cottage.
Arnold Machin, watercolour. *"A brick-built cottage down the lane was owned by Elsie Key, whose father had been a cobbler. When her parents died she locked up the house and left it for ten years. Pat went to see her. 'Would you sell it?' she asked 'I might, I might,' was the reply."* (ch. 9) ©Machin Archive

Chelsea Embankment and Albert Bridge.
Arnold Machin, watercolour. (RA Sch 2001 Ex Cat No. 192) ©Machin Archive.

Sketch book detail of a rose,
painted in the china-painting tradition, and later figure studies.
Arnold Machin, (no date), watercolour and pencil.
(RA Sch 2001 Ex Cat No. 232) ©Machin Archive.

Study from life of Her Majesty The Queen, 1963.
"I had four sittings at Buckingham Palace. I made drawings of The Queen's head, followed by modelling in Relief".
(RA Sch 2001 Ex Cat No. 128) ©Machin Archive.

Coins

(top) Final Design of The Queen's head, 1963, accepted for use on the new coinage.
(centre left) Silver Jubilee Crown, 1977, obverse.
(centre right) Silver Jubilee Crown, reverse.
(lower left) Coin effigy of The Queen's head, 1963.
(lower right) Silver Wedding Crown, reverse.

Designs for Reverses of Bahamas Coins, 1965.
Arnold Machin, pencil and white paint on green paper.
(RA Sch 2001 Ex Cat No. 154.) ©Machin Archive

damaged. Fortunately I had just enough time to finish it before 'sending-in-day' at the Royal Academy. I was by this time so determined not to let it out of my sight until it was safely delivered, that I bought a small farm trailer to tow behind my car and drove it down to London myself, not trusting anyone with the final transportation.

To my great relief 'Spring' was accepted for the Exhibition. It was given a central position in the room and was later purchased by the President and Council of the Academy under the terms of the Chantrey Bequest for £1,000 - an enormous sum of money in 1947 – eventually going to the Tate Gallery. As a result of this I was elected an Associate of the Royal Academy and was able to exhibit work there regularly at the Summer Exhibitions.

1947 was the year that paintings were submitted for the first time by an artist calling himself 'David Winter' and after they had been accepted by the selection committee, the President of the Academy, Sir Alfred Munnings, exclaimed: "Good job you passed them – they're Churchill's!" Only he had known that 'David Winter' was the pseudonym of Winston Churchill who had been a keen amateur artist for three decades. The following year Churchill was appointed 'Honorary Academician Extraordinary' – a unique honour which had been voted by the General Assembly.

On the day before the official opening of the Summer Exhibition exhibitors are invited to a special preview and it was during this that I suddenly noticed, amongst the hundreds of people attending, a young woman with glorious raven hair. On looking more closely I realised that it was Patricia Newton whom I had not seen since our days at Derby Art School. I went across to speak to her and found that she was exhibiting at the Royal Academy for the first time and had brought her sister Pam with her, who was now married. We all chatted animatedly, but Pat and I hadn't much time to compare our experiences since student days so consequently we decided to meet again. Whenever I was in London I took the opportunity to visit the art galleries which had re-opened after the war, in particular the Tate Gallery which was a favourite of mine. Coming out of the gallery at high tide, the Thames barges were above the level of the road; there was a retaining wall holding back the water and it was a most unusual sight, so we chose the steps of the Tate Gallery as a convenient place. We met as arranged, and I remember that two girls who had been with me at the RCA happened to pass by at the time, and looked astounded to see the rather quiet man they had known talking animatedly to a most attractive woman!

We had a great deal of catching up to do. Pat had been in the Army during the war, but after demobilisation she was able to get a grant to continue her art studies. Much later she reminisced:

> When I came out of the ATS, my only ambition was to join an art school and quite a lot of places were suggested including the Royal College of Art. A young Art critic named Michael Middleton proposed Goldsmith's

College, so I went along there for an interview, took a few drawings and was accepted. The first year there was very stimulating, because my eyes were opened from being a complete amateur into the business of painting with all that is involved; being thoroughly engrossed by the excitement of the vision of still-life and the thrill of getting to know the Old Masters, which has held me ever since.

At this time I submitted a painting of my dressing-table, (I had previously painted it a flamboyant yellow especially for this purpose) which was accepted by the Royal Academy for the Summer Exhibition; also a not nearly so exciting painting of fishes on a plate – which my tutor, Leonard Applebee, liked a lot. His subject is Still-life and we students have been greatly influenced by him. His teaching so excited my imagination that I was well away and for the next year or two made quite a lot of progress; also with portraits and a certain amount of landscape, but it was always Still-life that held me. It suited my particular way of thinking and I have worked very hard.

Pat was living in a very primitive attic in Earls Court while she continued her studies, but she had made it into her very own studio and loved it. She was thrilled to hear of my success with the terracotta 'Spring' but extremely disappointed for me that the Coventry job had come to nothing for, as she said, it would have been wonderful to work on such a lasting memorial. We reminisced about our time in Derby and she told me, to my surprise, that the other students had been somewhat in awe of me and knew that one day I would become an artist of distinction.

Pat had served as a Captain in the ATS, but did not regard it as a waste of time. She felt that it enabled her to free herself from the restrictions of provincial life – a small world from which she would have found it impossible to escape, such was the pattern of life for women in the thirties. Even the deplorable conditions of the Victorian barracks to which new recruits were sent, did not dismay her. Whilst most of the girls felt acute misery, Pat said that she never felt freer or happier in her life. On her top corner-bunk, in a hut of thirty noisy recruits, with her little collection of books, some paper and pencils, there was not a more contented person to be found. Even the first terrible breakfast of lukewarm cocoa, tripe and onions did not dampen her spirits! It was only later when she had to share a bedroom with two or three very incompatible ATS officers that she felt imprisoned. Pat was enjoying her course at Goldsmiths tremendously and still had another year to do. Whenever I was in town we arranged to meet. We found that we had a great deal in common and enjoyed one another's company so that by degrees our friendship developed. Periodically we corresponded, and when Pat and her sister had their first holiday after the war, I wrote to her from the studio in Barlaston:

My dear Pat,
I envy you going off to Ireland. I have only been in and near Dublin

so I know nothing of Kerry. I shall be in London from 29th March until April 6th so 1 hope I can see you on your return from Ireland. Yes, the world does seem to be in a shocking state and, if I believed only in material things, life would appear completely hopeless. A friend of mine once said that we are in for a hundred years of war, which began in 1914, and I am inclined to think he is right. Thoughts in time become realities so the less we think of war the better. I am sure that creative thought is the only answer to the terrifying problems which confront us today.

We can arrange about your visit to Barlaston when we meet in London. I hope you get lots of painting done in Ireland.

Yours ever,
Arnold.

However, in December of the following year whilst in London, I was suddenly taken ill: I could not control my muscles and my foot would shoot out for no apparent reason. Pat managed to get me on to the train for Stoke and I returned to the studio at Barlaston. As I was getting worse I visited an osteopath who advised seeing a doctor. He recommended a specialist, an awful man, who was annoyed that I had visited an osteopath, since the medical profession at that time did not approve of osteopathy. His comment was: 'Well, you've asked for it and you've got it!' He stuck pins all over my body, but I couldn't feel anything, and he sent me to a little hospital in Yarnfield, just outside Stone in Staffordshire.

This was the period when polio was uppermost in people's minds and at first it was thought that I had contracted this illness. I remember hearing an iron lung being wheeled into the room but fortunately I never had to use it. My muscles became useless and when my leg dropped out of bed the weight of it was so intense that it felt as though my legs were being torn apart. I tried to lift the sheet but it felt as heavy as a sheet of lead. The night nurse was a Roman Catholic and I couldn't always get her attention if I wanted anything as she was a very devout woman and prayed for me incessantly. Looking back I believe that I had a complete nervous collapse.

My friends were all concerned and showed extreme kindness. Josiah Wedgwood sent an enormous bunch of black grapes which were my lifeline and which I felt were helping me to improve. I was most distressed when they had all gone and begged people to bring more. I had a letter from Gilbert Ledward RA, who was a Potteries man like myself, in which he expressed:

.... my sincerest hope that your recovery will be speedy and complete; and also to let you know that these thoughts are echoed by many of your friends who were at the (*Royal Academy*) meeting. I saw your charming terracotta group at the exhibition of the Chantrey fund purchases which is now being arranged for the winter exhibition. It is rather a mixed collection but it will be interesting to see the changing fashions in art during the past century. I only hope that you will be well enough to visit it and see the work yourself before the exhibition is over.

Pat used to come and see me in hospital and when, eventually, the power came back into my limbs she took me to her parents' house in Derby to convalesce. It was a disastrous visit from the outset.

Pat's father was one of a large family; her paternal grandfather had been a schoolteacher, as also had her grandmother, who was Scottish and very ambitious for her sons. They became engineers and started an electrical engineering firm, Newton Brothers – Derby, which still exists today although there are now no Newtons associated with it.

Pat's father served with the Sherwood Foresters as a Lieutenant-Colonel in the First World War, where the deplorable carnage led him to experiment with bits of scrap metal in a hut behind the lines. From these he invented the first hand grenade which was nicknamed 'the Newton Pippin' and as a result of this he was sent to the War Office to continue with his inventions.

Her sister, Pamela, whom I remembered from art school days in Derby worked for the British Council, and Pat of course had also served her country in the Army. Now she had become friendly – too friendly in their opinion – with a man who was not only from a lower social background but had been in prison as a conscientious objector as well. It was all too much for them to accept and relations were very strained.

However, they did bring over a healer whom they knew to see if he could help in my recovery. He spent some time manipulating the back of my skull and then said, "That's got it!" He was not allowed to charge for treatment, but I gave him what I thought was appropriate payment. After this I certainly began to improve. Although I was grateful for their assistance it was not an easy time for us, and Pat was in a difficult position, being rather distressed by her parents' attitude and becoming rather distant towards me. I left as soon as I could and went back to my studio, while Pat went to Devon to stay with her sister.

Eventually we met up again in London and decided to go to a registry office and get married, with just a few friends as witnesses. It was a big decision for Pat who hated the thought of being ostracised by her parents, and she decided not to tell them until after we were married. They were horrified of course and Pat did not go to visit them for some time. Josiah Wedgwood was a staunch friend and always came to the rescue, not only of me but of anyone whom he felt he could assist. On learning that we were married he gave us £25 as a wedding present, which was a generous gift in 1949.

In 1948 Josiah, who was now chairman of the board of governors at the Royal College of Art, had recommended Robert Baker for a new post there as Professor of Ceramics. The Bakers sold the house at Moddershall to Robert's sister, Louisa, and moved down to London. His sister was a formidable woman who had been a hospital sister and was now married to a country squire who once owned two manor houses and whose family built the

Manifold Valley railway in North Staffordshire. When he died some time later Louisa continued to live there alone, intimidating any callers with a shotgun which she always carried. She used to send messages to me via a postman who sometimes came to the area where I was then living. When eventually Louisa died, Rosalind Baker told me that a niece, who had been caring for her, being unaware of the value of the antiques, sold them all to an antique dealer. The house was in a bad state of repair and has now been demolished.

Knowing how very hard-up Pat and I were, Josiah next persuaded Baker to take me on as a tutor at the Ceramic School at the RCA for three days a week. I taught pottery and figure design. This was an absolute godsend and so, for the next seven years, I worked part of the week for Wedgwood and for three days at the RCA. It is essential for an artist to have his own private place where he can work undisturbed, have his tools to hand and, like a conversation with a good friend, pick up the threads where they were left. I found a minute studio which I rented in Callow Street, Fulham. It had a small kitchen, a lavatory and a bed as well as space to work which was quite sufficient for my needs, and eventually I was able to buy it.

Before long, Pat found that she was expecting a baby so that it was imperative to find a suitable house to live in. We discovered that a house at The Villas, in Stoke, was for sale and went to see it in great anticipation, for I had always admired these lovely buildings. Number 15 was a detached house halfway up the steep hill on which the estate was built. Today they are listed buildings but they had been neglected over the years and were not very highly thought of when we decided to take up residence there. Stoke-on-Trent was not a place where people chose to live unless they had work there. Throughout the entire area smoke rose from the bottleneck kilns in black clouds and the Michelin tyre factory, quite close to the Villas, deposited grey particles in the air and produced strange smells. Buildings in the Potteries were completely shrouded in black soot so that fine churches, imposing town halls, houses and Georgian potteries were hardly noticed. We rarely had a drink in our garden as specks of soot landed in our cups or glasses, and children soon got covered in soot when they played there. Nevertheless, the views across the city were uniquely dramatic and the people were charming and very friendly. The bottleneck kilns with their clouds of black smoke have now disappeared and, as someone remarked recently: 'Stoke becomes cleaner and uglier every day!'

Number 15 and a good many of the others had been horribly treated inside. French marble chimney pieces which had been put in for the French emigrés had been replaced by 1930s style ceramic slabs with mean little grates that could not begin to warm the rooms. However, the rooms were nicely proportioned and our only problem was that we could not afford to furnish them and the house was extremely cold. I used a rather long, narrow greenhouse for a studio and Pat had a room at the top of the house, which had been added as a billiard room, for her own studio. Even in Stoke we managed to make a nice garden: the brick walls and paths and the ancient apple trees were an asset, even though they had their share of grime. The inhabitants of The Villas – twenty-one houses and some of them sub-divided – were quite a cross-section of urban society in those days. In the houses at the top of the hill lived a few of the wealthier families, one of which had a long established shop in Stoke. 'Is that a boy or a girl?' demanded the lady from that family when she saw Pat for the first time with Francis, aged two, who had curly hair. 'Then he must have his hair cut!' was the order when she was told. I do not think that she ever spoke to Pat again, probably thinking that, with our barely furnished house, we were not an asset to The Villas and rather outside our sphere. Lower down the hill lived Peggy Mitchell-Smith, daughter of the founder of Hartshill Orthopaedic Hospital and she became a close friend of ours. Opposite her lived Miss Pratt, last of the line of the famous Pratt ware. Her house was full of wonderful samples of her family pottery – all museum pieces. The house was quite unspoilt: the front door had beautiful painted glass in the style of Burne-Jones.

Pat and I made Stoke our centre but kept on my small studio for use when I was in London. Each week I drove down to the RCA in my little Morris and enjoyed the journeys. As yet there were no motorways and the roads wound through lovely countryside as they had done for centuries. There are so many ways of approaching and leaving London and I was able to stop here and there to discover the delights of many small villages hitherto unknown to me.

In London itself, when I found time, I looked for favourite haunts of my student days: some had been obliterated by the bombing, others had miraculously survived. I had always found the houses in Kensington most interesting with their basement rooms and coal-holes under the pavement, so that the coalman could remove the circular cast-iron lids and tip the coal straight through the hole. John Betjeman also found these lids intriguing with their varying designs and wrote about them, as well as the street signs made of cast-iron.

For decades London has been infamous for its thick 'pea-souper' fogs: radiation fog which tends to occur on cold, clear nights in wintertime. In a densely built-up area with coal fires belching black and sulphurous fumes, particles of matter mix with the fog to produce a highly toxic 'smog'. I vividly recall the yellowish pall which blanketed London in December 1952. It was dark for three days and the pavements were covered with thick black mud which accumulated out of the atmosphere; it was quite unbelievable. It was difficult to breathe and about four thousand people died during this period.

When working for Voluntary Service for Peace, I had wandered a lot through the East End of London and I found the Londoners fascinating. They reminded me of the Potteries people amongst whom I had grown up: poor and desolate but very much alive because of their community spirit. Inside their homes it was intriguing to see little collections of ornaments, treasured in the same way that my father had loved his precious Victorian glass domes. Adults and children made their own amusements as they had in the days of Dickens' characters, and even before that. Now that I was back in London for three days a week I was able to study these people in their gargantuan efforts to rebuild lives and homes.

However, modern thinking decided that the old terraced houses were outdated and that a fresh approach should be taken when replacing the old 'slum' dwellings; consequently tall blocks of flats began to spring up with modern amenities, and the re-housing of the Londoners began. The old 'village' atmosphere where everyone had their own patch of garden and got to know their neighbour over the fence, and where the children played together in the street had disappeared, and people found themselves isolated in towers with nowhere for their children to play and the area below devastated by vandals. I was talking to one of the tenants one day and she said, "One of the awful things is having to travel up in the lift with people you detest."

During the war, in order to stimulate an interest in the war-effort, a large photographic exhibition was arranged in London showing all the fine architecture that we were fighting to preserve. How exasperating to see that much of this heritage was being destroyed *after* the war by modern planners and architects who designed modern monstrosities far exceeding all that the German bombing achieved. Thousands of tons of handmade bricks and tiles were thrown away which would be priceless today, and Euston Arch was broken up without a second thought and pitched into the Thames. The post-war age has been a mad one with false values, and the Arts have been dominated by critics and spineless artists who propagate their theories through articles in the press, magazines and television – all with unimaginable arrogance. They profess to understand the Arts without practising them and imagine themselves to be endowed with judgements superior to those of artists. It is like advice given to an all-the-year-round swimming club by a non-swimmer. I remember John Skeaping saying that you will never see a monument to an Art critic!

I enjoyed teaching. It was good to be back at the Royal College of Art where Professor Garbe was still Master of Sculpture, and it gave me a great deal of satisfaction to be able to pass on my knowledge and skills to young people who were keen to learn. One of the students, Tina Serjeant, came to live in Staffordshire after her marriage to the son of John Adams, and became a great friend of Pat and myself. Recently, whilst reminiscing about her student days, she reminded me of my insistence that the students should be honest with their work, encouraging them to draw sensitively, with a searching understanding of what they were doing and with no fashionable gimmicks! Later, when Tina's daughter Louise began to show great aptitude for drawing, I encouraged her and watched her go on to the RCA also. Louise is now Chief Design Director for Royal Crown Derby and is the only woman on the board.

At lunchtime the Staff generally met together in the common room where a great deal of chatter went on, and also a certain amount of backbiting. Garbe, a small, retiring and normally timid fellow, was at times criticised openly about his work, but I remember one occasion when Barnett Friedman, a teacher of design, who tended to be cheeky and aggressive, riled him so much that he replied angrily, 'What about you Friedman? All you've done is design a bloody postage stamp!'

Robin Darwin, a cousin of the Wedgwoods, had succeeded Jowett as Principal of the RCA. He had come from teaching at Eton and brought in some of his students as tutors including Christopher Isherwood and Roger de Grey, who was to become President of the Royal Academy in 1984. They were all very pleasant to work with, although Darwin himself was rather abrasive and on one occasion Josiah Wedgwood admitted to me that he regretted recommending him as Principal.

Pat eventually took Francis to Derby to show to his grandparents. They could not help but love him and he helped to heal the family rift, as is so often the case in circumstances like these. As the tension eased amongst us we found that we had more in common than we had ever realised.

Pat's artistic abilities had doubtless been inherited from her mother, a most attractive woman, who played the piano beautifully and also drew very well, although sadly she had done very little after her early marriage at the age of nineteen. She had been sent to boarding school in Hampstead as a girl in order to have painting lessons from Savage Cooper, an artist her mother thought of very highly and whose works she collected.

I was shown a lovely pastel portrait of Pat and Pam, done when they were aged about five and seven, by the well-known Derby artist Townsend. They have one brother named Ancel who, after taking a degree in music at London University, stayed on at home to manage the garden and about seventy acres of woodland for his parents which he looked after most efficiently and almost single-handed. The house had been built between the wars and during the construction Henry Newton and his wife lived in a railway carriage resting on brick piers on a steep woodland slope. One of Pat's uncles, Frederick Newton, had died, but I came to know his widow Margaret who was very interested in art. The widow of the third brother, Charles Newton, was named Molly and some time after her husband's death she married Vincent Jobson, inventor of the Qualcast lawnmower. I remember that I did a portrait of him when he retired. Vincent became extremely wealthy, producing very elaborate castings but making much of his money from the manufacture of nails. He had a principle that you could make far more money producing millions of small items than a few large and more expensive ones. He was extremely proud of his wealth and always boasted that, paying 98% Income Tax, it cost him £1 to offer a cigarette and the same amount to buy a 2p stamp. They lived in a large house and also had a yacht on the Mediterranean. Molly herself was quite a character. She owned a mynah bird with a most irritating shout which lived in the kitchen and picked up phrases from the servants rather than the drawing room including, when the bell rang for upstairs attention, its raucous rendition of: "What's she want now? What's she want now?" She also had a dachshund which had damaged back legs resting on a trolley. It used to speed around the house with its forelegs, travelling at breakneck pace across the polished floors.

Pat's cousin Fenella, daughter of Margaret and Frederick, gave me some interesting information about her mother's family and their connection with William Morris. Her great-grandparents had lived at Compton Hall (which at that time was on the outskirts of Wolverhampton) and when their son, Laurence Hodson, married he brought his new wife to live there. He was a wealthy North Derbyshire brewer and became one of the best patrons of William Morris, employing Morris amongst other things to paint the ceiling of the dining room. Eventually the house was bought by the Wolverhampton Eye Hospital and used almost exclusively by the Matron, but it is now a hospice. Fortunately the Morris ceiling is still there to be admired and hopefully always will be, as the house is now a Grade II listed building. Morris also created the 'Compton' design of fabric and wallpaper, named after the house. Fenella inherited a child's high chair showing her mother's initials, which she understands was made in the Morris workshops. All the family had their own chairs, except the youngest, Martin, who had his mother's chair as they had the same initials. Her grandmother worked four panels for a screen designed by Morris, one for each of her first four children; Morris then made the actual screen to incorporate the panels. Fenella is proud to have a pair of curtains – too fragile to hang – with the Morris workshop label in them and a pair of original Morris wool curtains in her dining room which, in a hundred years, have never faded. As she commented: 'It must say something for vegetable dyes!'

We now regularly visited Pat's family in Derbyshire and Francis still has vivid memories of his grandfather, even though he died when Francis was about eight. He particularly remembers the intriguing workshop where Grandfather Newton still did experiments: the collection of boxes filled with bits of old bomb fuses, bullets and other souvenirs; the tobacco plants which he grew in the herbaceous borders and tobacco leaves hanging to dry in his study; the air raid shelter, now used to store the apples which he grew with such enthusiasm. On a steep slope in the woods he saw the old railway carriage resting on the brick piers where his grandparents had lived while their new house was being built. Previously they had lived in an old Victorian house on the outskirts of Derby, and here they kept hens.

Grandfather, ever inventive, had a pipe laid from the hen house under a footpath so that the hens could have access to the garden on the other side. They shared a love of cars and he told Francis how he used to save petrol by freewheeling two miles down the hill and over the level crossing to the factory without starting the engine; and of the big old car which had mice living in it, eating the leather bodywork.

Francis also absorbed avidly the stories which were told of Grandfather's exploits in the Great War: inventing the Newton Pippin hand-grenade; designing a lightweight military supply vehicle with tank-like tracking which he built from readily available motor parts and which was ordered in thousands by the War Office, only to be cancelled when the armistice was signed. During the Second World War he continued to experiment with weapons, testing his invention of using mortars to fire incendiary drums of petrol by filling the drums full of water and firing them across the wood and terrorising the neighbours. There was still a huge bomb-casing in the wood which was used as a pressure vessel for a water supply system, using water from a nearby spring. Visits to Grandfather were always full of adventure, and on one occasion Francis thought he would play a trick on him. His grandfather was an avid reader of The Financial Times and was never to be disturbed, but on one occasion he found a large blob of ink on the pristine page and Francis, hidden from view, heard a terrific shuffling of paper and angry ejaculations. He was disappointed to find that Grandfather was not particularly amused, even when the joke ink slid off the page!

Grandmother he remembers as elegant, frail in old age, and for making weekly visits to an osteopath for treatment for her arthritis. She was fond of her Persian cat and used to make very delicate pencil drawings of it and in youth she was an accomplished singer and pianist. and now made an annual pilgrimage, with a lady companion, to the Aldeburgh Festival, established in 1948 by Benjamin Britten. Aunt Margaret Newton had a cottage in Wales which shocked Grandmother by its simplicity as she was used to living in greater comfort. Francis recalls being on holiday there with them and discovering a cow's skull whilst on a walk. It had been picked not-quite-clean by crows but he was determined to have it, so it was secretly wrapped in newspaper and hidden in the boot of Grandmother's car. She continued to live in the Derbyshire house after her husband died and it was here, in the old workshop, that Francis built his first car, aged about eighteen.

On the way home through Derby it was customary to call on my old friend 'Tommy', where we generally had a quick cup of tea. Francis found her, and her house, most intriguing. Each room was packed up to the ceiling with every newspaper she had ever bought and with cardboard boxes full of her collections and 'useful things'. She seemed to know where everything was and to a small boy it was a mine of treasures. She gave him a box of collectors' minerals and fossils; also the mechanism of an eighteenth century pocket watch which began his lifelong interest in watches. She lived in the kitchen at the back of the house and her dining table was a utility metal table produced in quantity during the war; these were bolted together and used to shelter underneath during bombing raids. Francis was fascinated by the fact that everything was draped in home-made lace or homespun fabrics and that Tommy wore several layers of hand-knitted leggings as she shuffled about, for by now she was about eighty.

The back garden was completely overgrown, with bird-feeders hanging from the trees. She grew tomatoes and he used to watch her wrapping the green ones in brown paper before keeping them in a cupboard to ripen. In the tiny front garden was a huge tree whose roots now grew under the house and he never forgot the enormous hump which had pushed up the Minton tiles in the hall. Tommy used to be fetched every Christmas Day to spend the day with us, and on other occasions too. On one of her visits to us she went with Francis to see the pony which he kept in a field nearby, and leaning over the fence, she began to tell it how it ought to be eating the grass. Suddenly it took a tremendous bite at her arm, causing a huge bruise. Her greatest failing was that she couldn't help instructing people – and animals – what to do!

I had another reason for visiting Derby again. In 1951 I was approached to teach modelling part-time at Derby School of Arts and Crafts and for almost four years I motored there one evening a week to take classes. A student at that time was John Fineran who recalls that, 'As a natural painter but poor modeller I must have disappointed you, for despite your best efforts I could not then work effectively in the round… I recall your soft tones, almost a purr, as you quietly discussed the work in progress and gave a few tactful words to each student.' John also remembers belonging to 'The Graphics Club' and reading copies of the 'Art Herald'. He has fond memories of Francis Hounsell, whom he describes as 'A man of great charm and integrity, the last of the 'hands on' type of tutor'.

It was John who gave enlightenment to the derivation of the name 'Via Gellia' which had intrigued me in my own student days at Derby. Apparently it was named after the Gell family of nearby Hopton Hall, who were Parliamentarians in the Civil War. John says,"Later members of the family were classical scholars who did the Grand Tour and were lovers of all things Roman – hence the 'improvement' to the ancient trackway and its 'Via' nomenclature".

Workers from Crown Derby were given the opportunity to attend the School of Art on day release. They were known as 'trade' students and I recall being asked to lecture to them on Art and the Pottery Industry, an extract from which I include here:

> For 20 years I have watched with regret the gradual widening of the gap between the industry and the schools of Art which has proved detrimental to both. In the industry they have concentrated mainly on the technical problems relying on their old designs with the occasional

introduction of some modern novelty to stimulate sales and in the schools we have seen how the students have buried their heads in the sand, wilfully shutting themselves off from all experience and knowledge that has been accumulating for thousands of years. In Architecture, when we see pseudo-Tudor or confectioners' Gothic it is easy to see the stupidity of it and it was rightly abhorred in the schools but it's wonderfully strange that a parallel approach to pottery should be applauded in the very same schools. Every school in the country from the north to the south where pottery is taught has been producing 'ye olde slipware', or crude stoneware with a glaze poured over it and hanging in festoons like treacle sauce over a steamed pudding. It was considered a very desirable thing to take clay that had been carefully prepared by the industry and coarsen it with sand or grog which, being such a coarse and gritty material, may be permissible for certain articles but is the height of perversity and stupidity to use to produce drinking vessels and bowls that are to be eaten from.

The purpose of pottery has been confused and obscured and its field of activity narrowed by all kinds of false doctrines; the faintest hint of colour – either under-glaze or on-glaze – was looked upon with horror and any refinement in the glaze or body was the last word in vulgarity, while so-called 'studio pottery' became more and more crude. As the colour became more drab and unenterprising it was called 'sensitive' and any fortunate accidental blemish was looked upon with great awe and reverence. The process of throwing and firing became a subject of profound mystery and philosophical discussion; every ill-formed pot was heralded as a work of Art.

After two or three years brooding in some Art School another student would go away complete with Diploma. A knowledge of coarse throwing and a few metallic oxides, some experience of firing a muffle kiln, a Chinese painting brush with which he had learnt to make a few curls and flourishes – this, together with an abundance of confidence, seemed to be the only requirements of a pottery. If my observations appear to be rather harsh and somewhat exaggerated believe me it is not out of malice that I make these statements but because I believe that any influence which produces such a restricted point of view is bad and will only lead to constipation of the mind. The principle on which you work is likely to be as false in proportion as it is narrow. A lecturer in this subject, if he wants to raise a laugh, has only to mention The Victorian Period; but we would do well to reconsider it, if only for its exuberance and vulgarity. Whatever we think about the Victorian age we must admit that there was a vitality often misdirected no doubt – but no matter, it did exist.

J.Walter Thompson, a large advertising agency in London, had a director named George Butler who engaged many artists to work for them, including myself. This was very useful because there was little work at this time for people doing my type of sculpture and commercial work was quite highly paid. I remember that I was asked to do sculpture portraits in terracotta of famous fashion models and film stars for soap advertisements. My brother-in-law, Ancel, had one of these terracottas of the model Susan Abraham, and I have one of Ann Todd, the actress. George Butler was an unusual director, not slick and superior as one might have expected, but interested in the countryside, as I was. He has always kept a cottage in Bakewell in Derbyshire as well as a London flat, and over the years we have become good friends. I made a terracotta portrait of his daughter, Tania.

After we had been at The Villas for a few years I was requested by George to design an ash tray for a firm, showing its logo in bas-relief. A large quantity was needed but we could find no one to manufacture them. Therefore, making full use of our unfurnished dining room, we bought a small electric kiln and made them ourselves. My sister Hilda, who was always so good to us and generous with her time, came to help. We rewarded ourselves for all this hard work with a truly stunning Citröen Light Fifteen, one of the last to be made and the only car for which we have ever had any feeling. It was a wonderful metallic peacock blue and it amused us to see the looks of astonishment on the faces of The Villas hierarchy when they drove past number 15 and saw it parked outside.

On each side of the main drive at The Villas were stone pavements with Victorian gas-lamp standards at intervals, and in the very centre of the drive was a fine arrangement of circular stone steps, culminating in an elaborate cast-iron column on top of which was a copper gas lamp. We were extremely attached to these attractive old lamps which fitted in so well with the elegant buildings; they were part of the ambience of the estate, which one could never imagine being lit in any other way. The gas had always been paid for by the occupiers of the house but, in 1956, Stoke City Council enticed them with free lighting if they would agree to replacing the old lamps with modern concrete posts and electric lighting. Only Pat and I and Peggy Mitchell-Smith objected – but in vain.

In desperation I decided to make a public protest and on a hot day in July I chained myself to the central lamp standard. When a gang of seven workmen arrived to remove it they found me sitting at the base with Pat with a large umbrella to shield us from the sun. The city surveyor was called and as they attempted to make me move I said: "I forbid you, as a token of protest on my part, to remove this ornamental gas-lamp centrepiece! "Then a police inspector and a sergeant arrived in a car, and one or two newspaper reporters, so I announced, 'This is my protest against the destruction of all the beautiful things, which is going on in this country". A mobile crane was put in place to remove the lamp, so Pat had then to unlock the chain. This delighted many of the other residents who danced round the lamp-post because they had defeated me. However, the protest attracted enormous attention and I had many letters of support, some from abroad, including one addressed to: 'The Lamp-post Protester of England'. I wrote to the press:

> I am still receiving letters and telegrams from all parts of England and from abroad supporting this action, including those from the President of the Royal Academy, Sir Hugh Casson, Mr. John Betjeman, the Architectural Review and a representative of the National Trust. In view of this I feel that this quotation of William Blake's is particularly appropriate: 'A fool's balance is no criterion because, though it goes down on the heaviest side, we ought to look what he puts into it.'

In a gesture of appeasement the city surveyor allowed me to keep the old lamp to erect in the garden, but I informed him that I should put on it a plaque recording the day's events as a memorial to the stupidity of this modern subtopian age.

This was the beginning of our disenchantment with the place and one reason why we began to think of moving; but this final 'victory' of the City Council was much publicised and led to others making similar protests, eventually helping to bring about a complete change of attitudes. It is difficult for people today to realise what wholesale destruction of beautiful things took place after the last war and ironic that now, half a century later, The Villas has become a conservation area in Stoke and the concrete lamps have been replaced with replica Victorian lamps, similar to the ones removed! When people worship old things it is not just sentimentality; there is a living force there which attracts and, whether they recognise this or not, each hand-crafted object produces its own vitality which penetrates and has an effect on them. I remember the awful period when the first machine-made furniture was produced; people grew wildly excited about it and my sister Hilda took out all their lovely old chairs, tables and dressers to buy this modern mass-produced rubbish. New cookers and fridges were produced in dead white, reminiscent to me of the psychologically disturbing medical cells in 'The Scrubs'.

At the end of this century young people seem to be turning away from man-made fibres, concrete buildings, clinical white plastic, and are beginning to appreciate the appeal of natural fibres and textures and the age-old joy of wood in its enormous variety, avidly searching out Victoriana for their homes in order to express their own personality.

In February 1956 I had been elected as a full member of the Royal Academy of Arts and Pat and I arranged a private celebration dinner at the Crown Hotel in Stone, Staffordshire, to which we invited Josiah Wedgwood and my old friends Edmund and Anna Hart. My Diploma Work, which I presented to the Academy on election, was a terracotta which I entitled 'The Fallen Angel' and this was on display at the Summer Exhibition in 1957.

8

The Royal Academy of Arts was founded on 10th December 1798 and 'The Instrument of Foundation' was signed by King George III on this date. It decreed that there should be: '… forty Members only, who shall be called Academicians of the Royal Academy … Painters, Sculptors, or Architects, men of fair moral characters, of high reputation in their several professions; at least five-and-twenty years of age; resident in Great Britain; and not members of any other society of artists established in London.'

Vacancies were to be filled: 'by election from amongst the exhibitors in the Royal Academy' and a new member was to deposit in the Academy, to remain there: 'a Picture, Bas-relief, or other specimen of his abilities, approved by the then sitting Council of the Academy.' Upon the presentation of this specimen the new member received his 'Letter of Admission' which was, in effect, a Diploma signed by the Sovereign and the specimens are still known as 'Diploma Works'.

The home of the Royal Academy eventually became Burlington House in Piccadilly, once the private London residence of Richard Boyle, first Earl of Burlington, and it is set in its own beautiful grounds. This unique building has wonderfully harmonious rooms with marble fireplaces and, in one room, an eighteenth century ceiling painted by Angelica Kauffmann, a founder member of the Academy. There is a 'Diploma Gallery' containing a prodigious record of the work of previous members including Turner, Gainsborough and Joshua Reynolds, who was a founding member and first President of the Academy at its institution.

Officials are The President, elected annually, and a Council of eight, half of whom retire each year so that membership may circulate amongst all Academicians. The Council is concerned with the running of the Academy and from it are elected a Treasurer and a Keeper. A Librarian has always been employed and since 1873 the post of Secretary has been held by a layman, though formerly he too was a member of the Council. A General Assembly and an Election Assembly of all Academicians are held annually; although a General Assembly can be called if thought necessary by no less than twelve members. The Royal Academy is thus a most democratic institution which has run very well for over 200 years; every aspect of life and work being organised by members.

From the very beginning 'Visitors' were appointed on a termly basis as visiting Masters to the Academy schools. They were drawn from full and associate Academicians, but this idea was discontinued in the 1930s, and teaching has since been the prerogative of the Keeper and a permanent staff of Masters and Professors. However, extra classes are also given regularly by other Academicians and visiting artists. As in the days when it was a handsome town house it retains a butler who checks the silver and the wine cellar and organises luncheons and dinners. The President as his name implies, presides, but the next in line is the Keeper who has his own rooms within the buildings. Years ago one particular Keeper was rather touchy about his models being seen, so they used his private staircase to reach his studio, reminiscent in some ways of the subterfuge attached to the art work being done secretively during my days with Minton. Originally the Keeper was able to live in this private accommodation during his tenure of office but when Charles Simms, the Keeper in residence, died in 1928 his wife refused to move out of the flat and obstinately stayed on. Because of this embarrassment, permanent use of the flat was disallowed. The Keeper is now able to stay overnight from time to time and use the studio, but not to set up house there. To me, this is tiresome because it has upset a long tradition.

The President from 1944 to 1949 had been Alfred Munnings who was a great character and one of the few who made a stand against Modern Art. He was quite fearless and in spite of considerable opposition from many of the members he managed to get his own way. During an exhibition of Picasso's work in the V&A Museum, Munnings stood on a chair and roundly condemned it. Picasso was clever but a terrible showman and I think he allowed money to influence him. The story is told of a man to whom Picasso had given a picture and who, some time later, brought it to show him. Apparently their conversation went as follows, with Picasso saying, "It's a fake." "But you gave it to me!" 'I do fakes sometimes". Munnings was very interested in horses and painted them often, particularly in natural surroundings, as with gipsies or at race meetings. He was also concerned about their ill-treatment. I remember on one occasion hearing his comments on a horse whose heart had burst, "You'd be amazed at the amount of blood," he said. Unfortunately he was thought to be too outspoken about Modern Art and was eventually obliged to resign the Presidency. Whatever his contemporaries may say about him, he was a real artist and the value of his work will continue to increase.

I remember Philip Connard, who had been Keeper of the Schools from 1945 to 1949, when he was already in his seventies. He originated from Lancashire where he had been working as a house-painter but, like myself, he attended evening classes in art and won a scholarship to the RCA. After this he went to study in Paris and then, for a time, became a designer in a carpet factory in Liege. He began to exhibit at the 'New English Art Club' in

London where Wilson Steer and Henry Tonks supported his membership in 1909. After active service in France in the First World War he was invalided out and was elected RA in 1925. He was a delightful painter of pastoral landscapes with figures, and portrait groups. One of his best paintings, presented to the RA as his diploma work, was 'Apollo and Daphne': spontaneously painted in poetic mood, it depicted the lovers with cherubs and goats in a silvery glade. When I first knew him in the forties he already looked very old and slightly whimsical, but ten years later he was still attending Academy dinners and on one occasion he collapsed, much to our concern, and looked in a very bad way. However, we heard next day that he had eaten his usual breakfast and seemed to be perfectly all right. He died at the age of 83.

In 1954 the possible President had been Charles Wheeler, but he was not universally liked, and Albert Richardson, aged 73, had been elected to keep Wheeler out. However, because of his age, this meant that he could hold office for two years only and I became an RA in his final year. He was an unusual and eccentric man who lived like an eighteenth century gentleman in an eighteenth century house near St.Albans. The house was lit by candles and he sometimes dressed in costume of the period and used a sedan chair. He was a friend of the poet, John Betjeman. Meetings during Richardson's presidency were always held by candlelight and his eccentricities were ridiculed by some of the members; but the blazing fires in winter, the wonderful paintings, the green baize and silver, with silver candelabra on the table gave a tremendous atmosphere in my opinion. In one of the rooms was a bust of the Academy's first patron, George III, and on one occasion when our young Queen had been invited to the Academy, Richardson arranged for a rose to be put in the King's hand. In a charming gesture he then took it from the King and gave it to the Queen as a link between the two monarchs. One of his sayings was 'The Academy always does the right thing.' During this period he was often severely criticized, but he had great personality and I always considered him to be someone 'in the round,' compared with his critics who were 'in low relief'.

The Academy gains some of its income from the annual exhibitions held there and the highlight of these is undoubtedly the Summer Exhibition which has become part of the 'London Season'. In other words, if one lives in London or comes up for the fashionable social events like Royal Ascot, Wimbledon and the Chelsea Flower Show, visiting this exhibition is the thing to do.

Beforehand however, a great deal of work goes on behind the scenes. Members of the Academy are allowed to exhibit six works and non-members three, but even so about one thousand artists now exhibit and many more submit works for this popular exhibition. Most of the entries are for sale, so that it is an excellent opportunity for artists to advertise, and the Academy benefits from a proportion of the sale price. Originally a 'Selection and

Hanging Committee' was chosen annually from members, but in recent years the Academy Council was appointed to oversee the organisation which is on a vast scale.

It was traditional in the early days for artists to 'touch-up' their work and often varnish it after the pictures had been hung but, as they chose their time to do this on a whim, it became a great nuisance to the organisers. Ill-feeling often erupted when pictures were hung in places not deemed suitable by the artist! So in 1809 it was decided to limit these 'Varnishing Days', as they became known, to the three days prior to the exhibition and artists were not permitted to move their pictures from the allocated position. The story is told that Turner once went in after the hanging of the pictures and saw his hanging alongside one of an interior with a brilliant red carpet. He then set to work to brighten his own ! The following day his neighbour made an overlay pattern on the red in order to subdue the tones of the carpet. Turner's must have looked excessively bright in comparison.

There are many anecdotes at the Academy about Turner, who came from a very poor family. His father was a barber and Turner did sketches of his customers. He lived in Chelsea Reach and hung around taverns looking for women and doing his extraordinary landscapes of the river. One day a woman looked over his shoulder as he was painting and said, "I don't see it like that." "Don't you wish you could?" replied Turner.

Before the exhibition opens the exhibitors are invited to a splendid strawberries-and-cream tea. This is followed by the Annual Banquet for the hundred or so Academicians (there were about seventy when I first attended) and invited guests from the City. It is a wonderful gathering in the great hall where the exhibition is held and I always found the general air of excitement very enjoyable, although I was at first rather nervous of talking to many of these people. I remember that I once sat opposite to Sir George Solti. After the meal there was always an interesting speaker – Winston Churchill in 1954.

I didn't especially enjoy London life apart from visiting museums – the Victoria and Albert Museum in particular, as it was conveniently situated – or the National Gallery exhibitions. I still had very little money to spend on myself and so didn't visit anywhere unless it was free. I can recall my first visit to the opera with friends: it was La Bohème and I found it very romantic and exciting. I enjoy opera, particularly the marvellous aria in 'Samson and Delilah' – 'Softly awakes my heart'.

I had an old wind-up gramophone in my studio and I bought records of Beethoven's violin concerto and the Beethoven Quartets which I find remarkable and full of tremendous feeling. I found that these put me in the right mood for work, though I couldn't always manage to wind up the gramophone with clay on my hands! I remember modelling once to a background of rather lively music by Mozart and when Keith Murray saw it later at Barlaston, he commented that this particular piece of sculpture seemed to evoke music. I find Elgar's cello concerto spellbinding. In this way I suppose I educated myself to appreciate music in the same way that, as a child, I was introduced to poetry, literature and the arts by avidly studying the Children's Encyclopædia.

In 1958 I was invited to put my name forward for a vacancy at the Royal Academy Schools. I was elected Master of Sculpture in 1959, taking over from Maurice Lambert who was retiring. Lambert had not been at all well and the sculpture school had suffered in consequence with only four or five students remaining. This was very sad because he was an interesting artist and a good teacher. In his younger days he built up quite a reputation with his modernistic stone carvings but latterly he had given up this work to produce rather erotic nudes for fountains in the Middle East. I remember being very impressed by these beautifully designed figures and I could not help thinking that this was where his natural talent lay and, had he continued in his younger days with figure sculpture, I feel certain that he would have achieved something quite marvellous.

In those days the salary at the Academy was negligible, but I did have a private studio with a connecting door to the one used by the students. My own studio was heated and lit free of charge so that it was quite a valuable asset. A colleague of mine at the Academy, Henry Carr, a painter who was already established at the Sydney Close studios told me that the one next door to him was available so I took it over, as he particularly wanted someone whom he knew as a neighbour. The studios were splendid converted mews and mine, on the ground floor, was huge, about 25 feet in height, with enormous double doors about 15 feet high in order to move out large works of sculpture. During the war a woman named Emily Court had lived in this studio, but she could not afford to black out the enormous skylight, so she built herself a small tent in which she somehow existed, lighting it with candles. Prior to her some Russian fellow had lived there but disappeared at the outbreak of war. He could have been a spy I suppose as there was complicated electrical wiring still installed when I took over. The studios at that time were owned by Smith's Charity Trust which owned quite a lot of property in Kensington and the trustees were retired gentlemen who interviewed me before deciding if I would be a suitable occupant. It was the policy of the Trust not to overcharge, which was fortunate for artists. I used to travel from the studio to the Academy, and vice versa, by number 14 bus which came from Wimbledon.

Emily Court had died and her niece was left in charge to wind up the estate. She sold some very good pieces of furniture to Henry Carr but there remained stacks of old paintings by her aunt which were quite unsaleable, so she left them to me and amongst them I found a small study of hands by Sir William Nicholson which she gave to me. I found the studio left in an awful mess, but as the agreement specified that I was to clear it all and redecorate, I had to set to. The trustees generously charged me a mere peppercorn rent until I had redecorated. There was a tiny kitchen boxed-off with plywood at one end where Emily Court had obviously cooked all her meals on an ancient gas stove, as there was a heavy deposit of thick brown grease covering the ceiling at this end. One of the earlier occupants had been a sculptor who had mirrored the bathroom all round and masked the water tank with a pierced grille. This formed a screen over the bath which he decorated with pierced filigree plaster showing the leering head of the Devil. One day, quite unexpectedly, his widow turned up and asked to see it.

Nearby in Brompton Road was an old saleroom, where Christies is today, which I often frequented. The owner used to sell items in bulk. I once bought some large boxes of pastels and, when I went to collect them, I found that there was included a lady's bicycle, a small bookcase and a great box full of the most interesting things, some of which must have belonged to an Army officer in India. Amongst all the old razors etc. I found a collection of several mediæval taper-holders of most beautiful workmanship. I was delighted with this unexpected treasure for I find the refinement of mediæval work quite extraordinary. I have always been interested in old-fashioned candlesticks and oil lamps and these taper-holders were an intriguing acquisition which I still have today. Once, in this Kensington saleroom, there was a colossal mahogany bookcase with glazed cupboards which would have fitted very well into my studio and would have been most useful. No one wanted to buy it and when I went next time, it was still for sale. I could have had it, but couldn't afford to have it moved and eventually it went for £2. However, I did manage to buy for about £6 a beautifully shaped marble table with elegant legs and a huge mirror which fitted behind. I have this in my present studio.

On my way home from London I sometimes stopped to browse around antique shops. In Towcester I bought a set of four church candelabra holding about twenty candles each. I couldn't afford much in the way of pictures, but I had catholic tastes and bought something because I was attracted to it; I didn't care about 'names'. Somerset Maugham was the after-dinner speaker on one occasion at the Royal Academy and I remember him saying that: An old lady once gave this advice on buying at the Academy, "Walk round the exhibition and then, if you like something and the price is right, buy it!" By using this technique she amassed quite a large collection of valuable pictures.

Although the Royal Academy is often criticized right and left, it is still a power in the art world and exercises enormous influence. Applicants to the Schools are already well-advanced when they apply for the three year course. They submit examples of their work and references from previous schools of art and are then chosen after a personal interview. There are many courses offered, including painting, engraving and architecture, with no more than fifteen studying one subject, so that the opportunity for concentrated tuition is unsurpassed; they are in fact the élite of the country. Some of them win scholarships within the Academy for travel abroad, enabling them to visit Italy, Greece, France, India and so on, generally during the summer vacation.

Because I had not been able to take up my travelling scholarship awarded by the RCA, I had never visited the British Schools of Art in Rome, but an opportunity presented itself and I was able to go to Italy, staying at the Schools for a time. There was excellent student accommodation and marvellous studios for sculpture, painting and architecture but I was depressed to find that, in spite of being surrounded by a wealth of Italian art, the students could find nothing to sustain their interest – not even the work of Bernini, the greatest seventeenth century exponent of all these art forms. I remember saying to some of them one day: "I know you might hate the sight of Bernini's sculpting, but have a look at it – you *must* be impressed by the astonishing skill and the vast amount of work he achieved." I don't think any of them took up my idea, for I heard no comments from them. I think they were more used to making shapes with welding equipment in backyards in Birmingham. It is very sad that Modern Art has closed their eyes to everything else.

Discipline in the early days of the 'Royal Schools' was extremely strict: students were to remove their hats whilst in the schools and comments were not allowed during lectures. Lots were drawn for seating positions in the modelling class and each student, who worked by candlelight, was reminded to 'put out his Candles' upon completion of his work. A model sat for two hours, not counting rest periods, and was timed by hour-glass. I found that the present day students had 'admission tickets' which were ivory disks inscribed with their name and date of entry to the schools. They were known as 'bones' by the students and most likely this idea dated from the earliest days.

Within the Royal Academy is a first-rate library where students can study, and a wonderful collection of antique casts. These casts from Greek and Roman moulds were made by a famous family of Italian casters working in London who, I believe, were named Brucciani. Because the students are mature – in their early twenties (although I recall one who was only eighteen, but this was unusual) – they are able to get on with their work on their own, thus developing an individual style, with advice and suggestions from the tutor. Sir Joshua Reynolds had said to his students, "We can teach you here but very little, you are henceforth to be your own teachers."

I stuck to traditional training methods; we did stone carving, woodcarving, and life-drawing in pencil, chalk – any medium which the students preferred. They were encouraged to visit places of interest and I suggested sculptures which they should see in London, as there is a tendency to neglect places near at hand and living in the capital was a tremendous opportunity. I managed to get quite a few commissions for them which they carried out in the schools.

A new building was being erected at Wye Agricultural College in Kent and the Principal approached me to ask if my students could carry out large terracotta panels illustrating the work being done at Wye. There were six panels to be made and I directed them in the use and design of terracotta relief work. The panels were completed and much appreciated. Some years later, after I had resigned as Master of Sculpture, an extension was being put up at Wye and the college wanted six more terracotta panels but there was no one to direct their manufacture. Peter Greenham, the Keeper of the Schools at that time, asked me if I would return to oversee the work. I agreed and the panels were successfully produced and now decorate the new building.

The tool manufacturer Stanley, (who began his career as an apprentice in a stone-carving workshop and invented mechanical tools to help him in his work), was erecting a new factory and came to see me about a suitable logo for it. I suggested that he had a piece of sculpture based on the saying of Archimedes: 'Give me a fulcrum and a lever long enough and I will move the world'. I asked Edwin Russell if he would like to make it and he was very thrilled, setting about this more than lifesize figure with gusto. It was completed and paid for by Stanley who also presented a valuable set of tools for use by the RA students. Edwin later married a fellow student, Lorne McKean, who has been most successful modelling animals, birds and figures and has had many commissions. One of these, which I found of particular interest, was a huge, eye-catching seagull to stand on a small island. All the students had the ability to make a living at sculpture if they so desired, but some went into teaching. A teacher at the Academy named Eyres, who used to assist me periodically, had a son, James, who was a student there. James wrote very well about art and eventually became the Director of the American Museum at Bath.

Another student, Rosemary Barnett, had a great affinity with animals and wished to include horses in an exercise she had been set to do. I suggested that she go down to the Royal Mews at Kensington and approach the aide-de-camp, which she did, and was given permission to make sketches with such alacrity that I wondered if it was her attractive looks that gained her admittance. Rosemary made a terracotta relief panel, approximately six feet by two feet, depicting the Life Guards riding down The Mall. It was an excellent piece of work which she displayed at the students' annual exhibition and, thinking that he might find it interesting, she decided to invite the aide-de-camp. The Guards have a military chapel at Whitehall, within which each Guards regiment has its own small chapel and altar. It had been badly damaged during the German blitz on London, leaving only the apse intact. At about this time it was being restored and the officer thought that the panel might make an interesting and appropriate reredos to erect behind the altar, but it could not be his decision alone. He was discussing the possibility with Rosemary when The Queen suddenly walked into the room and, seeing the panel, immediately said, "I like that!"

So the decision was made for him and to our delight the panel was eventually installed in the chapel.

Rosemary now has her own school of sculpture in Stoke-on-Trent as well as carrying out interesting commissions. She named her school after Elisabeth Frink, who became an RA in 1977, and I believe it is very successful. Recently she brought another of my old students to visit me. He had taken up teaching and somehow became influenced by Modern Art. He brought with him a pamphlet about Modern Art theories, showing some of his work – two stones standing upright and that sort of thing – to me it was meaningless stuff. I couldn't help but remark, 'Rubbish! Why don't you concentrate on portraits instead of playing about with this muck?' He wasn't at all pleased with my reaction.

The most astonishingly successful student was Jonathan Kenworthy. He came from the RCA where he had started aged eleven, under John Skeaping. When he first came to the Academy it was clear that he had a great interest in movement and saw animals as excellent subjects for portraying this. I advised him to go to London Zoo and he also attended the Royal Veterinary College where he dissected and studied anatomy. He was devoted to his subject and worked painstakingly throughout his time at the Academy. After leaving in 1964 he continued with his research at University College, Nairobi. Jonathan has since become acknowledged as the leading sculptor in his field both here and in America, with all the attendant success that this would naturally bring.

After I had been there three years I had about fifteen students in the Sculpture School and at the end of the diploma year we put on a huge show of their work at the Academy: figures, designs and so on, but there was very little response from anyone. I knew then that Modern Art was taking a stranglehold on our endeavours.

The Royal Academy has always supported itself, mostly by proceeds from the annual exhibitions, but also from legacies and trust funds; consequently it is a very independent establishment. One remarkable aspect of this is that tuition has always been free, with the schools being maintained by grants provided by the Academy. Not until 1977 did some of its students become fee-paying and this is often subsidised by Local Education Authorities. Students find their own accommodation, but again this may be helped by an LEA grant. Members of the Academy will sometimes introduce students whom they know. The exhibition of their work at the end of the three-year course, and displays arranged at some London galleries, provide very good opportunities for their skills to be more widely seen and appreciated.

It has always been a tradition that the Scottish Schools of Art should have their students' work assessed by outsiders – one for design, one for painting and so on. As Master of Sculpture at the Royal Academy I was appointed as Visitor to Glasgow, Edinburgh, Aberdeen and Dundee and motored up once a year to make a final assessment of the work of the sculpture students and often to open exhibitions of their work. I kept the notes of my talk on one of these occasions:

> If there is one lesson to be learned from life it is that it is no use trying to evade things. I am quite sure the desire not to be here is mutual and you will understand that this mutually shared interest, this wanting to be apart brings us together in a way that nothing else can. All my life I have wanted passionately to be associated with youth and in a desperate, not to say breathless attempt to keep abreast of the times I have acquired a bicycle. Any of you young people could have told me that the bicycle as a mode of transport has long since been relegated to the realms of antiquity. I now know to my sorrow that students use motor cars and motor cycles for that purpose. While we are on the subject of movement I will tell you an amusing episode in the life of a young student of Art from Scotland. In the twenties, students of Art were not well off and in any case Scotsmen as you know are conspicuous for their careful habits where money matters are concerned. This particular student wanted to get from Charing Cross to Fulham, so he went to the tram stop and before getting on he asked the conductor in a broad Scots accent how much to Fulham. I must admit that Fulham could have sounded like a word struggling through a mouthful of porridge, at least to a Cockney. Whether or not he found this dialect incomprehensible or whether it was just his natural economy in the use of words we shall never know, but he just said "sixpence". The Scots student looked at his money and said he could not afford it. When the tram started off he followed behind as fast as his legs could carry him. Eventually it stopped and the Scotsman came running up and in a breathless state said to the conductor "How much is it to Fulham now?" I don't know if the conductor had got a bit more used to the Scottish accent by now but he certainly was a little more explicit and said "A shilling – you are running the wrong way". The odd thing about this is, the other day I was reading the discourses of Sir Joshua Reynolds – now I don't for one moment expect you to know who Sir Joshua was. He lived a very long time ago, and you will realise how inconsequential he was when I tell you that among his many friends he could list Johnson, Garrick, Goldsmith, Burke, Romney, Gainsborough, and dozens of others besides. You can always tell what a man is by the company he keeps, and you know what a lot they were – it is quite obvious that he must have been – shall we say – if I may be permitted to coin a phrase – slightly off-beat. But reading these discourses which were delivered to the Royal Academy students I came across this piece of advice. I don't suggest for a moment of course that you take any notice of it, I just put it to you simply because that silly story reminds me of it and I thought you might be amused. He said, "The danger with moving too fast is that you might discover too late that you have been travelling in the wrong direction."
>
> I must, on a different level, tell you about something that happened fairly recently. I have a colleague who helps me in my school. He was

> educated in that earlier age when everything moved slowly and all abbreviations in speech were shunned and abhorred, and the whole tenor of his life was more formal and serious and terribly lacking in a sense of humour. Now I said to him one day, "I see that some young artist has produced a painting by collecting a lot of worms, dipping them in different coloured paints and setting them to wriggle about on the canvas." While I was willing to admit that it was rather a novel and singular idea I was a bit annoyed that creatures should be treated in that inhuman manner, and in order to bring home to him the miserable plight of the worms I suggested that it would be much more interesting if the artist had used students instead of worms. Now you and I might have said that's a damn good idea, but not a bit of it – he said, "Though I readily admit that the idea is wholly commendable on that account, I think there is one vital point you have overlooked." I said, "Oh and what is that?" to which he replied, "I doubt if the students these days would wriggle enough!"
>
> But enough of this nonsense – I came here specifically to open your exhibition and open it I must. I therefore have the greatest pleasure in declaring this exhibition open.

Some fifteen years later I was again to assess the work of Scottish students and was able to speak in favourable context to my views on Art teaching in England:

> It was of great interest to me to be asked to assess the work of the sculpture students again after a lapse of some years. The situation in the southern schools is so depressing that I wondered how far this influence had affected the schools in Scotland. I was agreeably surprised to see that some sanity in Art training still remains.
>
> Judging by the work that I saw, which on the whole was good and in some cases very good indeed, it would seem that the teaching staffs have a genuine concern for the students and the development of their individual talents.
>
> The obvious encouragement of serious study, good craftsmanship and industry is quite refreshing to see; not only the quality but also the amount of work that some of the students produced was impressive, and this in itself is no small matter in these days. All this is in marked contrast to the situation which at the moment prevails in England where it would seem that the students are used like performing seals to amuse the critics and Art masters. These encourage every absurdity and excess of which the students are capable, in undisciplined conditions.
>
> It is not without significance also, that the doodlings of the subnormal, psychopathic and the incompetent are now looked upon as works of Art.

Each college has its own interesting art collection and Edinburgh has wonderful botanical gardens with displays of sculpture in the conservatories. I also met some notable tutors during this time: Bliss, the

Director of Glasgow School of Art, was an accomplished wood engraver and, at Edinburgh College of Art, Gillies was Head of Drawing and Painting – later becoming Principal – and Schilsky was Head of Sculpture. I introduced Gillies to the Royal Academy where he became a full RA in 1971. Glasgow School of Art, where Anna Hart had been a student, had been designed by Charles Rennie Mackintosh, the very well-known architect. The entire building had been planned by him including every detail such as light fittings and seating. He had original ideas concerning the girders used in the construction of the building. In the basement, for instance, instead of hiding the girders he left them exposed with the H-shaped ends cut and bent so that each one formed a different pattern. It must have been quite expensive to do, but he obviously thought it worthwhile.

On my way back from Scotland I took varying routes in order to make the journeys more interesting, sometimes doing watercolour sketches during rest time. On one occasion I stopped at a small village where there was an open area and one or two old cottages, and whilst walking round I found one where Thomas Carlyle had been born, and which is now a museum. I had been to his London house in Cheyney Walk a year or so before this, which is a museum displaying all his books, and where they were intending to plant trees and re-create the original garden. I was pleased to be able to look round his birthplace, finding everything as it was in his day.

Mysticism, religion and churches influenced me a great deal during my life, so that the architectural climate of our post-war 'brave new world' did not appeal to me at all, especially the concrete buildings which were in vogue. The French are clever with concrete: they make 'rustic fencing' in concrete which is rather effective, and Le Corbusier designed a church completely moulded in concrete which had all the publicity he could have wished for in the architectural papers. Basil Spence went to see it and his comment afterwards to those of us at the Academy was, 'It leaks all over the place, but it's bloody marvellous!'

I recall an exhibition of architectural drawings at the Academy when John Betjeman, who sat on the Fine Arts committee with Spence, teased him by saying about a fine traditional drawing, "Look at that Basil! If that had come before us at the Fine Arts committee we would have turned it down wouldn't we?" As well as coming into contact with Spence at the Academy, we also met at the Chelsea Arts Club. I found him conceited, self-opinionated and arrogant – not a pleasant person at all.

Another abrasive colleague was R.O. Dunlop. He was a rugged and heavily-bearded fellow and painted somewhat as he looked, with heavily loaded, thick paint on canvas, though quite skilfully. Being so vigorous and avant-garde, I think he considered himself rather superior to us lesser mortals. I was once walking behind him down the galleries when he dropped his wide-brimmed hat, which I picked up and handed to him. He took it without thanks and without the slightest appearance of recognition, before sweeping away.

On one occasion James Gunn and I were lunching together during the Summer Exhibition when Dunlop joined us. Gunn did much more refined work and after a while Dunlop remarked in his outspoken way, "Well Gunn, I like you but I hate your bloody paintings!" To which Gunn, with quick wit replied: "I'm sorry to hear that Dunlop. I rather like your work, but it's just as well that one of us left his cudgel behind when we left the caves this morning". I happened to be drinking a glass of wine and almost exploded at this brilliant riposte.

James Gunn bought one of my terracottas, of Leda and the Swan, and Russell Flint bought two, of angels, one for himself and one for his doctor. Charles Wheeler had already bought one of my figures when I was still a student at the RCA. It was very unusual for Academicians to buy one another's work and this was therefore a great compliment to me.

Sometimes I used to stay at the Chelsea Arts Club and frequently had tea with Henry Lamb, who was a very good portrait painter in oils. He had painted portraits of the Packe children and he introduced me to Lady Packe who wanted a memorial to her late husband at Prestwold Hall in Leicestershire. She commissioned me to make an angel for their private chapel. It was in terracotta, about five feet tall, and then gilded. I pierced the wings with holes and let in coloured glass. I stayed at Prestwold several times and found Lady Packe a charming person. She was very pleased with the angel and hoped that, after she herself had died, I would make a tablet to commemorate her. I worked on a design for this but it never materialised as her son was not at all keen on this idea – I think he had plans to pull down the chapel, so that her wish was never granted.

Henry Lamb was getting quite old by this time and I recall one occasion when he told me that Augustus John was making sentimental journeys to visit him in order to talk about old times. Henry had a rather dry sense of humour and when I asked him if he had seen Kenneth Clarke's recently published book on 'The Nude,' he replied, "I have read it with interest, but without profit". Kenneth Clarke had also done a series of much-talked-about lectures on television entitled 'Civilisation'. Lord Methuen's succinct remarks on the programmes were, "It must be always raining – he always wears a mac," and also, "His head's too large", which was something of a 'double entendre' since Clarke had physically a rather large head. Although he was exceedingly familiar with great works of art, I believe that he was not very direct and honest in his opinions because, at the same time as making these programmes, he was also supporting the Modern Art movement. When Clarke was lecturing in Edinburgh, the sculptor, Schilsky, told me, "They say that he is the man who has the influence and ability to *condemn* Modern Art, yet he does not – but I suppose it has got to work itself out."

At one time I sat on the committee of The Constance Fund which had been established in 1944 by Sigismund Goetze in memory of his wife. His aim was to place water sculpture in public spaces – either indoor or outdoor, and throughout the years a number of interesting fountains have been erected under the auspices of the Society of British Sculptors. The sculptor William McMillan was a colleague on this committee. He was over seventy but very fit and upright and lived at Richmond where he enjoyed walks along the towpath. He told me that he always carried a heavy, knobbly stick as he thought it might be useful if he was assaulted by ruffians. Tragically, at the age of ninety, he was indeed to be attacked by a gang of vicious muggers when coming out of his bank, and died later in hospital.

These were very interesting times for me, meeting and rubbing shoulders with so many experts in their own field of art, and gaining commissions of various kinds through some of them. Lord Methuen bought my work, and when we both sat on the Hanging Committee we got to know one another better. In fact, it was the beginning of a long friendship and from time to time Pat and I were invited down to his home at Corsham Court in Wiltshire, where he had a wonderful gallery of pictures – Gainsborough, family portraits and many interesting objects. He himself painted in oils and had been taught by Sickert. I remember a reporter once asking him if he had been elected to the Royal Academy because of his title, to which he replied, "What a bloody silly question!"

Methuen's father was at one time British Ambassador to Portugal and in the picture gallery at Corsham Court was a carpet, woven in Portugal, made to copy the ceiling design. I believe that this idea was also used at Chatsworth. However, Methuen designed this pattern himself, copying the ceiling, and I remember the carpet being laid. There was always excellent port wine to drink, and another interesting Portuguese drink which was kept in a fascinating little case containing the bottle and glasses. These visits were enlightening but never overawed me, since Methuen was a person who soon put one at ease. He had been an officer during the war and one of his tasks was to inspect abbatoirs; apparently it made him feel so nauseated that he became a vegetarian and he was pleased to hear that I was also.

Lady Methuen, who had been an interior designer, was very ill at this time and sadly died soon after our first meeting. Her husband found a Polish sculptor to make a death-mask and together they designed a rather fine full-sized monument in alabaster: at her feet was a paint brush and other tools of her trade. This was erected in Corsham church and Methuen remarked to me after her death, "She's perfectly all right – I've been over to the other side." This was during one of the séances which he attended. He was an unusual man and had a wry neck. He said that this had come about through his involvement with mysticism, which had affected his nervous system in some way.

On top of the house at Corsham, along the gable end, were several 'Methuen bears' and a phoenix, taken from the family coat-of-arms, some of which were in a poor state of repair. I worked in London with an Italian sculptor on their restoration. I also helped with a little marble sleeping cherub, about 4 feet in length which Methuen thought might be a lost Michelangelo. King Charles I had brought over an enormous number of items from Italy, some of which had disappeared after his execution and Methuen was very keen to establish the validity of his cherub, but no one would support him. It was certainly in the vein of Michelangelo but had been so much altered that I think it doubtful. I worked on restoring the hands and feet which had been damaged but it seemed to me that the hair had been re-carved in the Victorian period to make it more attractive – as they thought. Even so, the original has still not been discovered.

The first house at Corsham had been demolished and replaced with a Victorian building, Corsham Court, but in the grounds is a rather splendid eighteenth century bath-house designed by James Wyatt. Water was diverted from the stream nearby to a covered water tank, but one cannot imagine that it was much used unless the weather was hot. Leading from it was a rising corridor decorated with wooden laths and cones in a very formal design, and at the end of the corridor – which led into a garden at a higher level – Methuen had a stone gazebo built, which had been lying about in the yard for a long time. The wall round the estate had been deliberately lowered at one time to give a good view of the bath-house which had spectacular roses climbing over it. Methuen was a great gardener and when in Kenya he had collected plants for Kew gardens, especially orchids, which he also grew at Corsham. Garden design has long appealed to me and these visits were of tremendous interest both to Pat and myself.

Lord Methuen was particularly interested in conservation and in preserving old buildings. He owned a number of houses nearby, one of which had a barn attached, and this he had incorporated into the house to make a studio where he installed an eighteenth century stone fireplace. When I was down there once I found that Michael Tippet was staying in one of these houses, so I went to see him. When I returned and Methuen and I were chatting about Tippett I said, "How did you get on with him Paul?" "Oh, all right," he replied, "but he held my hand a trifle too long." This was the first time I realised that Tippett was homosexual; such things were never of public interest in those days, whereas today homosexuals are much more brazen.

Pat and I were staying one weekend when there were also quite a few guests from London, including two women writers, and also Methuen's Aunt Maud who was an odd creature – a recluse who lived in one part of the house with her many cats – and we would often see her strutting across the garden. There were some interesting portraits in the dining room: one, by Gainsborough, of an ancestor wearing exquisite jewellery. When we sat down to dinner I noticed that the same jewellery adorned Aunt Maud. The two writers were chatting about their books in a rather conceited manner and one could tell that Aunt Maud was getting bored as she stooped lower and lower in her chair. Suddenly she remarked, "And have you read my book?" "No – what is it?" "Dry as Dust" replied Aunt Maud, putting them in their place and immediately drooping even lower.

On another occasion, Edward Maufe and his wife were also there. He was a successful architect and had built a Scottish church in Kensington. I found him rather overbearing in his manner. At the Academy he would drive up to banquets in a chauffeur-driven Rolls Royce, wearing a cape.

When I became Master of Sculpture, the President of the Academy was Charles Wheeler. I had always got on well with him; we were both Midlanders and he was the first person to recognise my worth as a sculptor when I was still a student at the RCA; consequently it was unfortunate that I should have a serious disagreement with him over an important event at the Academy in 1962.

There had been a considerable loss on the recent exhibition, 'Primitives to Picasso', and due in part to this the finances of the Academy were found to be in such a parlous state that, first the Council and then the General Assembly agreed that the only way out of the difficulty was to sell one of their possessions – but which? For various reasons the Leonardo da Vinci cartoon of 'The Virgin and Child with St. Anne and St. John the Baptist' was decided upon, with the proviso that it must at all costs be kept in this country. If it were to be auctioned it would most likely go abroad and it was fervently hoped that the Government would buy it for the nation. I was absolutely opposed to this sale, for I felt that any money which it realised would be frittered away. I think myself that the Secretary, Humphrey Brooke, engineered the sale and that the President was easily influenced. Lord Methuen also opposed the sale, but at the last Council meeting for final approval he changed his mind and voted in favour. He apologised to me saying, "I'm afraid you won't understand that Arnold." I felt isolated, but would not renege on my firmly-held opinion, and I asked Humphrey Brooke to record my objection in the minutes. For some reason he refused adamantly and when I insisted he leapt from his chair and shouted, "You get out!". The President sat silent and the Council said nothing. I left the room saying, "To hell with the lot of you – I shall never come back into this building!" I never attended a Council meeting after that, although I continued teaching in the Schools for a few more years. Brooke was inclined to be a volatile man: I believe that Alfred Munnings had found him a job at the Academy after a previous altercation of his with the Tate Gallery. He wrote a letter of apology to me later and finally came down to the Schools begging me to go back to the Council, but I said, "Not until you go".

The Government declined to buy the cartoon and when the country as a whole learned that it was to be sold at auction there was an outcry, with many people condemning the Academy. It was suggested in The Times that a national appeal be launched to buy the cartoon and this idea gained momentum, resulting eventually in the cartoon being sold for £800,000. Over half this amount was raised by public subscription and the remainder by the Government and the National Art Collections Fund. The 'Leonardo' had been on display in the National Gallery during this period, and there it remained. The money from the sale paid debts owed to the bank, financed repairs to the Academy building and other maintenance work and the bulk was invested. I believe that part of the money was required to enhance pensions paid to some Academicians. I was determined that some of the cash should benefit the Academy Schools and I managed to get the President and Council to support my wishes to buy a kiln so that clay models could be fired by the students in the schools. At the time, Humphrey Brooke accused me of putting it in for my own convenience! I went to a lot of trouble to find a good kiln builder in the Potteries, eventually choosing Litherland. Together we designed what I think was a very good kiln. A 4 foot truck on wheels was also designed which could be loaded and packed externally and then, like a trolley, wheeled into the kiln. Any student making a large terracotta could push the truck into the studio, use it as a modelling stand and then, without further lifting or handling could push the model into the kiln for firing without causing any damage. Uppermost on my mind when deciding on this method was the traumatic firing of 'Spring'. I think this new design had been lying dormant in my mind ever since then. In the early 1990s I heard that this kiln had been dismantled and taken to the Royal College of Art. I can only trust that it is still in use there.

I found that being an RA was a unique and quite unusual experience because members of the Academy are appointed across the whole spectrum of society, the only criterion being that they are absolute experts in their own field. We therefore met as equals, but I found that there are some people who cannot accept the concept of equality so that there was a certain amount of snobbery. I also had my eyes opened to intrigue and jockeying for position and discovered that artists are pretty ruthless over the work of others. I did not let it affect me; my work is, and always has been, the most important part of my life – with reverence for tradition and excellence in whatever era it is created.

9

Sir Hugh Casson had been Professor of Environmental Design at the Royal College of Art since the early fifties, so I knew him very well. He had been responsible for the interiors of the Royal Train and the Royal Yacht and in 1960 he was commissioned to supervise the internal decoration of S.S.Canberra, now being built in Ireland. One day he contacted me and, to my surprise, invited me to do the mosaics for the swimming pool and restaurant on the ship. I had never done a mosaic in my life and told him so, but his reaction was, 'Oh have a go!'

Before committing myself I worked on a mosaic panel in my London studio. Edward Bawden RA, who was a draughtsman and had also been approached by Sir Hugh, asked if he could come and see what I was doing and his comment was, 'It's clear that you have done some of this mosaic work before.' which rather amused me. When I finally made up my mind to accept the commission I used designs reminiscent of marbled end-papers in books, which were very effective, deciding to use ceramic mosaics for the dining room and glass mosaics in varying shades of blue for the swimming pool. Sir Hugh arranged for two experienced Italian mosaic tile producers to advise and I travelled to Italy to discuss my specifications with these experts.

The glass mosaic factory was in Venice and I spent several days there. A mosaics importer from England flew out there, and when he discovered that I was staying in second-class accommodation he moved me to The Loona Hotel where he was staying. It was an impressive place, having once been a palace, and there was a preservation order on the building. The main room, which had been turned into a dining room, had an ornate ceiling elaborately painted with allegorical figures but unfortunately the central one – a naked female – had a modern fan shaft thrust through her abdomen! I found the Italians most helpful and hospitable, and on one occasion the English importer and I were taken out to dinner at a splendid restaurant by the factory directors and their wives.

It was a delight to find that I had time enough in Venice to see some of its priceless sculpture and paintings, its wonderful architecture and bridges, before all the business arrangements were concluded. I then had to take a train to Siena and from there by bus to Montepulciano, a very isolated place up in the hills between Rome and Florence, to meet Professor Carotti – a producer of ceramic mosaics. This delightful little town was completely

Arnold Machin's preliminary sketches in 1966 for initial Stamp design.
"I did endless variations of the portrait and decorative borders since I saw my task as creating both a likeness of The Queen and an image of monarchy. In all I made fifty-two preliminaries, but eventually the design was submitted".

Final plaster Relief of The Queen's Head.
Used on over 170 billion stamps from 1967 to the present day.

Arnold Machin with the Victorian camera used to photograph the plaster cast of The Queen's head. Photograph taken in 1987 at the exhibition of his work at the National Postal Museum. *"It was essential to obtain a Master photograph which would show up the relief in detail before the technicians began to work on the flat photographic image. After many trials and many rejections, the final photograph was produced on a misty autumn morning* <u>*outside*</u> *the factory, using a mahogany Victorian camera and a photographer with a black sheet over his head! It was excellent and quite suitable…"*. (ch. 9)

fig. 1

fig. 2

fig. 3

fig. 4

fig. 5

Illustrations refer to 'The Machin head of The Queen' by Douglas Muir. See text page 163-165. photos © Royal Mail Group plc

fig. 1 Photograph of the mould made for the Royal Mint for coins
fig. 2 Photograph of Machin's first plaster cast based on the coinage head
fig. 3 April – May 1965. Essays of designs using the first coinage head
fig. 4 August 1965. Simplified version of the first head with tiara
fig. 5 September 1965. Essays of the simple tiara head

fig. 6

fig. 7

fig. 8

fig. 11

fig. 10

fig. 9

Illustrations refer to 'The Machin head of The Queen' by Douglas Muir.
See text page 163-165. photos © Royal Mail Group plc

fig. 6 October 1965. Essays of the first diadem head
fig. 7 Corsage added to an enlarged essay photograph
fig. 8 The colour chosen by The Queen for the basic inland letter rate, and the first 4d essays
fig. 9 1968 The engraved version used for high values
fig. 10 1968 Photograph of the head with laurel wreath used at reduced size for commemorative stamps
fig. 11 December 1967. Essays of the laurel wreath head

HRH The Prince of Wales. Arnold Machin, plaster original bas-relief for Wedgwood Medallion, late 1970s. *"I designed a cameo bas-relief of Prince Charles, but for this he gave me four sittings at Buckingham Palace in his office. He was very friendly and chatted away about the countryside that he loves so much, whilst I was working. As with all cameo work, Wedgwood would take the image and reduce it in size to mass produce their blue jasper plaques. It has been said that this profile of the Prince of Wales is very much liked by The Queen"*. (ch. 9)
(RA Sch 2001 Ex Cat No. 197) photo ©Machin Archive.

(Left) **'Autumn'.** Arnold Machin, one of 'The Four Seasons', modelled for Royal Worcester, 1966-1968. *"I always experimented with various types of clay and body compositions in order to use the most suitable for the mood of the sculpture, and these partioular figures, 18 inches high, were produced in porcelain and mounted on ormolu bases. They were most successful, described by Royal Worcester as 'possessing extraordinary sensitivity and grace'. They were a limited edition and they became collectors' pieces".* (ch. 9) (RA Sch 2001 Ex Cat No. 102) photo ©Machin Archive.
(Right) **Rosemarie Timmis, 1970s.** Terracotta bas-relief portrait by Arnold Machin. photo ©Machin Archive.

'Spring' , late 1960s. Arnold Machin, 3 ft statue in terracotta.
(RA Sch 2001 Ex Cat No. 223) photo ©Machin Archive.

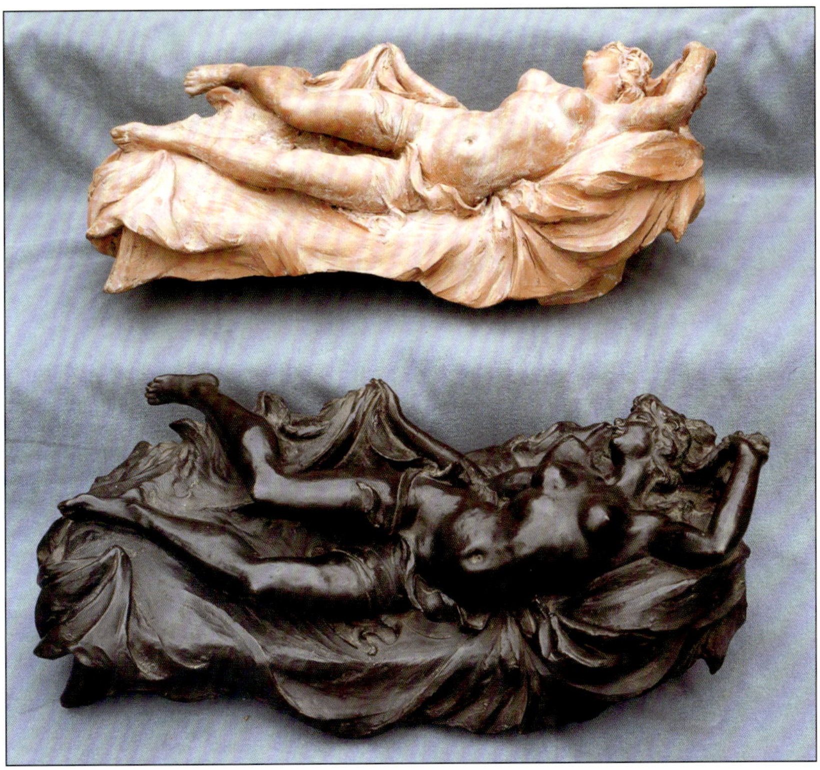

Life drawing, terracotta model and bronze casting of reclining figure, 1967.
Arnold Machin, terracotta model and bronze cast. length 23.5 inches.
(RA Sch 2001 Ex Cat No. 200, 180, 181) ©Machin Archive.

'Janice', 1965.
Arnold Machin, bronze.
(RA Sch 2001 Ex Cat No. 194)
photo ©Machin Archive.

(upper) **'Mother & Child', 1970s.**
Arnold Machin, bronze bas-relief, originally modelled for Royal Worcester.
photo ©Machin Archive.
(lower) **'Mary Magdalene', 1993.**
Arnold Machin, terracotta bas-relief.
(RA Sch 2001 Ex Cat No. 186) photo ©Machin Archive.

Design for a grotto fountain at Henbury Hall, 1986.
(RA Sch 2001 Ex Cat No. 219) ©Machin Archive.
The completed work photographed in the studio, Staffordshire, 1986.
(RA Sch 2001 Ex Cat No. 221) photo ©Machin Archive.

Drawing: 'Tristan & Isolde'.
Arnold Machin, pencil and watercolour.
Exhibited at Royal Academy Summer Exhibition, 1992.
(RA Sch 2001 Ex Cat No. 121) ©Machin Archive.

(Upper) **Drawing: Cupid and Venus.**
Arnold Machin, R.A Exhibition 1998, pencil and gouache.
(RA Sch 2001 Ex Cat No. 122) ©Machin Archive.
(Lower) **Drawing: 'One Last and Sad Farewell', from Dante's Inferno.**
Arnold Machin, R.A Exhibition 1998, pencil.
(RA Sch 2001 Ex Cat No. 120) ©Machin Archive.

(upper) **View from the garden Offley Rock, showing fountain at head of cascade.**
photo ©Machin Archive.
(lower) **'Girl in Hat',**
the figure that used to be recessed in the holly hedge at Offley Rock.
Arnold Machin, terracotta, 1940s, 27.5 inches.
(RA Sch 2001 Ex Cat No. 240) photo ©Machin Archive.

Arnold Machin ascending the stone steps of the grotto which he built in the 1990s.

unspoiled. I have not been there recently but, with the new motorway across the hills, access has been made very easy and I fear that foreign infiltration will destroy its timeless beauty.

The mosaic factory was on a site that had once been used as a retreat for previous Popes, but almost all signs of it had disappeared. Professor Carotti had built a house in the middle of what had originally been the Papal villa, with his factory situated nearby. He was a flamboyant Italian who employed quite a number of young people copying Old Masters in mosaic on to table tops. I considered them pretty awful artistically but the Professor himself seemed very efficient. On the morning after my arrival I was taken to a spot which overlooks all the surrounding landscape but to my astonishment, and even more to that of my guide, there was a very thick mist and we could see nothing. He remarked that he had never seen anything like it, being what one might expect to see in England but rarely in Italy. We remained there for some time, knowing that gradually the sun would eliminate the mist, and eventually I saw the most amazing sight: a small opening appeared in the clouds and, almost like a cinema picture, everything else was obliterated except the brilliant jewel-like effect of a small town revealed in the distance. It was an experience which I frequently recall with pleasure.

I stayed there for a few days and was conducted round the town by an employee of the Professor, a beautiful Italian girl – which added to my enjoyment of the exciting things to be seen! One of the most outstanding sights was the impressive church built in honey-coloured stone. It had a cruciform plan with a large dome in the centre and one of its unusual aspects was that the architect had used all three classical architectural styles – Doric, Ionic and Corinthian. It was quite remarkable how he had managed to blend these different styles together. Inside I was shown a very fine tiled pavement in the middle of which was a large round stone exactly under the centre of the dome. The acoustics were extraordinary and this was demonstrated by the guide who flicked one finger against another, and this could be heard for quite a while circulating the vast dome above. The town mainly consisted of a single street running very steeply from bottom to top, the street being enclosed with houses and shops all the way with, periodically on either side, an archway opening up a view across the valley to mountains in the far distance. The town had one small hotel which specialised in delicious cheeses and a very good local wine.

I recall my return journey from Montepulciano to Siena very well indeed. A small bus began to load up with people and when it seemed impossible to fit in any more passengers the conductor still packed them on board willy-nilly; but the most surprising thing to me was that he was able to squeeze himself through the packed throng to collect the fares, and that the vehicle managed to accelerate at all. In Siena I had to connect with a train to Florence, but I had time to spare and looked for a church where I knew that Carotti had done a mosaic panel over the entrance archway. Whatever one may think of orthodox decoration one could not fail to be impressed by the enormous signature of the Professor, which eclipsed all the other work on display. It reminded me somewhat of Graham Sutherland's signature at the base of the tapestry of Christ in Coventry Cathedral, which, when woven, turned out exceedingly large. Before returning home I managed a short visit to Rome where I saw the house on the Spanish Steps where Keats had once lived. I also visited the graves of Keats and of Shelley. It stirred my imagination to think of what these men had been in life and of their memorable poetry, which will live for ever.

Hugh Casson was delighted with the completed mosaics and said that they were some of the best designs on the ship. I certainly enjoyed the experience of working in this medium, although I have not done any since. The Canberra was to eventually serve with distinction in the Falklands War of 1982 and now, almost four decades after her commissioning, she is to be broken up. I have seen the beginning and end of her useful service.

When Queen Elizabeth the Second came to the throne in 1952 it was necessary to produce new coinage, and Mary Gillick designed a very attractive head depicting the Queen as a young woman. The Gillicks were both sculptors and lived in a most intriguing place in London. In the centre of Chelsea is an acre of Moravian burial ground, behind a very high wall, which was a gift by one of the English kings to Moravian refugees. Gillick was allowed to rent it and used the chapel as a studio. He had a row for some reason with the Academy – before my time – and only sent a small amount of lettering each year in order to keep his ARA status. He never became a full RA. The Government had been planning for some time to change the coinage in readiness for decimalisation in the late sixties, by which time The Queen would be forty. This seemed a good opportunity to produce a new effigy of Her Majesty and in 1963 a competition was launched to find a suitable design.

The Royal Mint had established, in 1922, an Advisory Committee of twelve people knowledgeable in the History of the Realm and in the Arts, to advise on matters connected with the designing and preparation of Seals, Coins, Medals and Decorations. It was the task of the present committee to draw up a list of suitable artists and sculptors, to examine their work and to decide on a shortlist to compete for the final design. This distinguished company included The Duke of Edinburgh (President), the Deputy Master of the Mint (Chairman), John Betjeman, Sir Robert (Robin) Darwin, Principal of The Royal College of Art, Maurice Lambert RA, and Milner Gray from the Council of Design .

Charles Wheeler, President of the Royal Academy, was one of those appointed to engage suitable artists and he chose himself, William McMillan (who was well over eighty) and myself, all of us being RAs. Sir Robin

Darwin had recommended Christopher Ironside who had been a student of his at Eton and who taught under him at the RCA. As it happened we three Academicians and Ironside were on the shortlist. Darwin from the beginning had imagined that Ironside would have no competition and fully expected that he would be chosen to design the coinage.

Stage two was to produce a plaster relief, and we were to receive photographs of The Queen taken by Lord Snowdon, from which we would work. Robin Darwin, who was always keen to get publicity for the college and for himself, was able to arrange for the competitors to meet at the RCA so that Lord Snowdon could be briefed by each of us in turn as to the type of photographs we wanted. I was the last of the competitors waiting to speak to Lord Snowdon, and when the others had finished Robin Darwin said: "I think that should meet all the photographic requirements that we need", leaving me out. "Not at all Robin", I replied, "I would like Lord Snowdon to listen to my requirements also", which of course he did. I asked him if I could have a series of photographs of The Queen taken at every angle from the front of her head to the back, with The Queen seated on a revolving chair. Lord Snowdon produced an excellent set of photographs for me and the competition then began in earnest. With our applications for entry into the competition we had to state our aims when designing the coin, and mine were as follows:

> To produce a design with charm and dignity and yet without sentimentality. To create an illusion of strong relief thereby counteracting the stringent limits of the actual projection essential in Coin production. To attempt to recapture something of the richness and vitality of the earlier Coins which has not seemed possible with the limiting techniques of modern mass production.

I heard later that John Betjeman, looking at my portrait of The Queen, liked it and thought I had 'made her look a bit sexy.'

Each competitor had to make designs in plaster of both sides of the coin, working on a disk six or seven inches in diameter. Some people can knock off this type of work very quickly, but I have always worked slowly and painstakingly and I spent a long period producing various plaster models. Eventually my portrait was chosen for the obverse side, together with Christopher Ironside's reverse. He was a distinguished-looking man with a very pleasant personality and we had become quite friendly. I remember that when the results were announced he said, "You're heads, and I'm tails!"

I now had to produce a true likeness of The Queen, and for this I had four sittings at Buckingham Palace. I made drawings of The Queen's head, followed by modelling in relief. Usually when I am doing this I work direct on to a board with clay; but such is the security at the Palace that I had everything taken from me and investigated before I was allowed to meet The

Queen. It is astonishing that many years later an intruder managed to get into her bedroom. The room where I worked overlooked the front gates of the Palace and The Mall, which was a particularly interesting view. The Queen seemed rather excited one day and told me that a man outside had a dog which had come through the gates, and when the owner came in after it he had been pinned to the ground by one of the guards with a bayonet. She had observed all this through the window!

This was the first time that I had worked on a coin design and I found it a challenging and different technique; the problem was to get the relief levels right. You can't really model true form; you have to make a depression where the ear comes, because that is normally the highest point, and then you work back from there. On one occasion the Duke of Edinburgh came to watch me at work and remarked, "It wants a bit more on the chin." The following day Her Majesty was sitting again, this time for a portrait by Peter Greenham, the Keeper of the Royal Academy Schools, and he told me later that The Queen had chatted to him about me. She said, "The Duke came in to look at my model and commented that the chin wanted to be stronger and needed more clay, which Mr.Machin did – but as soon as the Duke left he took it off again!" I found The Queen to have a great sense of humour. One day she asked my opinion of Lowry and I said, "Well, his paintings have a poetic quality, but what I can't understand is how he can reach that age and not improve on the feet of his figures." She didn't say anything, but a tiny smile came on her face. Speaking to someone in the Academy later, I discovered that she had bought a Lowry not long before. I particularly remember the day that Her Majesty had a trayful of tiaras brought in so that one might be chosen to be included in the portrait. She put them on, one after the other, asking which I liked best – that was really quite a thing to see. As it happened she liked one while I preferred another.

From these studies I built up the image, working at my London studio for a long time. I had returned home for a short respite, but the coin was always uppermost in my mind and I finally decided in the summer of 1963 that I would need one more sitting. I contacted the Mint, who telephoned The Queen's private secretary; but it was the summer break and the Royal Family were staying at Balmoral. Her secretary spoke to the Duke of Edinburgh, who immediately said, "Tell him to come up here," to which the secretary added, "When you come, bring your dinner jacket." In consternation, I realised that my dinner jacket was in London, so I borrowed one from a friend who was inclined to be rather flamboyant in his dress with artistic and unusual taste: velvet this, and velvet that, which wasn't my style at all.

I met The Queen in her sitting room on the day of my arrival at Balmoral. She greeted me with, "How good of you to come all this way. I understand that you would like another sitting? Where would you like it to be?" It was arranged for the following morning in the same room. In the meantime I discovered that there was to be a special dinner party that night to celebrate the announcement that The Queen was expecting a fourth child. I was put at the top end of the table with The Queen and the Duke. The way in which they have all the information to hand regarding their visitors is amazing, it makes every guest feel that they are already known, and both chat in an informal way which soon puts one at ease. Scottish pipers played round the table at dinner. It was wonderful to see the Victorian marbles, paintings and sculptures in their proper setting. Afterwards we all retired to the drawing room where The Queen sat knitting, surrounded by many of her Scottish friends and cousins. There is a chair in this room which only Queen Victoria was allowed to sit in; I don't think even The Queen herself used it.

I was waiting to begin our sitting next morning when I suddenly saw The Queen coming down the staircase with curlers in her hair. Apparently this was not an unusual occurrence, but it was somewhat startling for new visitors. The Queen said, "I hope you don't mind? – because John Ward was horrified when he came to paint my portrait!" The modelling took about an hour. It must have been a bit of a bore for her, but she always found something to talk about. There was to be a large shooting party for guests, but The Queen said to me, "You won't want to go I suppose?" Instead she arranged for her secretary to take me by car to see the estate. There is a splendid carriageway laid out to Queen Victoria's instructions, so that she could drive round the estate in her pony and trap, and immaculate gardens perfectly set out, including the kitchen gardens. I was enthralled by it all, in particular the marble statues and, inside, the very impressive collection of Winterhalter engravings taken from his original paintings. People criticize Victorian Art, but when seen in its proper setting it is outstanding.

When I arrived back home there was great excitement at our small local Post Office because a parcel had arrived for me from Balmoral. It was a brace of grouse, which we had to give away as we are all vegetarians.

I still continued to work on the effigy, and did several versions, because I made it a classical design which was a symbol of royalty, rather than a portrait. The pearls round the neck were done a number of times in order to give perfect detail, so that I was submitting designs for some months. However, to my astonishment, I was sent for by an official of the Royal Mint who told me that although my portrait had been chosen and Ironside's reverse, Ironside would supervise the production of both sides of the coin. I suspected that Robin Darwin had a hand in this decision. "Then you had better begin to look for a new designer," I replied, "because if you or the committee insist on my work being carried out by Ironside I will withdraw it." That decided it of course and Ironside and I each looked after our own design. My final portrait was handed over to the Mint which, at that time, was still at Tower Hill where it had originally been put for protection by soldiers. Here it was reduced mechanically with a pantograph machine to coin size. I visited two or three times to supervise the final engraving in the dies. It was a long process from beginning to end but once the dies were finalised the work proceeded quickly ready for the set date.

The first two coins with the new effigy of The Queen were in circulation in 1968 because in size they were compatible with sterling. These were the 5 new pence and the 10 new pence, made of cupro-nickel, and being the exact weight, dimensions and value as the shilling and florin. A year later a 50 new pence piece was introduced, interchangeable with the ten shilling note which was to be gradually phased out. The remaining coins became available as legal tender on Decimalisation Day, February 15th. 1971. I remember that Cecil Thomas, for whom I had worked in my student days, and who had also been one of the competitors, wrote to congratulate me on how well I had adapted to the coin technique.

In March 1965, the year after I had designed the coin, I was awarded the OBE, which I received from Her Majesty at Buckingham Palace. We all gathered beforehand in the Picture Gallery where there is a marvellous collection of pictures. Pat and Francis were with me of course. The Queen had quite a long talk with me. It seems to me, looking back, that after creating a design I have always had a battle to get things done the way I want, or a disagreement of some kind afterwards. A monetary prize of £300 went with the competition but Charles Wheeler insisted on having it for himself and William McMillan, saying that I had the job and the prestige! This was amusing in the extreme as they were both quite wealthy. However, on my award of the OBE, Wheeler sent me a congratulatory card which read:

> My dear Arnold,
> I missed your name in the New Year's Honours List but having just been told of its inclusion I write to send you my congratulations. The award should have been higher, I think, but that will follow. All good wishes,
> Yours Ever, Charles.

In 1972 I competed in designs for a commemorative crown to celebrate the Royal Silver Wedding, and again in 1977 for Her Majesty's Silver Jubilee. I won both these competitions and had to go once more to the Royal Mint to discuss the final finish with the engraver. The Silver Jubilee crown depicted The Queen riding side-saddle and I needed someone to sit for me whilst I made models in relief. As luck would have it my wife's friend, Margot Phillips, had a saddle rack and a saddle, and she very kindly agreed to sit for me. She perched herself side-saddle on top of this contraption but almost had an accident as the saddle hadn't been strapped on securely and she only just managed not to fall off.

My success with the coinage designs brought commissions from various quarters and I was invited to design coins for Australia, Malta, Hong Kong, Brunei, the Guernsey Jubilee and the Bahamas, which was Crown property. I was invited to go there by the Governor, Sir Stafford Sands, who had built himself an Italianate villa with beautiful gardens. He gave a lavish party to which I was invited together with John Coddrington, the representative of The Queen, and his wife. There was dancing outside with flares illuminating the flowers and fountains – all of it quite spectacular. I don't dance myself, although Mrs Coddrington persuaded me to try. It was a most interesting visit and the journey there and back, via New York, on Cunard Line's 'Queen Elizabeth' was unforgettable. On my way out I sent the following note home from on board:

> Wed. 16th 1964
> Made a good start – very cold frosty morning but beautiful and sunny. The cabin is very comfortable. I have a double one to myself so it is quite roomy. Just going to lifeboat drill.
> PS. F would love it on board. Don't forget the water drain for the car. Joe will tell you its correct name.

The return trip was especially eventful. In the middle of the Atlantic there was a frightful storm, so violent indeed that the ship had to be turned into the wind and stayed stationary for nearly two days. As it turned I fell out of my bed and I heard that a great deal of crockery was broken.

The Bahamas, however, decided to have its coins made in the United States, using my design, so of course neither I nor the Royal Mint benefited financially as we should have done. It reminded me of Dickens and his novels which were taken by the USA and printed there because there was no law of copyright at that time. It took the author 50 years to obtain copyright.

During this period I was asked to produce portraits for various reasons and Wedgwood dealt with all my moulding. For instance I produced cameos in bas-relief of The Queen and The Queen Mother, and a portrait medallion of Princess Anne to commemorate her wedding. For the latter I worked from portraits specially taken by Lord Lichfield. It was a limited edition of 2000 individually numbered medallions measuring four-and-a-half by three-and-a-quarter inches. They were produced in pale blue and white jasper with a gold inscription on the reverse; Princess Anne has the first copy. I designed a similar one of Prince Charles, but for this he gave me sittings at Buckingham Palace in his office. I particularly recall a great board on one wall showing all his appointments for the year, looking quite formidable. Prince Charles was very friendly and chatted away about the countryside that he loves so much whilst I was working. Wedgwood would take each image and reduce it in size in order to mass-produce their blue jasper plaques. It was said that this profile of the Prince of Wales was very much liked by The Queen.

In 1966 another competition was initiated, by the Royal Mail, to produce a new definitive postage stamp and at the head of the committee was James Fitton RA. A number of designers, sculptors and painters were invited to participate, including the painter John Ward RA, David Gentleman and myself. It has always been assumed in the philatelic world that the Penny Black is the finest stamp ever introduced and the committee was anxious to produce something of comparable quality. Apparently I was invited because the Penny Black was an engraving taken from the coinage designed by William Wyon RA, that is to say – not a direct portrait. They thought that, like Wyon, I could refer to my coin image of The Queen rather than to The Queen herself.

In the first instance all the designers, as well as the Stamp Advisory Committee, thought that the format of the existing stamp would continue, that it would include some sort of lettering such as 'Postage Revenue' or 'Postage' together with the portrait and the value of the stamp. It was therefore necessary to link all the information into a suitable frame enclosing the portrait, so that all my original designs submitted to the committee, and I think those of the other competitors, used this format. There was very little information conveyed to us, so I produced a number of designs based on my coinage portrait but enclosed with various devices to link all the lettering together and to form, if possible, an attractive frame. The committee then decided that, instead of the existing portrait where The Queen was wearing a simple tiara, she should be depicted wearing a diadem, which is a lightweight, jewelled, royal crown. This has been in the possession of the Royal Family since it was made for the Coronation of King George IV in 1821, and a City Medal of 1837 shows the 18-year-old Queen Victoria wearing the same diadem. The medal was designed by Wyon, chief engraver at the Royal Mint.

I saw my task as creating both a likeness of The Queen and an image of monarchy and over a considerable length of time I did endless variations of the portrait and decorative borders. In all I made fifty-two preliminaries, but eventually the design was submitted. The committee, however, could not come to a final decision over whose work was to be chosen. At last the Postmaster General hurried them along, saying that it was imperative to decide so that production of the stamps was not delayed. They chose my design and Fitton telephoned me, rather reluctantly I thought, with their decision, but at the same time saying that all the work was to be carried out by the RCA. When I objected, Fitton said that surely I did not want to be involved in all the technical preliminary work? I felt sure that this was again at the instigation of Robin Darwin, who would simply claim all the merit for himself and the college, so I warned James Fitton that I would withdraw my design if the committee insisted on such a course of action.

After he had discussed the situation with his committee he telephoned me again (there was of course nothing in writing), saying that I would be invited to carry out the work at the RCA, because they had all the equipment and expertise to carry it through, and would I come to the college to have lunch and discuss it with all those concerned? I agreed to do this, but before going to the lunch I went to see a senior Director of the Post Office with my designs. I explained the situation to him, saying that if they insisted, I would withdraw my design and they could start all over again. He was most interested and asked me to come and see him after the meeting to let him know what took place. During lunch at the college everyone was very friendly and persuasive, but I insisted that once the portrait was satisfactory there was little else to do to complete the stamp and that I was perfectly capable of that myself. I then went back to see the Director. He immediately took matters into his own hands, taking full responsibility for the outcome, and told me to go to Harrison's, the printers at High Wycombe, 'to push on with it.'

At Harrison's I met R.F. York, the Works Director, who was to supervise everything from now on. He was always known as 'George', no doubt after King George V1 when he was Duke of York. Fortunately, from the beginning we got on very well together, although I did not realise at the time that he came from a similar background to my own. His first job at the stamp factory had been to sweep the shop floor, but he was obviously very interested in the production of stamps and very talented. He eventually progressed to being a manager and finally a director of the firm. His intimate knowledge of all the processes of stamp production put him in a unique position. All the men working under him realised that he knew more about the requirements of each department than those who were supposed to be experts. He was also involved closely with the Trade Unions and was usually able to sort out any of the problems that arose from time to time, consequently the factory was run very efficiently.

Until now it was still thought that the stamp would follow a similar format as before, incorporating lettering in a frame containing the portrait, but when we looked at the image that was to be used I commented to George York, "It looks so fine and so dignified without a frame or lettering, is it really necessary to include them?" He spoke to the Post Office and to our delight it was agreed that everything could be omitted except the values. So the stamp design was then concluded. I am convinced that had I not been allowed to work out the design with the manufacturers the final result would have been very different and far less successful.

At first George York advised on the production in the normal way. All the equipment was first-rate, with the very best cameras of enormous size running on railway tracks, and with brilliant lights everywhere ready to be switched on and off during the process to produce an original Master photograph. However all this equipment, although most efficient in dealing with designs on a flat surface, was soon seen to be utterly wrong when dealing with any embossment such as my two bas-relief portraits in plaster. It was essential to obtain a Master photograph which would show up the relief in detail before the technicians began to work on the flat photographic image. After many trials and many rejections the final photograph was produced on a misty autumn morning *outside* the factory, using a mahogany

Victorian camera and a photographer with a black sheet over his head! It was excellent and quite suitable for the technicians to produce a flat photographic image.

Harrison's employed a skilled artist to produce the Master image from which all subsequent productions would be made. His technique was to work over every fraction of the photographic image with a very fine stipple, but I was concerned to find that the finished work obliterated any liveliness and spontaneity. All stamps are produced by this method and George York believed there was no other way of arriving at the perfect image, so he insisted that my design went through the same process. I had to be very tactful because he intended to submit these treated stamps to Her Majesty for approval. "Now George," I said, "What you have to do is to produce another set of essays from the untouched photographs." This he agreed to do, and when both sets were examined together there was no doubt in my mind which was the best, but George insisted on submitting both sets to The Queen. Fortunately she chose the one that had been untouched by Harrison's artist, so all was well; some say that it is one of her favourite portraits. Finally I chose all the original colours because the three-dimensional effect varies according to the colours used and some colours bring out the desired effect more than others. The stamp was then ready to be launched in 1967. Later I was to receive a pleasing letter from George York in which he wrote:

> I shall always look back with great pleasure on my association with you in this particular job, and I do hope that some time in the future I shall be lucky enough to be associated with you again in a similar venture. From the first day I met you in this production, I was stimulated and refreshed, and in spite of all the quite fantastic amount of work that was being done at the time, the happiness of working with you was a major factor in overcoming the problems associated with the production.

The stamp itself was an immediate success and many letters of appreciation were received from around the world; the new Postmaster General, Edward Short predicted that it would become a classic design; but the proof of the pudding is in the eating, as they say, and the stamp is still in use after more than thirty years. I regard the stamp as my greatest achievement and it has been described as: 'the finest British postage stamp of this century.' After twenty years the Post Office gave me an engraved bowl but chose to ignore the stamp's 30th anniversary. However, a small stamp firm in Kent produced a First Day Cover, copies of which they asked me to autograph.

In 1969 a National Postal Museum was opened by Her Majesty and, with her agreement, Wedgwood were asked to produce small trays with cameos of her head, which I designed.

Unless one is involved with the production of an item it is rarely known what battles and intrigues go on in the background. Several times the Post Office has tried to alter the stamp without consulting me and I have had to write to the Palace about it. On one occasion Geoffrey Matthews was employed by the Post Office to help with the lettering on some commemorative stamps: he altered the shape of the stamp, added his lettering and gave his own name to the design. I have never signed any of my work, not even the coin. Once a collector bought a piece of terracotta and sent it to the Academy for identification, but they realised at once that it was mine. I feel that an artist's work should be instantly recognisable by his style.

10

When we lived at The Villas in Stoke, we found it to be a very cold house and I developed a serious rheumatic complaint. Pat's father came to visit us, but he was elderly and it was so cold that all he could think about was central heating. He died when our son was aged eight. Pat and I had to decide about future schooling for Francis and as we had a great desire to live in the country we began to explore the area nearer to Shropshire. On one outing we visited Newport, on the Staffordshire-Shropshire border to look at the Adams Grammar School, which is a Haberdashers School, founded in the seventeenth century. When I saw the pleasing architecture I said, "This is it!", for it seemed to be the perfect environment in which to educate a child. There was a preparatory school conveniently close, which Francis could go to beforehand, so that we decided to come and live near enough for him to travel daily.

In 1956 a property was on the market at Walk Mill, near Eccleshall, which I was very keen to buy as it had a fine watermill nearby and the interesting house overlooked a mill pond. Years before I had passed it many times on my rounds with the Capewells. It belonged to Mr & Mrs. Lowe of Sugnall Hall, who owned a number of farms in that area. Interestingly, Mrs Lowe was one of the first women to become a doctor.

For some years the house had been let to the Hon.Mrs Bowyer, who had been a Lady-in-Waiting to Queen Victoria. After the death of her husband she lived there with her son who, according to local people, was a good musician and also had a very generous nature, loaning his car if ever there was an emergency. He later developed cancer, and the story is told that on more than one occasion his mother walked the considerable distance to Eccleshall to catch a bus in order to visit him in hospital. When he died she moved away from the area.

We looked round the house which had an atmosphere of elegance in a state of decay. An unusual feature was a little chapel at the top of the building and there was also an ice-house in the garden near to the pool. We were unfortunate not to be successful in our bid for the house, but we managed to buy some interesting items from the sale of its contents, including a fine kitchen dresser and mirror, several oil lamps, some traditional garden seats and a viola which had belonged to the Bowyers' son. At the sale we also acquired some interesting books, which were given to us, including a family photograph album of Victorian times and a nicely bound book of rather racy poems by the Earl of Rochester. Losing the house was a disappointment to me and I was distressed when the new owners cut down two splendid yew trees which stood either side of the path facing the mill, as I have a deep love of ancient trees.

If one continues along the country road linking Walk Mill with Bishops Offley there is an intriguing outcrop of red sandstone which, over many years, has been cut through to form roads and quarried to provide building stone. It is possible to travel through by car and hardly notice the delights which lie hidden on either side, except for one small sandstone cutting towards the top of the hill; but at the cross-roads there is an abrupt descent to the right leading down a deep cutting, known as The Dark Rock, to the infant river Sow at the bottom. Ahead is a more gradual incline to Croxton and Sugnall, passing on the right Greatwood House, where the sturdy twin brothers of my Capewell rounds helped themselves to our produce, and we to their milk. So the wheel had turned full circle and I was house hunting in an area which I knew very well indeed. At every turn I had a memory to recount to Pat.

However, before reaching the cross-roads at Bishops Offley, there is a narrow hidden lane, almost a cart track, winding up a tree-covered slope and here we discovered, at Offley Rock, an old sandstone cottage with a few acres for sale. As we explored we found that the land overlooked an ancient disused quarry of deep red sandstone, overgrown with trees and incredibly beautiful. It occurred to me that this might be the quarry where Tom Wedgwood had drilled his Homeguard when he was living at Greatwood. The cottage, although well-built, was very primitive, but the whole area had great potential and we decided to make some enquiries. The property was owned by a Miss Fowler who lived at Bishops Offley, just below The Brown Jug public house. She was a very tall melancholy woman, a recluse, who had a large number of dogs and she could be seen walking the lanes with dogs of all sizes straining at their leashes: there must have been seven or eight of them. Miss Fowler lent us the key to look round. Then we discovered a newer, brick-built cottage a little further down the lane which was owned by Elsie Key, whose father had been a cobbler. When her parents died she locked up the house with most of its contents, and there she had left it for ten years. Pat went to see her. "Would you sell it?" she asked. "I might, I might." was the reply. We left it a day or so for Elsie to think about it, but almost immediately Miss Fowler sent us a letter to ask for the return of her key; she had heard on the grapevine that we were interested in Elsie Key's cottage and thought we didn't want hers.

In the event we were able to buy both cottages, living in discomfort in the brick-built one for a long time whilst the stone one was being made habitable. Elsie Key's cottage, after being abandoned for ten years, was covered with brambles and it was quite exciting when we were given the key to unlock it. It was in a terrible state of neglect; Elsie took what she wanted, but we had to burn the rest. There was a grandfather clock which had been too tall for the low ceiling, so a hole had been dug in the ground to accommodate it.

Eventually we were able to move into the stone cottage, and here I had made a bay window which the local carpenter panelled in special brown oak which he happened to have. Both cottages had their own well and I found a man at Newport to make wooden well-heads for them. The well serving the stone cottage was very close to the quarry and was 90 feet deep; originally it had been much less, but quarrying had affected the water level and it had become necessary to deepen it. We later used the brick cottage as a studio and to accommodate visitors. One of these was Jane Best-Shaw, a very good friend of Pat's from student days at Goldsmiths College and who took over Pat's Earls Court flat when we married. Jane came to stay several times and was full of enthusiasm for the garden we were planning. She recalls with amusement that her bedroom was also used as a museum for Francis's colections.

We could not sell our house at The Villas at that time, so we made three large flats which we let to students. When they left, usually after a year or two, Pat had to go back there from Offley Rock to clean in readiness for the next tenants. The council eventually bought the house and I believe it still houses students to this day.

This was a busy decade for me and one of my most productive. I met again 'Tim' Timmis whom I had known at Burslem School of Art, finding that he was living nearby at Johnson Hall in Eccleshall with his wife, Mollie, and their three daughters. In 1963 he asked me to model busts of his twin daughters, Anne and Rosemarie, then about seventeen and their younger sister, Patricia. It was at the time when I was enjoying working on the relief portrait of The Queen and I suggested that he might like bas-relief portraits of his daughters, to which he agreed. I began with a terracotta portrait of Rosemarie and she has reminded me recently that I was working on it during the December of an extremely cold winter, also that we talked a great deal about art and that after it was completed I gave her a book about Benvenuto Cellini, which she has treasured ever since. Her portrait was exhibited at the Royal Academy Summer Exhibition in 1964 where it was seen by the father of the painter, John Merton, who asked me to model a similar portrait of his grand-daughter.

Rosemarie herself showed great talent as an artist, which Pat and I both felt should be encouraged so she came to us as a private pupil – in fact, one might almost say she became our protégée and we were very fond of her. After some years of training she has become a well-established portrait painter.

In later years Rosemarie expressed her thanks to us both in a letter, which moved us very deeply:

> …as a fellow vegetarian I was greatly influenced by your strong ideals, your respect for life and your example as a pacifist. Your constructive criticism, intelligence and humour always raised one's spirits; you opened the doors into the traditions of the Old Masters, particularly Gainsborough and Reynolds; your search for and absolute belief in form was a huge strength to me, when it was totally unfashionable to admire either form or beauty. All conversations with you both inspired me towards excellence rather than novelty… Will you mind if I say that the partnership between you both is a great example of two complementary artists working together? Pat's exquisite flower paintings and your own sensitive sculpture …

I was still working in my London studio but had by now been appointed Master of Sculpture at the Royal Academy Schools, travelling down each week in the peacock-coloured Citroën along the A5. In 1964, I was attending a dinner at the Academy and found myself sitting next to James Butler, a newly-elected Associate, who was himself an enthusiastic sculptor. I asked if he would like to assist me in the Academy Schools and was pleased when he agreed to become a visiting tutor. I remember James being particularly interested in the installation of what he called, 'the vase-kiln'. However, after about ten years of teaching there, because of my disagreement with Humphrey Brooke, the secretary, I resigned my post, but James has remained a very good friend over the years.

My old friend Robert Baker, who had left the Royal College of Art the year after I had, was now director of design for Royal Worcester Porcelain, and in 1967 he asked me if I would design figures for them of 'The Four Seasons.' I have always experimented with various types of clay and body compositions in order to use the most suitable for the mood of the sculpture, and these particular figures, 18 inches high, were produced in porcelain and mounted on ormolu bases. They were most successful, being described by Royal Worcester as 'possessing extraordinary sensitivity and grace.' They were a limited edition which were immediately bought by Thomas Goode of London and they became collectors' pieces. I then designed a number of limited editions for the company including a plaque of The Queen, based on my relief portrait for the definitive stamp.

At Offley Rock, over the years, I made a most exciting garden in the old fields. One field was long and sloping so I created a pool at the top which overflowed into a small cave and then cascaded 50 or 60 yards down the slope into another pool at the bottom. Here I installed an electric pump underground which pumped a good volume of water back to the top pool, to make a fountain and then cascade down again. A gravity-fall pipe in the upper pool created a jet of water in the lower pool. It was a very ambitious project and I felt extremely pleased when I had completed it successfully and edged it round with a clipped hedge. All through the years I had very little help, except for a local farm lad, Cedric Bostock, known to all as Cedy, who came when necessary to help with hedges and tree planting. I was strong and could dig, and lift and move stone relatively easily. Pat's father had given us a small 'wheel horse' mower, like a miniature tractor, which was most useful. In the days when I had divided my time between the cottage at Hanchurch and the studio at 'The Lea', Tom Wedgwood's gardener, Bowers, gave me part of a wild root which Lord Wedgwood had brought back from Africa. The very first thing to come out is a cluster of white, star-like flowers, rather like garlic but not edible. It has a broad leaf and is very prolific and I brought some of it to Offley Rock.

Pat says that her happiest times have been spent in gardens, and memories of the Victorian garden on the outskirts of Derby where she spent her childhood still fill her with pleasure. She can recall every detail even now, from the abundance of grapes and tomatoes in the old glass houses to the great shady chestnut trees, lawns and flowers, and vegetables of every sort presided over by an old gardener who grew everything to perfection. To her it was a little paradise.

Although our childhood days were very different we both have so much in common in our deep love of art and the satisfaction brought by hours of dedicated work, both in our studios and in gardens. Pat loves flowers and wherever we have lived, she has delighted in growing flowers of every kind for her exquisite illustrations – lilies, oriental poppies, hyacinths, tulips and morning glories – but in particular, roses – her favourite being centifolias like Juno and Fantin Latour. Other roses which she frequently portrays in her pictures are the gallicas Rosa Mundi and Jenny Duval, and the damask, Madame Hardy.

At Offley Rock the walls of the tiny cottage studio were eventually smothered with old rambling roses and the Old English flowering pea. While I was occupied with my 'sculptor's garden', clipping alcoves into holly hedges to display sculptures and creating the Grand Cascade, Pat was busy providing the colour and perfume which complement my work. She also found time, in her busy life, to continue with her own artistic career, conserving for all time the beauty of the flowers she grew, especially her beloved roses, in still-life paintings reminiscent of the Dutch masters. One of our favourite places in London is the Victoria and Albert Museum and in the 1970s we became intrigued by the beautiful flower designs painted on papier maché trays on display. Pat wondered if it would be possible to have tin trays produced, and decorated in a similar way with her own paintings. She approached the Metal Box Company, who were interested, and eventually a small industry was developed displaying attractive illustrations of her flowers on metal trays, tea caddies, bins and containers which are mass-produced and sell all over the world. The technical aspect of printing these trays has improved enormously since she started and now, at first glance, the printed design can be almost identical with the original painting.

The land beyond our boundary, which was known as 'The Delves', was two or three acres in extent and encompassed the old sandstone quarry. It belonged to a farmer named Cornes who lived at the top of the lane and eventually he sold it to me. I gave him the price he asked but said that he could have full grazing rights for life. However, sometime afterwards, he fenced it off from his own land and said that we could use it. It was a fascinating place with intriguing mounds of rubble covered with bracken and twisting paths between, until they reached the road where the quarrymen had once loaded their blocks of stone for transporting. With the cattle gone, when we looked one day in spring, The Delves were full of bluebells, which had appeared like magic and were an extra treat for us.

I began work on the quarry by extending our garden down secret winding paths of grass under the great trees, all the pathways forming ramps to lead upwards to a series of different levels, bordered by ferns, bracken, hawthorn and wild roses. Sculptured heads were placed on columns to peer at one as corners were turned. Natural rivulets of water dripped down the rock to form small pools which glinted in shafts of sunlight, and on one large angle of rock-face I carved a huge, winged head. Then I constructed a high rustic bridge to span a 15 foot ravine, with a pagoda-like summerhouse in the centre of it. Here we could relax on our own, or with friends, in complete solitude. The air in summer was full of the scent of wild meadow flowers, gorse and wild roses. Pat says that her best memories of it are of dawn in early summer when the sun rose through the mist across the valley, and evenings when the setting sun lit up the red rock to a fiery brilliance and it was wonderfully silent. There was a tumult of birdsong in the early mornings: in fact it was a haven for wildlife.

In the 1970s the BBC arrived to make a film of the garden, and it was also featured in a gardening magazine when Norman Painting came to interview us. He was very impressed by Pat's paintings of which he wrote, 'Flower paintings often fail to stand up to close scrutiny. Pat Machin's glorious paintings of flowers are an exception – in urns, or still lifes with grapes, lemons and onions they reveal a close study and intimate knowledge of the subject. Her roses have the feel of roses, the bloom on her grapes is almost tangible. She knows, and shows, how an oriental poppy – say Perry's White – differs in colour, structure and texture from, say, a Blanc Double de Coubert rose, or a floret of a white hyacinth. Flowers are presented in her paintings, not merely as beautiful things, but as individuals which have been tended, weeded round, fed and cherished by a gardener who understands them. He described the garden as, 'One of the most thrilling and brilliantly designed gardens I know, a garden of stone and water… I know nowhere in the world quite like it, where one can enjoy so green a paradise in such soothing, enveloping silence.'

It was distressing, therefore, when a new neighbour came to live close by who had dogs barking throughout the day, and kept foreign birds which were very noisy. Our peace and quiet was shattered almost overnight and I found it impossible to concentrate on my work. I approached the man, but he was unpleasant and would not co-operate at all. Complaints to the local authority brought someone with a machine to measure sound, but they said it was not excessive, and as I was the only complainant they would do nothing. Although we had done a tremendous amount of work on this marvellous site and garden over the last twenty years, we sadly concluded that we had to find somewhere more restful.

It is not easy to find something unspoiled by modern alteration but there was a fine house about two miles away, near Eccleshall, which was on the market at this time and we went to look round. The main part of the building was Georgian, but this had been attached to an earlier and much smaller farmhouse, probably in the eighteenth century, and a later Victorian wing had been added. It was a fascinating house and there would be plenty of room for us each to have a studio and to keep our collections and acquisitions. There was also a large and untouched farmyard to the rear with splendid outbuildings which could be used for a variety of purposes. At the side was the original garden, an old apple orchard and a pool, all of which appealed to us; but yet again we were not successful in our bid as it was bought by a property dealer. We shuddered at tales of the extensive alterations he was making to this lovely old house while we continued to search for a suitable place.

During our time at Offley Rock, Francis was attending school in Newport. Formal schooling was not entirely to his liking: he had wide interests, making inventive models and being passionately interested in engineering. He also kept extensive illustrated records of wildlife, amongst other hobbies. He did a little modelling in clay at home but was a much better draughtsman than modeller. When he was about fourteen he spotted a Rolls Royce Merlin engine, which was no longer required by the government, crated up in a scrap yard, and begged us to buy it for him. This was right outside our interests or understanding but he was so insistent that Pat offered to buy from him his collection of meticulously-drawn dragonflies for £30. Thus Francis acquired his engine but there was, however, nowhere to store it so he made a rough shed to cover it and there it stayed for some years. He also built a car with a Volkswagen chassis and a fibreglass and aluminium body. He seemed to be a natural engineer. On leaving school he decided to train as an architect and attended the Bartlett School of Architecture, which is part of the Slade School of Art.

News came to us after quite some time that the house near Eccleshall was on the market again. The new owner wanted to convert the old stabling into flats, but as he couldn't get planning permission he decided to sell and move on. We had not intended to buy it as we thought he had most likely ruined it but ,by a stroke of luck, a few days before the sale, we decided to go and have another look and saw that there hadn't been a great deal of alteration. We felt that without too much expense and energy we could put it to rights again. As we weren't keen on going to auction we made him a good 'take it or leave it' offer, which he accepted. We sold our home at Offley Rock, although it was a wrench to leave our studios and the lovely garden. I felt that I was selling a masterpiece when I took my last look at the Cascade.

The new house was actually old and had started life as a small Georgian farmhouse. Four steps led to a central front door originally covered with a porch consisting of two pillars with two pilasters and a single stone to cap it, which I think had come from a churchyard. I found the porch in a field, somewhat damaged but complete, and I planned to reinstate it. There was a staircase rising on the right of the hallway with a room on either side and a passage leading to a small kitchen and work-room where we found an old fashioned bread oven. Upstairs were two bedrooms and two utility attic rooms under the roof. It was completely symmetrical with gable ends of finely-shaped stone to enclose the tiled roof. Subsequently, in the early Victorian period, the owner, who must have been quite wealthy, more than doubled the size of the house and made a large garden. At this time some fine trees had been planted, including Wellingtonias, which are now home to treecreepers.

When we first visited the house I had greatly admired the impressive entrance with eight-foot sandstone columns surmounted by huge stone balls. However, I found that one of the gateposts was damaged and a stone ball missing: someone had obviously gone through with a bulldozer, caught the catch, rocked the pillar and the ball fell and smashed. I found the pieces in the shrubbery and managed to restore it by fixing the bits and pieces with cement. A local farmer, Bert Lowe, came to help periodically and with the help of his fork-lift and a scaffolding pole he very skilfully lifted the ball in a net which I had made of chicken wire and gracefully placed it in position. It was a most delicate operation. Now that the ball has weathered you would never know that it had once been destroyed. I have since designed wrought-iron gates to equate with the splendid pillars. The drive, which is lined with tall laurels, curves so that the house cannot be seen; while the side entrance between ivy-covered stone walls is enhanced in Spring by plantings of snowdrops.

The house has its own deep well which must originally have been situated in the open farmyard but close enough to the house for later extensions to cover it, so that it now lies under the kitchen floor in an intriguing maze of Victorian vaulted passageways. These are lined with stone and link the Victorian cellar with Georgian wine cellars and still-rooms. In one of these we found the old cheese and butter-making equipment. We were disappointed to find that the bells in the kitchen had been ripped out and all the amber handles to the bell pulls removed, but nothing had been done about the leaking roof, a leaking bay window and a problem with the drains.

In the large drawing room the ceiling had been painted purple and plaster mouldings fixed on the walls so that it was not possible to hang pictures; the old grate had been demolished and a stove with tiles put in its place. We set to work to renovate the room to its original style and replaced the fireplace, and those in the other rooms, with something more in keeping with the period. Pat has a wonderful feeling for colour, choosing paints and fabrics which have a warming effect on the spirit. Against this background we are able to display treasured paintings, one of which is a particular favourite of hers.

Pat describes it, "I have a painting by Savage Cooper of a very pretty but very sulky- looking young woman standing amidst apple blossom in an elaborate costume, her red chiffon scarf floating round her head, painted in 1906. I was the only one in the family who liked the painting, which had rather a rough passage over the years after it left my grandmother's house where it had pride of place in her drawing room. For some years it had to stay at The Villas when we let it to students and although the furniture suffered greatly, there was never the slightest damage to the picture. I think my family objected not to the picture, but to the very sulky model whose mouth I have slightly modified, otherwise I think she would have had to be hung in the attic, beautifully painted though she is".

Pat has called me 'a great hunter-up of junk', and says that in the days when Victorian was still taboo we would be laughed out of the salerooms, but that we have some lovely things to show for it. Certainly the house is a delightful setting for the personal treasures we have collected over many years. One of Charles Wheeler's greatest friends was Robert Swann, who had made some excellent drawings from the antique at the Royal Academy. I was able to buy these from him before he died, and I have them on display. When we were at Offley Rock, Francis found a lovely unbroken globe from a Victorian oil lamp thrown into a stream which he kept and which he still treasures.

In the yard some of the old barns had been restored and the roofs re-tiled, but luckily in the correct way, apart from the doors which they had only just begun to replace with modern ones; otherwise we found everything intact, including the old Victorian lavatories near to the house. The large barns at the end of the farmyard were known as drift barns, open in the centre, where – as the corn was being sifted – the strong West winds would blow the chaff away. The corn would then be stored above where bricks had been left out to provide ventilation, not haphazardly but in an attractive decorative pattern. I eventually restored or renewed the huge barn doors. Disappointment greeted us in the garden however. Having left behind our romantic quarry garden we viewed the flat, vandalised area with dismay. The Victorian flower and vegetable garden and the ancient apple orchard had disappeared and had been replaced by grass; but we were compensated by a spacious house which gave enormous pleasure over the years.

I decided to enlarge the pool. I felt sure that the Georgian bricks used to build the original farmhouse came from the clay ground which eventually formed the pool. The bricks would have been made on the spot, soft-fired, then rubbed together with water to true them all up. The lime mortar joints are only about an eighth-of-an-inch thick and this part of the building has not needed any repointing in 200 years. Some farmers had a secondary job and did a bit of potting from local clay during the winter, or made steens, these being brick-lined shafts for wells. This is how many potteries began, and if the pottery did well the farm disappeared.

Before leaving Offley Rock I had bought another stone cottage with an orchard, further down the lane, but the cottage was condemned and had to be demolished so we took the stone to our new home to use for future plans which I had in mind. Also at this time, a farmer nearby was pulling down his old farm buildings of decent bricks and stone, which I bought from him. I started to rectify the extreme flatness pretty quickly. In a desolate area beyond the old farmyard, where the prevailing wind was so fierce that it could be difficult to stand up, the ground consisted of broken brick and concrete. Here I made a sheltered walled garden, with a terrace on either side so that we could view the countryside.

My friend, Robert Baker, had retired by this time and had become a technical adviser for various heritage projects, particularly at the cathedrals of Winchester and Wells. I travelled down to Winchester to see his restoration of a mediæval tiled floor. He had built a kiln in his garden at South Newington, made tiles from local clay and glazed and fired them himself using wood faggots, all done as the originals would have been. He had made remarkable copies of these inlaid tiles and it was fascinating to watch him laying them. I had the opportunity to wander round the cathedral, and in so doing I came across a typical Henry Moore sculpture, with half its limbs missing. Two women were standing there, wondering what it was, and they asked me if I knew anything about it. I told them that it had been done by a sculptor who some believed had improved on Michelangelo and to be the finest who ever lived. 'Can you tell us', they asked, "What it means?" My reply was, "I don't think Henry Moore himself knew what it meant."

Still exploring the cathedral, I found the Prior Silstede chapel in which is a fine stained glass window donated, in 1914, by the fishermen of England and America in memory of Izaak Walton. I did not realise that there was any connection between Walton and Winchester but, as often happens, unusual discoveries are made in the most unlikely places. Apparently, after the Restoration of the Monarchy, Walton was appointed Steward to the Bishop of Worcester, Dr. George Morley, and accompanied him when he became Bishop of Winchester in 1662. Sadly his wife, Anne, died soon after they moved there, but his daughter married a prebendary of Winchester and Walton stayed on, living as one of the Bishop's household in the cathedral close and fishing in the river Itchen behind the cathedral. His son, Isaac, became a Canon of Salisbury. Izaak Walton died at the remarkable age of ninety and was buried in the Prior Silstede chapel. One light in the memorial window depicts him fishing with his friend, Charles Cotton, in the river Dove, and the opposite light shows him seated, reading, beside the river Itchen. Below the latter is the inscription: 'Study to be Quiet' – one of his favourite quotations from Thessalonians and used in his book, 'The Compleat Angler'. I have often noticed that if one becomes interested in a well-known figure, they seem to appear from time to time as if by accident. How much more interesting places become when associated with distinguished people.

Soon after our move, Robert Baker was commissioned to do the restoration work on the front of Wells Cathedral, and he asked me if I would talk to the conservators. I spent several days down there. It was a remarkable experience for me, being up on the scaffolding in close contact with some of the finest carving of the Middle Ages. I had to climb several flights of ladders to reach the topmost figures and initially it was a rather disturbing experience. The first ladder would be leaning towards the cathedral, but the next one was leaning in the opposite direction, pointing into space, with only the slender scaffolding poles to remind one of some support. As I moved higher and higher it became more and more terrifying to look into space at a great height. Strangely enough, after doing the climb several times, it was amazing how the fear diminished, so that finally it did not affect me at all. How privileged I felt to be in a position to be able to put my hands on these astonishing carvings, which are normally so remote.

The figures had obviously caused alarm in the Victorian period, when several of them were in danger of collapsing, for the Victorians had done some rather crude restoration work by filling in the niches behind the figures with cement and trying to hold them in position with iron bars. This eventually caused further corrosion and Robert Baker had the job of removing all the cement and ironwork before he could begin to restore them. He used a method which I think was his own invention. He prepared some lime water from rock lime and, over a long period, sprayed the figures with fine jets which automatically switched off and on. The theory was that the lime water gradually impregnated the stone and consolidated it. The figures were then drilled and fixed to the main wall with phosphor bronze rods. Of course these were not available to the Victorians who, I feel sure, would certainly have used them in place of iron. The new restoration was a great improvement and the figures, free from cement, look exactly as they would have done in the Middle Ages, when they were originally placed in their niches. I was intrigued to find that the West front has apertures put there in mediæval times, to enable the voices of the choristers to be heard by those outside.

What a wonderful cathedral Wells is! I wish that I could have had the time to investigate it in detail, but there are two features which I must mention. A magnificent central tower was added to the cathedral in the early 14th century, but the early foundations were not strong enough to support it, and after about twenty years, the tower began to tilt. A remedy was found by building inverted strengthening arches beneath, known as cissoid arches, which are unique and architectural connoisseurs come from all over the world to look at them.

The second feature which is so interesting is the staircase leading to the chapter house, which adjoins the cathedral on its North side. I have never seen anything so impressive. There is a wide flight of stone steps curving round and halfway up branching off to the chapter house on the left. This was originally used for daily meetings of the cathedral canons. These stones which are so well-worn with centuries of use are alive with memories and, in my opinion, are a work of art; they have to be seen to be believed, stirring the imagination and causing the mind to wander to thoughts of great poetry and music, like steps leading to heaven, 'to a state of calm repose and sweet tranquillity.'

I shall always treasure my experiences at Wells: the Bishop's Palace with its moat for protection and the swans which daily pull on a chain to ask for food; the wonderful row of lodgings built for the Vicars Choral, and the simple fountain in the town with water trickling over pebbled stones – so natural, but so effective. What a joy to visit Wells and how much more to be discovered. Later I received a letter of thanks from the architect in charge of the work, A.D Caroe, in which he said:

> I used at one time to visit your district fairly often since my father, W.D Caroe, had so many architectural commissions in that area, amongst which were Aqualate Hall near Newport and Eccleshall church itself, where the organ cases and memorial chapel below are his work.

This was of particular interest to me, since the memorial chapel which he mentioned was altered and furnished in memory of Susan Mary Lowe, one of the daughters of Mrs.Lowe of Sugnall Hall. Susan's niece, Anne Jacques, had inherited the estate on the death of her grandmother. Since coming to live near Eccleshall we had come to know Anne and her husband Greville very well, and greatly admired the exquisite carving in the 'Sugnall' chapel when we first saw it. Anne tells this interesting story concerning the alterations:

> My grandparents decided to refurbish the chapel – a dark and gloomy affair which was hardly ever used – and also to give a new organ which was particularly appropriate as Mary had been very musical and a talented pianist. A well known architect from London, Mr.Caroe, was chosen to plan the work. He decided to use limed oak for the panels and

> carving. This was a new medium in the 1930s, the attraction being its light colour and the lack of maintenance and polishing required. The hand-carving of the chapel and organ casing was hailed as a masterpiece of modern craftsmanship. The Lichfield firm of Bridgeman was entrusted with the actual carving. As a small girl, I remember walking up the church path and coming face to face with the two trumpet-blowing angels which were about to be lifted into position high upon the organ casing. They seemed the same size as myself, and I can remember desperately wanting to be put up there between them and spend the rest of my life playing a trumpet too. When I was told: 'All right, but you won't be wanting any tea then', I changed my mind.

About fifty years after the memorial chapel had been designed, Anne lost her mother very tragically. One of the original craftsmen still with Bridgeman added the carved inscription on the chapel screen bearing her mother's name: Margaret Ellen Hayes; thus the chapel is now dedicated to both sisters.

At our Eccleshall house, over the years, I increased the acreage and planted many hundreds of trees – hawthorn, beech and holly – and small copses, with the aim of creating wind-breaks and for conservation and wildlife purposes. After 17 years they are well established with a lot of quite good trees to admire. We had a German gardener at one time who had been a prisoner-of-war and had married a local land-girl. Like most Germans he was most methodical with his work and very thorough and accurate at clipping box and yew – but he was a great pessimist. Ten years ago when we were planting a plane tree he said mournfully, "You'll never see it fully grown"! My plane tree is now 15 feet tall and beautiful, reminding me daily, with its attractive pinkish bark, of the plane trees in London.

From the terrace we look down on to what is now a small lake and here, with the help of a builder I created six Gothic arches. In one corner I began to construct a domed grotto, inspired by the one at Chatsworth which is at the top of a large cascade. Mine was to include a stone spiral staircase, fountain and waterfall. Soil was removed from the lower level by the lake and an elevated walk made at the back to make a different level.

I found that more stone was needed than that which I had brought from Offley Rock, so I paid a visit to Hollington quarry to negotiate for a further supply. The manager was eager to tell me of the previous night's happenings when he had been called out by the fire brigade. It seemed that the quarrymen had reason to prepare some lime mortar but no one had any previous experience of the process, not knowing that the chemical reaction of water being poured on to rock lime is the generation of intense heat. The rock lime was in a metal skip resting on wooden baulks and the slaking process heated the metal to such an extent that it set fire to the wood. It brought back vivid memories of the lime mortar being prepared when we were children at Trent Vale and of the danger we had been in of falling into it. I have been working on the grotto for fifteen years and it is nearing completion. Finally there will be a few more additions and then the decorating. All of this has not only given much more interest to the garden but has been an on-going project which I have found most satisfying.

In 1981 Lady Collins, who was a friend of Pat's, asked her to illustrate a book of hymns to be produced by Collins the publishers, and later, she illustrated the 'Pocket Poets' books published by Webb and Bower. On one occasion the Duchess of Devonshire and her shop manager visited us to discuss a tray which was to depict Chatsworth House framed by roses. They walked with us round the garden and the Duchess admired four splendid Italian vases. 'They wouldn't look amiss at Chatsworth' she said.

The garden itself is embellished with box and yew, most of which I have grown from cuttings, and with old roses. Pat says that she follows on behind me wherever there is a spare bit of land to plant flowers for her paintings or special vegetables and herbs for cooking. She has commented more than once that all the flowers she paints, she grows; and that if she had to resort to florists she would never get good enough roses for her pictures. Some of Pat's flower beds are within the half-acre farmyard, now enclosed completely with walls. She observes, "It could only function today as a working farmyard if it were to be completely modernised and then it would lose all its old character." Instead we have now created enclosed gardens there – with Italian pots and espaliered trees – perfect as sun-traps and hideaways. When we first came the ancient pigsties were full of ash saplings which had seeded themselves; I transplanted these to train into a pergola over the path to the secret walled garden.

When we moved to Eccleshall, Francis made use of the barns by transporting his Spitfire engine to more sheltered accommodation and since then, although he had never had anything to do with aero-engines in his life, he has obtained information from a Rolls Royce manual, gradually collected the missing parts from dealers or ingeniously made them himself, set up the engine and got it going again. He has also filled up the barns with two French farm wagons and two other aero-engines which he managed to obtain. After completing his training as an architect he began his own business constructing conservatories. His very first one was added to the Victorian wing of the house, overlooking the garden, and is used as a sitting and dining room in summer. His attractive summerhouses have been erected as focal points as the garden developed, and by the lake is a brick-built boathouse to his design. Francis is full of creativeness and determination, working incredibly hard, but he still finds time to come and lend a hand and, with the grotto nearing completion, he installed a pump for me, being a good plumber. He is not only a very fine draughtsman, but a craftsman as well, understanding building materials and their uses.

In the 1980s there came an interesting and unexpected sequel to the history of the sculpture made by Edwin Russell for the Stanley logo twenty years previously at the Royal Academy. By now the Stanley factory had been bought by Ferranti and Francis had been commissioned by one of the Ferranti family to design a swimming pool for him. Francis asked me if I would like to accompany him on this trip to Basingstoke, and as we toured the garden I suddenly recognised Edwin's sculpture on display. I was astonished, as was its new owner when he heard the story.

We had brought many things with us to our new home which had been packed away in boxes for years and during an unpacking session we rediscovered the Derby dessert set. This was a splendid collection of Derby china decorated with roses and other flowers in soft shades of pink, mauve, yellow and green with a deep blue border and extraordinary gilding. At last we had room to exhibit them. After the onslaught of Dutch elm disease many lovely old elms were felled on the Jacques' estate and Francis acquired a number of them, slicing and maturing the wood. I designed a dresser and shelves which Francis had made for us by one of his joiners. Elm is one of the most decorative timbers because of its interesting grain. After the dresser had been made it was left for a period, as exposure to light affects the colour, and when the shade was exactly what we wanted, it could be waxed. The Derby plates and dishes were arranged on the shelves and the resulting display is beautiful.

Francis's career has changed direction in recent years and he spends a great deal of time abroad designing various complexes for clients, or developing a farm in France which he owns, but he still has a flat here where he can entertain friends and which he, his wife and three children Alice, Henry and Louis use when they visit. It is a great joy to us to have grandchildren. After Alice was born I approached an old friend from the RCA, Peter Wall, to make a dolls' house for her. Peter was studying Industrial Design under Robert Baker during the period after the war when I was teaching part-time at the RCA, and it was here that we met. Then, in the early 1950s, Peter came to work for Wedgwood, becoming Deputy Art Director under Victor Skellern so that our paths crossed once more and we have been good friends ever since. I had seen two of Peter's doll's houses and was most impressed by them. The first was made for his daughter, Annabel; the second was based on Barlaston Hall which stands on the Wedgwood estate. This was made at the request of the wife of the writer, Richard Adams, and is now displayed in Stoke City Museum.

The design for the doll's house for Alice was inspired by a lovely early Georgian house in Lucton, Herefordshire, now a Public School. Peter recalls that 'It was a happy working partnership for five years; we both derived a great deal of pleasure working on it together', and he remembers that I was particularly interested in the illusion created by mirrors in the drawing room and also the view created from the garden room. Every detail was carefully planned and Peter provided several examples for the colour of the bricks before we settled on the final effect. From the library one looks through to the kitchen with its blue tiled floor; there is electric light and imitation fires glow as small bulbs shine through crumpled orange paper. At the top of the house is a chapel where I painted a scene of The Annunciation for the reredos and on one wall an illusion of a cloistered walk beyond. I also painted designs on canvas to carpet the house. Pat contributed miniature framed pictures of her lovely rose paintings and photographs of her trays were reduced in size to adorn the walls.

The completed house was eventually given to Alice for her sixth birthday and she has kept the letter which I wrote to her on this occasion:

> August 1997
> Dear sweet Alice,
> Many happy returns of your (sixth) birthday. I have got some new furniture and a clock which keeps perfect time. I enclose a picture of them. What a big girl you are now. I hope you are very very good and have lots of sumptuous things to eat. Have a lovely party.
> Lots of love,
> from Arny xxxxx

Alice loves to show her house to people and is particularly interested in the numerous references to her which are incorporated. For instance, on the pediment is a monogram of her initials; the 'lead' spouting on either side of the building has hoppers which display the year of her birth on one side and her birth sign (Leo) on the other, and the clock below the cupola stands at 7-30, the time of her birth. The house itself has been named 'Augusta House', after her second name. The angel Gabriel stands with his horn inside the cupola, on top of which is a weathervane of a lion. On the roof is a viewing platform with a miniature telescope.

We visit our grandchildren whenever we can and they all come as a family when it is possible, making bonfires, lighting lanterns and fireworks in the wintertime; exploring the garden and having fun outside in summer. All three draw very well and Pat encourages them to make little booklets and illustrate them which they find more interesting than mechanical toys. People often fail to realise that children need adults near to them to take an interest in their work and show them what to do. Pat also makes up stories for them which she later copies into small books and illustrates as birthday presents. They call her Granny, but I am 'Arny', which we both like. All this brings us great happiness and continues our close family links, especially as we grow older.

11

When I look back over the years and see my life unfold I am amazed by it all. I realise how fortunate I was to be born into a good-living family with loving parents, dedicated to their children. Desperately poor we may have been, but with careful management we never felt deprived or envious of those in more flourishing circumstances; we accepted the situation and got on with the business of living, trying to make it as pleasurable as possible. It is not poverty that damages a child: often it becomes the incentive to work hard.

What simple pleasure we derived from our 'penny savings', carefully accumulated over the year to buy a special treat for Christmas – in my case, chocolate walnuts. I remember later on, at Minton's, someone gave me a small wallet to keep pound and ten-shilling notes, but I never had any to put in it! This did not worry me however, for I have never grabbed for money. Mother was easily persuaded to acquire the twelve volumes of The Children's Encyclopædia, books which broadened my horizons and gave me the opportunity to copy sculptures and paintings which interested me – thank goodness I had no one to tell me what was good or bad! I made a copy of Leighton's 'Athlete struggling with a Python', which has since been passed back to me by my sister Hilda. It seemed miraculous when Father saved enough money to take me on the exciting trip to Liverpool Art Gallery to see the real thing for the first time. What a child needs most in life is a responsive ambience in which to grow and I realise now that my parents always encouraged and supplied food for the soul as well as the body.

It is interesting to recall how others have influenced my life: parents, brothers and sisters, employers, tutors, friends – all had their part to play. A word of encouragement here, a kindness there, loyalty and opportunities given – these were the stepping stones that guided me. My marriage to Pat and the birth of Francis, and later of our grandchildren, have brought love and companionship in full measure. We have kept in touch with friends and students, many of whom come to see us from time to time. Recently we had a visit from our friend from Bakewell, George Butler, who is quite remarkable, with voice unchanged and still enjoying watercolour painting at the age of ninety-three. A deep debt of gratitude is due to those who help to shape our lives.

We are all born with our own unique abilities, but it is no good having ability if you haven't the *drive.* What is needed is integrity and the steadfastness to 'stick at it', then there's a chance to achieve something in life.

I am convinced that hard work is the key to success. So many people today are protected from reality and have become apathetic. I firmly believe that the secret of contentment is to accept what you have and to make the most of it – not stretching for the impossible but working to one's utmost for the possible. Above all, I am eternally grateful for God's help in my work and my enjoyment, for every move I have made in my life seems to have been dictated.

My lifelong interest in reading developed apace when I had the opportunity to look round the library at Minton's. My preferred reading then was Zane Grey, Jack London and Fenemore Cooper. I was transported to another world by 'Roping Lions in the Grand Canyon', or, 'The Last of the Mohicans'. Later on it was 'The Scarlet Pimpernel' by Baroness Orczy and years later when I rented the Sydney Close studio I discovered that at one time she had lived in the studio two doors away from mine. Here she had designed for herself a writing desk with bookshelves above, where she wrote her novels, and I was invited to see it by the occupier.

Later I began to explore the works of Plato, Pascal, St.Thomas Aquinas, Dante, Byron, Shelley, Scott and many more. I have read most of their works time and time again, especially Goethe, whose writings are like a great goldmine which one can dip into at will. I have always been grateful for the lighter side of life personified by Anthony Trollope and the inimitable P.G.Wodehouse, both so entertaining; but under the frivolity lie serious thoughts of the problems of life. In my opinion, P.G.Wodehouse books ought to be a remedy prescribed by the National Health Service!

When I discovered William Blake, it was so different from anything I had encountered before that since then I have been a constant reader of his work and admirer of his drawings. When I first opened one of his books it was like opening a gate into a secret garden of the mind – a garden of endless paths and hidden surprises where I have been privileged to wander ever since. In the haunting beauty of his 'Songs of Wisdom and Experience' what captivating blooms are viewed from a moss-covered path through a dark yew tunnel. The thoughts of William Blake became the inspiration for the gardens which I have since created.

Water has always held a great fascination for me, from the small stream bubbling under the natural stone bridge at Trentham to crossing the stepping stones in Dovedale. What a joy it was to roam along the side of the river Dove with its endless natural beauty, and how the imagination was stirred by the 'Strictly Private' areas on the other side! Somewhere on that further bank Charles Cotton's fishing lodge lay concealed, while above steep rocks rose up to a considerable height, covered with trees. Perhaps my problems with hair-loss when I was young caused me to choose solitary places, away from people. Certainly at that time I grew to dislike the lighter days of summer, and even now I prefer the shaded walks of woodland paths to open sunlit fields.

Man's harnessing of water intrigues me, for practical purposes or for elegant water features in gardens. When, as a boy, we moved from the house in London Road and had our first little garden I built a small pool, collected rainwater by gravity fall and made a tiny fountain. Years later, I was greatly impressed by the magnificent water display at Versailles, where an artificial hillside had been constructed and water was pumped up from the river in vast quantities to make cascading fountains. Men are wonderful in the way in which they solve problems of all kinds, and the Victorians in particular were admirable in this respect. One of the most evocative sounds in my life was that of a Victorian ram pump making its distinctive thudding, and it always made a good excuse to search out the direction and source of the noise. Before electricity reached remote areas there were hundreds of ram pumps raising water mainly, I should imagine, for irrigation and drinking troughs for cattle. The concept is very simple with the energy coming from flowing water: a chamber is dug about six feet below water level and a pump placed in the chamber; water from a stream is diverted through a pipe which takes it through the base of the pump, or 'ram'. When the flow reaches a certain speed a valve closes, stopping the flow out of the ram; another valve opens, allowing the water to be forced up into an air chamber when an immediate rebound occurs. For a short while the water is forced upwards through a narrow pipe to where it is required; as soon as this happens the outlet valve opens again, and the water once more flows through the ram until it reaches sufficient velocity for the process to be repeated. The amazing thing is that the entire process takes but a few seconds and is the nearest thing to perpetual motion.

If the sight and sound of water have brought delight to my life, the feel of clay in my hands has had an even more profound influence; certainly I have a great affinity with the land and all that it produces. From my father I learned the joy of growing vegetables and flowers and the wonder of creating from clay.

I think that I was born a terracotta modeller! It has always given me the utmost pleasure to work in this medium as one can produce much more spontaneous work. Whereas in stone-carving the sculpture is produced by cutting away and destroying the original stone, in work with clay one is building up and creating from the earth itself. I also feel great affinity with Italian works of art.

I recently visited the Minton Museum, sixty-five years after I had worked at Minton, and found that they had a single plate painted and signed by me, when I was about sixteen, of two cherubs on a cushion. It is a very modest effort compared with the French artists. In those days Minton had three separate factories, one making tiles, one earthenware and one fine china. In the museum some of the earthenware is spectacular: life-size blackamoors and peacocks displaying the enormous skill of their production; the making of the clay model, the firing and lastly the decorating. One of their peacocks was sold by Sotheby's recently and fetched over £100,000. As I looked round the Minton museum I was enormously impressed by the quality and variety of the work produced from the past to the present day. My own achievements in the world of art have brought me tremendous satisfaction and now, as I approach my nineties, I feel honoured to have been asked by the Royal Mint to compete in a design for a Millennium Medal.

At the close of the twentieth century I am bound to have concerns about so-called 'progress'. I believe that modern society has failed to tackle problems vigorously enough and has waited until it is almost too late to deal with global warming and other impending disasters. Certainly science is progressing at a tremendous rate, seemingly unstoppable; but in my opinion art has regressed – standards have deteriorated shamefully, both in training and in practice – free expression is rampant and it is now accepted that anyone can produce the highest standard of art, even young children. They are given a great bowl of colour and allowed to flick paint about with no control and, worst of all, with no training; but a child wants to become an adult, not remain as a child. In fact children's art is copied and acclaimed, which I consider 'childish'. I am reminded of the verse from Corinthians: 'When I was a child, I spake as a child, I understood as a child, I thought as a child: but when I became a man, I put away childish things'.

What is so appalling is the number of people persuaded to accept these standards by chatter on television programmes. Unlike the past the art world is now dominated by the critics who have enormous influence through magazines and television and they seem to manipulate the so-called 'Masters of Art' like puppets. I call them 'castrated artists' and the Courtauld Institute of Fine Art, where many of them were trained, 'The Courtauld Institute of Castration'. Sensible people simply dare not criticise because they are ridiculed, yet they are the ones who realise that the work of children and untrained artists cannot compare with the works of the Old Masters, and this above all condemns it. In 1986 1 had a letter from certain students at the Royal Academy expressing their concern about deteriorating standards, and this extract is from my letter in reply:

> I was interested to receive your letter and I share your concern regarding the Diploma Course and the library etc., but your dissatisfaction with the instruction you receive raises a more important issue and as I have been out of touch with the school for a number of years it would help me if I knew what changes and improvements you are seeking. Your statement that you want to make the RA School a great art school impresses me, implying as it does a degree of involvement which has been conspicuously lacking in the past; if I knew what sort of study and what facilities you envisage in order to achieve this, I would then know whether or not I could help.

I worry particularly about the future of The Royal Academy, a centre of excellence for over two hundred years, of which the first President, Joshua Reynolds, said at the inaugural meeting :

> An Academy, in which the Polite Arts may be regularly cultivated, is at last opened among us by Royal Munificence. This must appear an event

> in the highest degree interesting, not only to the Artists, but to the whole nation.

The more recent displays put on for public edification – in particular the 'Sensations' exhibition of 1997 – could not possibly be described as 'Polite Art', or even 'Art' at all! Sometimes I despair, until I am reminded of the words of Reginald Farrer, 'But what is the use of fighting and raving? The only thing to do for a wise man, is to sit under the wall while the dust storm of mortal folly drives by.' Or, as a friend of mine from the Academy remarked rather more crudely, 'It's no good fighting against it – it's like pissing against the Niagara Falls.' Some of these new approaches to art eliminate humanity, without considering that in the end what interests people most is the vital human touch, the creation of a rhythm in life which many cannot understand any more.

This was well comprehended by inspired preachers like John Donne, who fed his congregation by producing a vibrant atmosphere with words. Mediæval designers also understood this influence when they produced spectacular church architecture and stained glass windows; enhancing the interior with music, incense and oils – all designed to stimulate the senses and enrich the soul by creating auras of Paradise. Sir Colin Southgate,the Chairman of the Board of the Royal Opera House, has said, 'Without Art souls get undernourished… it is a comfort for the misery of the world' and, 'Good Art stimulates the imagination as well as ravishing the senses.'

Rudolf Steiner, an Austrian teacher and philosopher at the turn of the 19th century, believed that creative activities are psychologically valuable for teaching and healing. He filled a chapel with stained glass windows to illustrate his theory that colours in glass vibrate and stimulate the senses. He also carved benches deliberately with a chisel to give a sense of movement, and the 'Steiner Group' was founded to introduce rhythmic dancing. He considered it necessary that all aspects of life should be influenced by the healing power of creativity.

I remember reading that the first Josiah Wedgwood spent countless hours doing hundreds and hundreds of experiments with texture and colour in order to achieve something nearing perfection. Great artists go on experimenting because they have the vision and because they are inspired to help their fellows, not because they are filled with personal greed, as so many seem to be today. More than ever we need men of conviction, to open people's eyes to what is 'alive' – the different textures of wood, the individuality of stone compared with concrete, the soaring grandeur of magnificent trees – to appreciate the beauty of really great Art. Even old bricks made by hand have life in them and give back something to those who have the ability or training to appreciate them. D H Lawrence is not one of my favourite authors, but I am reminded of the following quotation from his work:

> Things men have made with wakened hands, and breathed soft life into, are awake through the years with transferred touch. For this reason some old things are lovely, warm still with the lives of forgotten men who made them.

The playwright, Alan Ayckbourn, has said, 'All great Art comes from people who recognise that there is something higher than themselves', and indeed I can subscribe to this, for all my thoughts and aspirations have been influenced by writers who acknowledged this great truth.

As I reach the end of a long and fulfilling life I continue to work to the very best of my ability, but I also have time to meditate a little more – on the past, on the future and on death. Anna Kingsford, that great mystic, was deeply religious and yet she said, just before dying, 'They all philosophise about the end, but I've never met anyone who wants to go.' We are all afraid of the unknown.

Perhaps it is because of this that I am reading again, with heightened poignancy, 'The Mystical Doctrine of St.John of the Cross,' concerning the perfecting of the soul. I find the words of his Spiritual Canticle devastatingly beautiful, and I can think of no better way to conclude my reminiscences than with my favourite stanzas, in which St. John describes the desire for the full possession of God.

My Beloved is the mountains,
The solitary wooded valleys,
The strange islands,
The roaring torrents,
The whisper of the amorous gales;

The tranquil night
At the approaches of dawn,
The silent music,
The murmuring solitude,
The supper which revives, and enkindles love.

Oh! who can heal me?
Give me at once Thyself,
Send me no more
A messenger
Who cannot tell me what I wish.

Quench Thou my troubles,
For no one else can soothe them;
And let mine eyes behold Thee,
For Thou art their light,
And I will keep them for Thee alone.

Reveal Thy presence,
And let Thy vision and Thy beauty kill me.
Behold the malady
Of love is incurable
Except in Thy presence and before Thy face.

Appendix (i)

Stamps: The Machin Head of The Queen

by Douglas Muir of Royal Mail Group's Heritage Services

(see illustration pages 36-37)

Design

Even before official invitations were sent out by The Post Office to selected artists in November 1965 the work of Arnold Machin was being considered for a new portrait of The Queen on postage stamps. This was because of his successful work for the Royal Mint for the new coinage. A copy of the coinage plaster cast was obtained from the Mint together with Machin's preliminary drawings as early as August that year and a preliminary briefing was given to Machin and Reginald Brill. Formally, invitations were sent out at the end of November to Machin, Brill, David Gentleman, Stuart Devlin and John Ward. All were to submit "renderings" of the Queen's head in profile by the end of January 1966 and were supplied with photographs taken by Lord Snowdon as a basis.

Arnold Machin had already received the Snowdon photographs which he had used for his sculpture of the Queen's head for the Royal Mint. When he approached the stamp brief he utilised them again for the portrait but also relied on personal impressions of The Queen and, most importantly, his previous work for the coinage.

From material extant it is clear that, for the head, Machin utilised a photograph of the mould made for the Royal Mint (or a reverse of the plaster cast). (*Fig.1*). This showed The Queen facing left which was required for stamps (facing into the envelope) rather than right as on the issued coins. After eliminating the coinage legend he then worked on the head and produced ink wash drawings with or without a tiara. This provided his "rendering" of the portrait. He then created more than 60 colour variations of frames to surround this.

First images from all five invited artists were shown to the Stamp Advisory Committee (of the Council of Industrial Design) on 26 January 1966. Several of the heads by Brill, Gentleman and Machin suggested a possible treatment by blind embossing, or by photography giving much the same effect, and these artists were asked to take their work forward. By the time of the next meeting, at the beginning of March, Machin had modelled his portrait in clay and cast this at Stoke-on-Trent. (*Fig.2*). Harrison & Sons Ltd, the stamp printers, had taken photographs, variously lit, of both the unworked plaster cast and the matrix and the Committee agreed that this approach held great promise and was preferred. (Other artists such as Andrew Restall and David Gentleman continued with their own work throughout 1966 often without reference to the Committee but rather to the Postmaster General – Anthony Wedgwood Benn – and this served as an alternative to Machin's sculpture.)

Work now centred on the stamp printers under R. F. (George) York with whom Machin worked closely throughout the coming year. Here essays, or trial stamps, were printed using a photograph of the plaster cast of the Queen's head within adaptations of one of Machin's frames. This incorporated symbols of the four countries making up the United Kingdom and the legend "Postage Revenue". A large number of essays were prepared during April and May in both single and bicoloured versions, and with variations of the frame design, but it was felt that more work was needed. (*Fig.3*).

Using photographs Machin now worked on his sculptured head to simplify it. This he did by cutting the neckline and omitting any legend other than the value (which had also been created from a plaster cast). (*Fig.4*). The resulting image was essayed in five colours and shown to members of the Committee. (*Fig.5*). These essays were compared with alternatives based on new photographs of The Queen which had been taken specially by John Hedgecoe in June and approved by The Queen in August. In the Machin portrait The Queen was wearing a tiara; in the Hedgecoe photographs a diadem. The new simple sculpture design by Machin was regarded as a considerable improvement, but the diadem was preferred to the tiara harking back to the Penny Black when the same diadem was worn by Queen Victoria.

At this point Machin reworked his clay model and a new sculpture was created with the diadem, as seen on the Hedgecoe photographs. Again a plaster cast was made and photographs taken under different lighting conditions. This was recognisably similar to the final portrait but with a simple cut-off neck. Acceptable bromides were sent to the printers on 25 October and essays without value were already prepared by the end of that month. (*Fig.6*).

When these essays were shown to The Queen she expressed a preference for a corsage. To achieve this Machin took an enlarged photograph of one of the essays and added clothing in China White and India ink. (*Fig.7*). He then translated this on to his clay model and a further plaster cast was produced. More than one cast was made and work on these created slightly different versions which can be differentiated on the issued stamps. Many photographs were taken in various lighting conditions both by Machin with an old camera at the printers and by others elsewhere. Subsequently, a large number of essays were produced in different colours and shades and with varying value positions.

The design was accepted and approved by The Queen who chose a particular dark olive brown sepia for the basic inland letter rate (4d). (*Fig.8*). This was a conscious imitation of the original Penny Black, whose classic simplicity Machin's design emulated. Other colours were suggested by Machin, with the assistance of the printers, for the other low values required and the first stamps appeared on 3 June 1967.

Printing the low values

All the first low value definitive stamps were printed in photogravure. The image was created as a photograph and repeated by a step-and-repeat camera to create the film of the printers' sheet. This was etched on to the surface of the gravure cylinder in the form of tiny square cells – the deeper the cell the darker the colour printed. Paper was on a reel rather than sheet-fed and the process was much quicker and cheaper for the long printing runs required.

Gravure was the printing method used for all low value definitives until the introduction of offset litho for some in 1980, which eventually needed new origination. Many developments have taken place over the years but despite the introduction of decimal currency, colour changes and standardisation, and more advanced methods of printing, the design has remained the same.

High value stamps

After the production of the new low values thoughts turned to high value stamps. At the time these were printed in intaglio from an engraving, rather than in photogravure from a photograph used for the smaller, low-value stamps. After the initial consideration of possible pictorial designs it was decided to use the Machin head of The Queen instead. (*Fig.9*).

The final plaster cast was re-photographed to give greater depth to the moulding as an aid to the engravers at Bradbury Wilkinson & Co. Ltd, the printers of the stamps. A master die was then engraved for each value (2s 6d, 5s,10s and £1), the image appearing in reverse. This steel die was hardened and under considerable pressure an impression (now right-facing) was taken on a roller and transferred 160 times to create the printing plate. These images on the printing plate were again in reverse. The plate was then hardened and curved to fit the sheet-fed rotary printing press. Later technology changed the form of the plate and subsequent designs and contracts superseded this printing method.

The Commemorative Head

For pictorial commemorative, or special, stamps a much smaller, simpler head was required which would not interfere with the design but still clearly represent The Queen. Machin reduced his definitive diadem head to commemorative size but this was unsuitable. Subsequently, he produced a version of the head with a laurel wreath in place of the diadem. This was also modelled in clay and created as a plaster cast (*Fig.10*) and photographed and essays at various sizes of head were printed in December 1967. (*Fig.11*). The model was approved by The Queen and from 1968 it has been used in three different formats: embossed, as a flat silhouette or with full features. Most often it has appeared as a silhouette, but it can face either left or right, satisfactorily superimposed on a design.

A Time for Change?

To mark the 30th anniversary of the coronation in 1983 it was proposed by The Post Office that a new definitive design be created. The Queen agreed in principle for work to go ahead but thought that a work of real quality would be required to replace Machin's symbolic representation. No accurate portrait proved successful and the Machin head has continued to this day.

In the period since the introduction of the design in 1967 more than 170 billion definitive stamps with this simple, timeless effigy have been printed.

Appendix (ii)

Glossary of Names.

➼ Adams, John, (1882-1953). Born in Bucknall, Staffordshire. Student at RCA 1909-1912, followed by three years there as a student-teacher. Taught at Durban School of Art, South Africa. Married Truda Carter and established 'Carter, Stabler and Adams', better known as Poole Pottery, where he was their designer and Managing Director.

➼ Ayres, James, RAS Cert. RA student in Sculpture 1961-1964. Director Judkyn Memorial and author of a number of Books on Art.

➼ Baker, Eve, (1906-1990). Painting student at RCA. Trained as conservator in Denmark, devoting her life to the restoration of mediaeval wall paintings. Worked in some 100 churches and in cathedrals.

➼ Baker, Robert, (1909-1992). Painting student at RCA. Worked for Rural Industries Bureau during the war. 1945, Superintendent of Art Instruction for Stoke-on-Trent. 1948, Professor of Ceramics RCA. 1959, Design Director for Royal Worcester Porcelain. After retirement, Technical Adviser for heritage projects; re-created mediaeval floor tiles for Winchester Cathedral; developed revolutionary conservation techniques in fresco conservation.

➼ Barnett, Rosemary (Mrs.Holmes), RAS Cert. FRBS. RA student in Sculpture 1960-1964. (Winner of Edward Stott Scholarship, Silver Medal and Landseer Prize.) Principal – The Sir Henry Doulton School of Sculpture; Director Frink School of Sculpture; Curator; Jerwood Sculpture Park.

➼ Besant, Annie (1847-1933) Became a Fabian, a trade union organiser and an enthusiast for birth-control. Later a theosophist and an active supporter of the Indian nationalist movement.

➼ Betjeman, Sir John (1906-1984) English poet, noted for his nostalgic and humorous verse and essays. Poet laureate 1972-1984. Also known for his concern for the preservation of historic buildings, especially of the Victorian era.

➼ Bevin, Ernest (1881-1951) British Labour statesman and Trade Unionist, later Foreign Secretary in Churchill's coalition.

➼ Birks, Alboin (c.1862-1940) Born in Fenton (Stoke upon Trent), son of Henry Birks, figure maker and later manager of Pratt's pottery of Longton. Apprenticed to Minton as a surface modeller and after this as a pâte-sur-pâte artist from 1876-1940. He was the last pupil of Solon to be employed on this type of work.

➼ Bladen, Alfred, ARCA. FRSA. (b. 1899). First Head of the Department of Drawing at Derby School of Art in 1931 and head of the Junior Art School. Exhibited at the Royal Academy, the Royal Institute and Royal Birmingham Society of Artists.

➼ Bliss, Douglas Percy, MA. ARCA. RBA. (1900-1984) Painter and Wood Engraver. Studied at RCA under William Rothenstein. From 1927 frequent exhibitor at many London galleries. He taught at Schools of Art in Blackheath, Hornsey and Harrow. Also illustrated 12 books, published 2 and wrote for 'The Scotsman' as London Art critic. 1946-1964, Director of Glasgow School of Art.

➼ Campbell, Colin Minton, of Minton's China Works, and Robert Minton Taylor founded the Campbell Brick and Tile Company in 1875 to produce encaustic and geometric floor tiles. Architectural decoration became their speciality.

➼ Caroe, Alban Douglas Rendall. (1904-1991) Considered one of the greatest Gothicists of the twentieth century; responsible for the restoration of Sunderland Minster and a pioneer in methods of preservation of stone and stone buildings, as were his father and son.

➼ Forsyth, Gordon Mitchell, RI, ARCA (1879-1952). Born at Fraserburgh and later studied at Gray's Art School, Aberdeen and the RCA, where he was awarded the Travelling Scholarship in Design in 1903. Designer for Minton Hollins in Stoke and in 1906 Art Director of Pilkingtons in Manchester. Appointed Superintendent of Art Instruction for Stoke-on-Trent in 1920 and Principal of the City Schools of Art.

➼ Gillick, Mary (b. 1881). Studied at Nottingham School of Art and then the Royal College of Art from 1902-1904 under Lanteri. She produced medals for a number of societies including the Royal Society, the Institute of Physics and the Royal Academy Schools. She won the competition to produce the first coin portrait of Queen Elizabeth II in 1952, which was in use until the introduction of the Machin head in 1968/1970. She was greatly influenced by her husband, Ernest Gillick, and their working partnership lasted some forty-six years.

➼ Gresley, Cuthbert, (1876-1963). Apprenticed in 1893 to Royal Crown Derby as a china painter, he became an accomplished designer-decorator with commissions for royal households and numerous individual pieces. His watercolours were mainly of landscapes and flowers.

➼ Gresley, Harold, DCM. BWS. NSA. (1892-1967) Watercolour painter. Attended Derby School of Art 1908-1914 and (after distinguished Army service) Nottingham School of Art 1919-1922. Lived at Chellaston, Derbyshire. Third generation of famous family of Derbyshire artists who specialised in the rural idyll, exhibiting at the Royal Academy, Royal Institute and Royal Watercolour Society.

➼ Hounsell, Francis William, ARCA (1885-1956). Painter, principally in water-colours. Head of Derby School of Art 1926-1948. Paintings exhibited at the Royal Academy and excellent drawings of the human figure in the Derby Art Gallery.

➼ Ironside, Christopher OBE, FSIA, FRBS (1913-1992). Sculptor and Designer. Trained at the Central School of Arts and Crafts. 1946-48 in charge of Education Section of Council of Industrial Design. 1953-63 part-time teacher at Royal College of Art. Designer of reverses for coinage abroad and known especially for the first British decimal coins.

➼ Jowett, Percy Hague (1882-1955). Painter, especially of landscapes in watercolour. Born in Halifax, Yorkshire, he studied at Leeds School of Art, winning a Royal Exhibition to the Royal College of Art in 1904. In 1907 he won the Prix de Rome which took him to Italy. He taught at Beckenham School of Art, and became Principal of Chelsea, then of the Central School of Arts and Crafts, and from 1935-48 of the Royal College of Art.

➼ Kenworthy, Jonathan. RAS Cert. FRBS. RA student in Sculpture 1961-1964. Landseer Travelling Scholarship (twice); President's Prize for Craftsmanship; 4 Silver Medals for Sculpture; Gold Medal and Travelling Scholarship for Sculpture). Numerous commissions and international exhibitions.
➼ Lowry, Lawrence Stephen (1887-1976) Painter, noted for his bleak industrial scenes of northern England, usually containing stylised figures.
➼ McKean, Lorne (Mrs.Russell), RAS Cert. RA student in Sculpture 1960-1964.
Public Works include: Girl and Swan, Reading; Swan Fountain, Horsham; 'Flight in bronze' for Norwich Union, Leeds. Also sculpture portraits of members of the Royal Family.
➼ Moore, Henry (1898-1986) Sculptor. Well-known for his massive, rounded figures to be found in churches, cathedrals and public places.
➼ Morris, Roy, ATD. (1890-1967) Taught at Derby School of Art in newly-formed Department of Pictorial Design from 1920-1955, principally teaching drawing, painting and printmaking.
➼ Morris, William (1834-1896) Influential designer of tapestries, woven materials and furniture in the Victorian era. Also a socialist writer and poet, he founded the Kelmscott Press in 1890.
➼ Murray, Keith Day Pierce, FRIBA, RDI (1892-1981). Born in New Zealand, moving to England with his family in 1906. In the 1920s he trained as an architect in London. He became extremely interested in the decorative arts and began to design ceramics for Wedgwood in 1932. In 1936 he formed the architectural firm of Ramsay, Murray and White which was chosen to design the new Wedgwood factory at Barlaston.
➼ Owen, Eric Raymond (1902-1974). Born Stoke-on-Trent and studied at Burslem School of Art, Stoke-on-Trent. Apprenticed to Minton Hollins Co. and moved to Minton's China Works in 1922, becoming Chief Modeller in 1928. Left in 1947 to become Wedgwood's Chief Modeller at Barlaston.
➼ Pratt, F.& R. of Fenton, run by Felix Edward Pratt (1813-1894). The firm produced multicoloured pot lids and bases as containers for products such as Gentleman's Relish, bear's grease, foodstuffs and cosmetics, including rouge. Known today as 'Staffordshire pot lids' their success led to over forty years' production of 'Prattware':
➼ Russell, Edwin. RAS Cert. FRBS. RA student in Sculpture 1959-1963. (Gold Medal and Edward Stott Travelling Scholarship 1960). Public Works include: 'Lion and Lamb', Farnham; 'History of London', Tower Hill. Also work on St.Paul's Cathedral; Westminster Abbey; Wells Cathedral.
➼ Sanders, John. MBE. FRSA. ATD. Born 1917 in Derby. Attended Derby School of Art at the same time as Arnold Machin. 1938-1939, London Central School of Arts and Crafts. 1946-1947, London University Institute of Education. 1947, Head of Art at Long Eaton Grammar School; 1958, Principal, Lichfield School of Art and President Lichfield Society of Artists. Founder Member Lichfield Civic Society.
➼ Skellern, Victor. ARCA. FSIA. NRD. (1909-1966) Artist and Designer first employed by Wedgwood in 1923 and made Art Director in 1934. Designed countless surface patterns, encouraged appointment of new artists and first proposed employment of studio potters – (Arnold Machin being the first).

Responsible for a number of paintings and stained glass panels depicting life in the Potteries.

➼ Thomas, Cecil, OBE (1885-1976). Born in London he became a sculptor and medallist, training under his father at the Central School of Arts and Crafts where he specialised in gem engraving. Portraiture in his cameos led to an interest in medals from 1910 onwards. His royal portraits made frequent appearances on official medals and the British Museum has a collection of his plaster models.

➼ Timmis, Rosemarie; private pupil of Patricia and Arnold Machin 1962-1964; studied Art in Florence 1964-1967; Byam Shaw School of Art (under Bernard Dunstan RA) 1967-1969. Now an established portrait painter in oils. Commissions include: H.M. The Sultan of Oman (1973); Sir Robin Butler, Cabinet Secretary (1991) and Lord Guthrie (2000).

➼ Tippett, Sir Michael, OM.CH. Kt. CBE. (1905-1998) English Composer, born in London. Studied at the Royal College of Music and became a conductor of educational organisations under London County Council. June 1943 imprisoned for 3 months as a conscientious objector. He had considerable success with operas and other works include symphonies, an oratorio and works for the piano.

➼ Wall, Peter. Born 1923. Studied at Woolwich Polytechnic; Wimbledon School of Art; Burslem School of Art; Royal College of Art (Silver Medal for work on molecular patterns for surface decoration – an idea promoted by The Council of Industrial Design). Became designer for Wedgwood in 1951 and later Deputy Art Director, developing many designs and shapes for earthenware, bone china and jasper ware. Head of The School of Ceramics and Glass at Birmingham College of Art and Design 1968-1988.

➼ Walton, Izaak (1593-1683) Born in Stafford and benefactor of that town, he was a London draper until 1643. In his spare time he became an experienced angler, author of 'The Compleat Angler or the Contemplative Man's Recreation', and also of biographies of eminent clergymen, in particular John Donne. He fished the River Dove with his friend Charles Cotton and the River Itchen when he retired to Winchester, where he was later buried.

➼ Wardle, Sir Thomas. (1831-1909). Textile manufacturer and silk dyer of Leek, Staffordshire and founder of 'Wardle and Co.' Well-known for producing printed linen and velveteen. Great collector of silks and embroideries from abroad, India in particular.

➼ Wedgwood, Josiah IV. (1892-1943). First Baron Wedgwood of Barlaston. Fought in the Boer War and at Gallipoli. Politician, involved with the transportation of Jewish refugees from Austria and Germany. Chancellor of the Duchy of Lancaster in the first Labour Cabinet. Father of Josiah Wedgwood V.

➼ Wedgwood, Josiah V. (1899-1968) Educated at Bedales and University College, London. Awarded PhD for thesis on the Economics of Inheritance. Became Wedgwood's Managing Director in 1930 on the sudden death of his uncle, Frank, and immediately rationalised the number of patterns in production. With his cousins, Tom, Hensleigh and John, and the Production Director, Norman Wilson, Josiah V masterminded the move from the old factory at Etruria to the present site at Barlaston in 1938.

=› Wenger, Albert Francis. 1837 Born in Lausanne, Switzerland. Served an apprenticeship at Nyon and became senior technician to a ceramic specialist in Milan. Emigrated to England to manufacture feldspathic porcelain at the Parker Street Works, Hanley, circa 1870s-1960s. The firm specialised in colours and became a supplier to other potteries.

=› Wilding, Dorothy (1893-1976). Photographer. Responsible for the photographic portrait of Queen Elizabeth II which appeared on all British definitive stamps prior to the Machin head.

Members of the Royal Academy of Arts referred to in text

=› Brooke, Humphrey, CVO. Born 1914. Secretary of the Royal Academy 1952-1968. A lay member of the Staff.

=› Butler, James Walter, FRBS. RWA. Born 1931 in London. Sculptor, RA elected 1972. Attended Art Schools: Maidstone, St. Martins and RCA. Taught Sculpture at City & Guilds of London Art School and was visiting tutor to the RA Schools. His first major commission, the twice-lifesize statue of President Kenyatta of Kenya in 1973, has been followed by numerous private and public commissions.

=› Carr, Henry Marvel, (1894-1970) Painter, RA elected 1966.

=› Casson, Sir Hugh Maxwell, CH. KCVO. (1910-1999) Architect, RA elected 1970. President of the Academy 1976-1984.

=› Connard, Philip, CVO. (1875-1958) Painter, RA elected 1925. Keeper of the Royal Academy (with responsibility for the Schools and Staff.) Connard's exhibits in the Summer Exhibitions were amongst the most popular in the 1920s and 30s, 'Pelicans' being bought for the Academy by The Chantrey Bequest during this time.

=› Darwin, Sir Robert (Robin), CBE. (1910-1974) Painter, RA elected 1972.

=› Dobson, Frank,CBE. (1888-1963) Sculptor, RA elected 1953.

=› Dunlop, Ronald Ossory, (1894-1973) Painter, RA elected 1950.

=› Fitton, James, (1899-1982) Painter, RA elected 1954.

=› Flint, Sir William Russell, (1880-1969) Painter, RA elected 1933. His paintings in the Summer Exhibitions were always popular, and he had a one-man exhibition during the Presidency of Sir Charles Wheeler.

=› Garbe, Richard, (1876-1957) Sculptor, RA elected 1936. Head of the Sculpture School at the Royal College of Art when Arnold Machin was a student there.

=› Gillick, Ernest George, (1874-1951) Sculptor, ARA elected 1935.

=› Gillies, Sir William George, CBE. (1898-1973) Painter, RA elected 1971. Head of Drawing and Painting at Edinburgh College of Art and later Principal (1961-1966) during Arnold Machin's tenure as Sculpture assessor.

=› Greenham, Peter George, CBE. (1909-1992) Painter, RA elected 1960. Keeper of the Schools 1964-1985.

=› Gunn, Sir James, (1893-1964) Painter, RA elected 1961. Died within a few weeks of being elected Treasurer in 1964.

=› John, Augustus Edwin, OM. (1878-1961) Painter, RA elected 1928.

=› Lamb, Henry, MC. (1883-1960) Painter, RA elected 1949.

=› Lambert, Maurice, (1901-1964) Sculptor, RA elected 1952. Master of Sculpture 1950-1958.

➵ Ledward, Gilbert, OBE. (1888-1960) Sculptor, RA elected 1937. Commissioned by The Leighton Fund to design a fountain for the centre of Sloane Square – erected in 1953. Bequeathed a fund for the benefit of the Sculpture School at the Academy.

➵ Machin, Arnold, OBE. FRSBS. (1911-1999) Sculptor, RA elected 1956. Master of Sculpture 1959-1966. It has been said that he opted for the classical approach, both as to technique and the use of materials. Later he would deplore the excesses of modernism and in 1996, as an elder statesman of the Royal Academy, he spoke out against the 'Sensations' exhibition and against the Academy's exhibitions secretary, Norman Rosenthal, for his part in staging it.

➵ Maufe, Sir Edward Brantwood, (1883-1974) Architect, RA elected 1947. Treasurer 1954-1958.

➵ McMillan, William, CVO. (1887-1977) Sculptor, RA elected 1933. Master of Sculpture 1929-1941.

➵ Methuen, Lord Paul Ayshford,(1886-1974). Painter, RA elected 1959.

➵ Munnings, Sir Alfred James, KCVO. (1878-1959) Painter, RA elected 1925. President of the Academy 1944-1949.

➵ Richardson, Sir Albert Edward, KCVO. (1880-1964) Architect, RA elected 1944. President of the Academy 1954-1956.

➵ Schilsky, Eric,(1898-1974) Sculptor, RA elected 1968. Head of Sculpture at Edinburgh College of Art during Arnold Machin's tenure as assessor.

➵ Scott, Sir George Gilbert, (1811-1878) Architect, RA elected 1860.

➵ Scott, Sir Giles Gilbert, OM. (1880-1960) Architect, RA elected 1922. Grandson of the above.

➵ Skeaping, John Rattenbury, (1901-1980) Sculptor, RA elected 1959. Training: Blackheath School of Art, Goldsmiths College, Central School of Arts and Crafts, Royal Academy Schools. 1920 winner of the RA Gold Medal Travelling Scholarship and in 1924 the Prix de Rome. Well known for his sculptures of animals, in particular of horses and was commissioned by Wedgwood to model a series of fourteen animal figures. His training was largely based on the classical tradition but in 1925 he married the sculptress Barbara Hepworth in Italy and he began to change the style of his work. Appointed Professor of Sculpture at the Royal College of Arts in 1964.

➵ Spence,Sir Basil, OM, OBE. (1907-1976). Architect, RA elected 1960.

➵ Ward, John Stanton, CBE. Born 1917. Painter, RA elected 1965. Studied at the Royal College of Art and received many prestigious commissions, including several from the Royal Family.

➵ Wheeler, Sir Charles, KCVO, CBE. (1892-1974) Sculptor, RA elected 1940. President of the Academy 1956-1966.

Acknowledgments

For their part in assisting the publication of this book, the publishers wish to thank the following: Francis Machin, photographer of the Machin Archive and Barbara Went for co-ordinating the written memoirs; for editorial contributions, research or verification – Pamela Adams, Tina Adams, Jane Best-Shaw, James Butler, Norma Davies, Stanley Davies, Martin Elkes of Stafford Library, John Fineran, Sharon Gater and Joanne Nutt at the Wedgwood Museum, Rosemary Holmes, Anne Jacques, Joan Jones of the former Minton Archives, Alice Machin, Patricia Machin, Ancel Newton, John Sanders, Rosalind Thomas, Mollie Timmis, Rosemarie Timmis, Peter Wall, Alan Wedgwood, Sally Wedgwood, Alexander Went, James Went, Norah West.

Description

Artist of an Icon is the story of the sculptor, Arnold Machin, OBE, RA, 1911-1999. The icon of the book's title refers to his portrait of her Majesty, Queen Elizabeth II, which appears on definitive British postage stamps. With over 170 billion copies, this is the most reproduced image in history. But the essence of this book is the life of the artist himself, as Machin tells his own story.

Machin considered the stamp to be his greatest achievement, though his whole career was remarkable and to read his memoirs, one takes a journey through eight decades of art history. He started as an apprentice in the Minton factory in the Potteries at the age of 14. Attending art classes he was accepted for Derby Art School, from where he gained a scholarship to the Royal College of Art. Further opportunities were curtailed by the outbreak of war in 1939. He spent a year in prison as a Conscientious Objector before returning to Staffordshire to work for Wedgwood. In 1947 he submitted a terracotta statue to the Royal Academy which won him the Chantrey Bequest, and returned to London to teach at the Royal College of Art. Elected to the Royal Academy in 1956, Machin then became Master of Sculpture in the RA Schools.

In 1963 Machin won the competition to model The Queen's head which appeared on all British Decimal Coinage until recently. The famous stamp design followed in 1967 and is still in use today. It is known as 'The Machin' and regarded as the supreme definitive stamp, valued and collected in all its variations throughout the world.

He writes enthusiastically about the gardens he created, which he regarded as a source of inspiration and calm. At this stage in his life, having countered modernism in numerous forms for seven decades, he was justifiably concerned for the future of contemporary art. In retirement, the sculptor spoke out against the Royal Academy's 'Sensations' Exhibition in 1996, which reflected disregard for artistic ability and the pursuit of excellence. Arnold Machin's memoirs refer to an ideological war in 20th century British Art, and he concludes his book by pointing to values in Art which pay homage to tradition, but are common sense even to the layman. His observations come with hindsight and wisdom and will inspire those who seek a thread of continuity in the great tradition of Art.

The book is complemented by extensive illustration of Arnold Machin's life and works. This includes terracottas, bronzes statues, drawings, ceramic figures from Wedgwood and Royal Worcester, and designs for British stamps, coins and medals. Finally, the appendices contain additional information about the sculptor's Royal Academy exhibits and his contemporaries named in the text, as well as a factual essay about the Machin head of The Queen, by Douglas Muir of The Royal Mail Groups' Heritage Sevices.

Cover photos:

Front: Arnold Machin and 'Spring', 1947,
purchased by the Tate Gallery, after winning the Royal Academy's Chantrey Bequest.

Back (left): Bust of fellow student, c. 1938
Polychrome terracotta.

Back (right): Final plaster Relief of The Queen's Head.

Index of illustrations

1-16 in between text pages 64-65
17-32 in between text pages 96-97
33-48 in between text pages 128-129

Index